THE CONSTITUTION OF

South Africa's 1996 'Final' Constitution is wi̤ ̤ ̤ ̤ ̤ ̤
ing achievement of the country's dramatic transition to democracy. This transition began with the unbanning of the liberation movements and release of Nelson Mandela from prison in February 1990. This book presents the South African Constitution in its historical and social context, providing students and teachers of constitutional law and politics with an invaluable resource through which to understand the emergence, development and continuing application of the supreme law of South Africa. The chapters present a detailed analysis of the different provisions of the Constitution, providing a clear, accessible and informed view of the Constitution's structure and role in the new South Africa. The main themes include: a description of the historical context and emergence of the Constitution through the democratic transition; the implementation of the Constitution and its role in building a new democratic society; the interaction of the Constitution with the existing law and legal institutions, including the common law, indigenous law and traditional authorities; as well as a focus on the strains placed on the new constitutional order by both the historical legacies of apartheid and new problems facing South Africa. Specific chapters address the historical context, the legal, political and philosophical sources of the Constitution, its principles and structure, the bill of rights, parliament and executive, as well as the Constitution's provisions for cooperative government and regionalism. The final chapter discusses the challenges facing the Constitution and its aspirations in a democratic South Africa. The book is written in an accessible style, with an emphasis on clarity and concision. It includes a list of references for further reading at the end of each chapter.

Constitutional Systems of the World
General Editors: Peter Leyland and Andrew Harding
Associate Editors: Benjamin L Berger and Alexander Fischer

In the era of globalisation, issues of constitutional law and good governance are being seen increasingly as vital issues in all types of society. Since the end of the Cold War, there have been dramatic developments in democratic and legal reform, and post-conflict societies are also in the throes of reconstructing their governance systems. Even societies already firmly based on constitutional governance and the rule of law have undergone constitutional change and experimentation with new forms of governance; and their constitutional systems are increasingly subjected to comparative analysis and transplantation. Constitutional texts for practically every country in the world are now easily available on the internet. However, texts which enable one to understand the true context, purposes, interpretation and incidents of a constitutional system are much harder to locate, and are often extremely detailed and descriptive. This series seeks to provide scholars and students with accessible introductions to the constitutional systems of the world, supplying both a road map for the novice and, at the same time, a deeper understanding of the key historical, political and legal events which have shaped the constitutional landscape of each country. Each book in this series deals with a single country, and each author is an expert in their field.

Published volumes

The Constitution of the United Kingdom
The Constitution of the United States
The Constitution of Vietnam

Forthcoming titles in this series

The Constitution of South Africa
Heinz Klug

The Constitution of Japan
Shigenori Matsui

The Constitution of France
Sophie Boyron

The Constitution of Australia
Cheryl Saunders

The Constitution of Ireland
Colm O'Cinneide

Link to series website
http://www.hartpub.co.uk/series/csw

The Constitution of South Africa
A Contextual Analysis

Heinz Klug

·HART·
PUBLISHING

OXFORD – PORTLAND OREGON
2010

Published in the United Kingdom by Hart Publishing Ltd
16C Worcester Place, Oxford, OX1 2JW
Telephone: +44 (0)1865 517530
Fax: +44 (0)1865 510710
E-mail: mail@hartpub.co.uk
Website: http://www.hartpub.co.uk

Published in North America (US and Canada) by
Hart Publishing
c/o International Specialized Book Services
920 NE 58th Avenue, Suite 300
Portland, OR 97213-3786
USA
Tel: +1 503 287 3093 or toll-free: (1) 800 944 6190
Fax: +1 503 280 8832
E-mail: orders@isbs.com
Website: http://www.isbs.com

British Library Cataloguing in Publication Data
Data Available

ISBN: 978-1-84113-737-7

Typeset by Hope Services Ltd, Abingdon
Printed and bound in Great Britain by
TJ International Ltd, Padstow, Cornwall

Contents

Table of Cases

Table of Legislation

National legislation

International Legislation

1

The Constitution of South Africa

Context and History

———

Introduction: A Constitution in Context – History – Political Context – Conclusion: Context, Continuity and the Problem of Path Dependency

I. INTRODUCTION: A CONSTITUTION IN CONTEXT

MORE THAN A decade into South Africa's constitutional experiment, many scholars have discussed possible interpretations of different clauses of the 1996 Constitution and analysed the Constitutional Court's decisions. Others have examined the political, philosophical and legal concepts that underpin its text. This book will provide another perspective by attempting to locate an understanding of the 1996 Constitution within the context of the many political, social and economic struggles that South Africa's first democratic government inherited. This book will pursue a contextual analysis of the 1996 Constitution by identifying a number of issues that have dominated the first 15 years of the new South Africa. While many of these issues have been identified as legacies of colonialism and apartheid, a number of important new issues have come to dominate social and legal relations in South Africa since 1994.

Instead of organising this study around each of these issues, however, the book will take up these issues intermittently in the context of a discussion of different constitutional provisions and institutions. I will use these issues to illustrate the role the Constitution has played, or failed to play, in addressing these questions. At a different level of abstraction,

I will also explore the relationship between the specific domestic issues that the Constitution attempts to address and the impact of globalisation—both actual economic globalisation and the longer-term and possibly more enduring process of legal globalisation—on the creation and development of the Constitution. In regard to this latter concern, I will explore the idea of legal continuity, as a form of path dependency, in the building and functioning of constitutional institutions in post-apartheid South Africa. The issues I have chosen to highlight, as a means to contextualise the Constitution, incorporate five general themes: the legacies of colonialism and apartheid; pervasive social problems, such as crime, gender relations and HIV/AIDS; legal pluralism; aspiration for a rights-based culture; and democratic governance. Each of these categories covers a number of specific issues, and will enable a general discussion of the ways in which the Constitution—through its creation of institutions, allocation of power, and proclamation of rights—attempts to address the past and construct a future society that transcends the often desperate, violent, unequal and unforgiving realities of the present.

South Africa's 1996 Constitution is heralded as the extraordinary achievement of the democratic transition that formally began in early 1990. In this sense, it is both a cherished product of that transition and a national plan or aspirational guide that attempts to address the past. It provides a roadmap for the construction of institutions, policies and frameworks within which South Africans will continue to struggle for their various visions of a brighter future. A contextual analysis will focus first on the issues that may be identified, in part, as legacies of colonialism and apartheid. I will explore these issues in discussions of how the Constitution, though the institutions it has generated, has addressed questions of inequality and violence. Inequality is manifested not only in the growing economic disparities that have outlived the apartheid era, but it exists most specifically in the unequal distribution of land ownership, which is a direct legacy of colonialism and apartheid, as well as in the extraordinary levels of unemployment and underemployment that rob nearly 40 per cent of economically active adults of the chance of a dignified life. The other major legacy, which is closely related to economic disparity, is the legacy of violence and lack of accountability that mark the ongoing levels of criminal activity in South African society. While the Truth and Reconciliation Commission was designed to address the legacy of past impunity, the Constitution continues to be buffeted by the high levels of violence and impunity that have characterised South African life.

The second category of issues involves the pervasive social problems that have either continued into the post-apartheid era or have arisen anew since 1990. Three particular issues stand out and serve to illustrate these questions for the Constitution: The first is a legacy of violence and crime that has dominated social life since the diminishment of political violence which followed the first democratic election in 1994. The second legacy is the high incidence of rape and domestic violence that pervade gender relations. While the Constitution and post-apartheid laws have sought to guarantee and promote gender equality, conditions for women have, by many measures, continued to decline. This reality is evident in the impact of the HIV/AIDS pandemic, which provides the third focus for discussing and evaluating how civil society has mobilised the Constitution to address a pervasive social problem despite the long failure of government to address the issue.

Legal pluralism—the recognition in the Constitution that South Africa has more than one legitimate source for basic legal rules and concepts—provides the third category of issues for discussion. This legal diversity is reflected in the Constitution's recognition of both the common law and indigenous law as co-equal sources of rules while simultaneously subjecting both these sources of law to the Constitution itself. This legal pluralism raises issues for both the creation of national identity as well as the institutional tension it creates among different sources of political and legal power in different localities and among different segments of the population. While the government has been committed to the creation of a single nation, 'united in its diversity', the very recognition of legal diversity raises questions about the dominance of any particular vision of the Constitution or the rights guaranteed in the Bill of Rights. Institutionally, the creation of houses of traditional leaders has both offered recognition to indigenous forms of governance and injected new vibrancy into forms of ethnic identity that are expected to be subsumed into the nation. This tension has been further exacerbated by the process of mass urbanisation that has followed the demise of apartheid and the failure of rural development that has resulted in parts of rural South Africa facing the dual burdens of HIV/AIDS and abject poverty.

Aspiration for a rights-based culture, which stands at the core of the Constitution, provides the fourth source of issues that will form the context for understanding the role of the Constitution in South Africa. From its inception, the struggle for national liberation in South Africa was characterised by claims of rights. As one of the enduring struggles for human rights over the course of the twentieth century, the struggle against apartheid and racism epitomised the global movement towards decolonisation and equality within the United Nations human rights system. The introduction of a fully formed Bill of Rights came quicker than the African National Congress (ANC) anticipated; the party argued initially that the interim Constitution should include only those rights essential to ensuring a free and fair election. However, once the committee negotiating this aspect of the interim Constitution proposed a fully formed Bill of Rights, it was impossible for the ANC to resist it without betraying the human rights claims of the anti-apartheid movement. Instead, the ANC would later push for the expansion of rights to include a range of socio-economic rights that were central to its constituencies' demands. The 1996 Constitution's Bill of Rights thus represents the highest aspirations of the global human rights movement, a set of rights—including political, civil, socio-economic and cultural—that are indivisible and enforceable.

The inclusion of such an extensive set of constitutional rights does, however, raise questions about their effective status in the political and judicial context of the new South Africa. Unlike earlier bills of rights—such as those included in the first 10 Amendments to the US Constitution, which are assumed to reflect the existing rights held by the citizens of the polity—there is no assumption that all South Africans presently enjoy the vast range of rights included in the Bill of Rights. Instead, it is assumed that the state and society are working towards the effective realisation of these rights. To this extent the Bill of Rights is aspirational. Yet, these rights are also fully justiciable and thus the courts are required to review the practices of government, and in some cases private parties, to ensure that these rights are being protected. It is this dual feature of the South African Bill of Rights that provides the contextual framework within which the government and civil society both seek to justify their programmes and claims, while the courts—and the Constitutional Court in particular—have sought to balance the problems of effective governance, reasonable government programmes and the claims of those who continue to strive towards the realisation of those human rights guaranteed in the Constitution.

The Constitutional Court has identified three core human values as central to the Bill of Rights: dignity, equality and freedom. As Justice Kate O'Regan argued in the Constitutional Court's first major opinion:

[r]espect for the dignity of all human beings is particularly important in South Africa. For apartheid was a denial of a common humanity. Black people were refused respect and dignity and thereby the dignity of all South Africans was diminished. The new Constitution rejects this past and affirms the equal worth of all South Africans. Thus recognition and protection of human dignity is the touchstone of the new political order and is fundamental to the new Constitution.[1]

This placing of rights at the centre of the post-apartheid project is daily challenged by the contextual realities of the new South Africa, where exposure to violence, poverty and government incapacity continue to shape the lives of the majority of the country's inhabitants.

The question of democratic governance forms the fifth and final category of issues that provides the contextual background for this book. The national liberation struggle in South Africa was at its core a struggle for democracy, which came to fruition with the 1994 election and the establishment of Nelson Mandela's government as the country's first truly democratically elected government. The 1996 Constitution's embrace of a supreme Constitution and a Constitutional Court with the power to 'make the final decision whether an Act of Parliament, a provincial Act or conduct of the President is constitutional',[2] means that South Africa is committed to a system of democratic constitutionalism in which the democratic will is enveloped within and constrained by the national pre-commitments outlined in the Constitution. This is the contextual reality that has given rise to increasing tensions and debates over the role of the judiciary in the new South Africa as well as raising concerns over the relationship between the government, whose choices and programmes are bound by the limits of the Constitution, and the ANC, the dominant political party, which has increasingly taken a turn towards populism. Simultaneously, the sheer weight of public need and a lack of experienced and qualified public officials have challenged the administrative capacity of the government. Despite the government's budgetary success over the first decade of democracy and its increased funding of social welfare programmes, the challenges of crime, unemployment and a rampant HIV/AIDS pandemic continue to frustrate government hopes of social and economic progress. The re-emergence of corruption and conflicts

[1] *S v Makwanyane* 1995 (3) SA 391, para 329.

[2] Constitution of the Republic of South Africa Act 108 of 1996 [hereinafter 1996 Constitution] s 167(5).

over access to government tenders as a significant source of economic gain and social mobility has only exacerbated the already daunting problems of democratic participation and governance. These issues are particularly troublesome at the local level, where delivery of government services must occur, and where the interaction of the whole array of law—from the common law through to indigenous law and traditional authority—comes into play.

II. HISTORY

South Africa's constitutional democracy has been more than a decade in the making. Despite the continuing burden of the legacies of colonialism and apartheid, the country's commitment to constitutionalism has provided remarkable stability in times of dramatic change. With the adoption of the 1993 interim Constitution the history of constitutionalism in South Africa could be summarised as the rise and fall of parliamentary sovereignty. However, the last decade has added an extraordinary chapter in which the government and opposition have accepted—and civil society has relied upon—the constitutional framework to resolve continuing political and social conflict. While constitutional law was a peripheral part of law in the colonial and apartheid eras, since the achievement of democracy in 1994, the Constitution, and its interpretation by the Constitutional Court in particular, has become a central pillar of South African law.

South Africa's Constitution is the product of a legal revolution unleashed by the democratic transition from apartheid.[3] Adopted by the Constitutional Assembly in 1996, Nelson Mandela promulgated the Constitution into law at Sharpeville on 10 December 1996; it went into effect on 4 February 1997. Since the creation in 1910 of the Union of South Africa, by an Act of the British Parliament, the country has had three other constitutions, in 1961, 1983 and 1993. The 1996 Constitution is, however, the first one adopted by a democratically constituted body representing all South Africans. Not only is this democratic South Africa's founding Constitution, but it also marks the shift, together with the 1993 interim Constitution, from parliamentary sovereignty to constitutional supremacy, thus fundamentally changing the role of the judiciary and the significance of the Constitution. While there are significant continuities

---

[3] See A Lewis, 'Revolution by Law', *New York Times* (13 January 1995) A15.

between the 1993 interim Constitution and the 1996 final Constitution, there are also important differences. These include such innovations as the idea of co-operative government and the explicit inclusion of socio-economic rights in the bill of rights, that mark the unique character of this Constitution as the crowning achievement of South Africa's democratic transition.

The hegemony of Parliament—supported by the doctrine of parliamentary sovereignty—was short-lived, compared to pre-colonial and colonial forms of governance based on participation by status-defined subjects or imperial command. Yet it was the rise and dominance of parliamentary sovereignty that shaped South Africa's modern constitutional history. The introduction of constitutional review, which empowered the judiciary to review democratically enacted legislation, was, in this context, a very new development. The democratic government has been required to reverse many decisions, including such sensitive and difficult issues as the HIV/AIDS pandemic and the national housing shortage, as well as proclaiming the duty of government to assist property owners whose lands have been occupied by homeless people. Yet, despite these reversals, the government and country remain proud of their internationally acclaimed Constitution.

Assertions of democratic authority by elected officials unhappy with particular judicial decisions are not unknown. But in stark contrast to the past, the judiciary—particularly former Chief Justice Chaskalson and his successor Chief Justice Langa—has vocally reminded the country of the value of the court's independence and of its duty to uphold the supremacy of the Constitution. In response, the government has publicly recognised the authority of the judiciary to interpret the Constitution and the importance of its independence. Even the opposition parties—which threaten at election time that the ANC government is intent on amending the Constitution to weaken individual rights—claim the Constitution. Consensus on the adoption of a justiciable Constitution, as one of the defining features of a democratic South Africa, may still be understood, in part, as a response to the historical experience of parliamentary sovereignty in the apartheid era. Yet a new layer of experience in which conflicts are mediated through litigation and fairly restrained judicial practice, is providing additional roots for democratic constitutionalism in today's South Africa.

A. Pre-democratic Constitutionalism

Historical legacies and legal continuity continue to have important effects on South Africa's constitutional order. In order to understand these effects it is necessary to review the constitutional history of South Africa prior to the democratic transition. From the seventeenth century onward a number of centrally governed polities, or states, emerged and existed for different lengths of time in the territory that is now South Africa. Most prominent of these was the Zulu Kingdom, whose armies dominated the northeastern parts of the area until late in the nineteenth century. Although these various entities—including the Griqua and Boer Republics, as well as other African polities—exhibited a variety of different forms of governance, it was the steady advance of British colonial power that eventually brought these different communities under a single political authority. Colonial power also provided the impetus for the political process that led the white settlers in the four British colonies—the Cape, Orange Free State, Transvaal and Natal—to agree to form the Union of South Africa in 1910.

i. *Colonial Constitutionalism and the 'Bifurcated' State*

Formally, the South Africa Act of 1909 brought together four settler colonies into a single Union of South Africa, but in effect it created a bifurcated state.[4] On the one hand, the Union Constitution granted parliamentary democracy to the white minority. On the other hand, it subjugated the majority of black South Africans to autocratic administrative rule. When they were excluded from the National Convention, black leaders protested against the refusal to extend the Cape franchise to the former Boer Republics,[5] but these leaders were rebuffed as not being representative of African society. Instead, African society was presented as essentially 'traditional', to be governed separately by chiefs in a system of

---

[4] See, A Ashforth, *The Politics of Official Discourse in Twentieth-Century South Africa* (Oxford, Clarendon Press, 1990) 34; see also Mamood Mamdani, *Citizen and Subject: Contemporary Africa and the Legacy of Late Colonialism* (Princeton, NJ, Princeton University Press, 1990).

[5] With the establishment of representative government in the Cape Colony in 1853 the right to vote was granted to every man, over the age of 21, who was a British subject and owned property—in land or buildings—worth at least £25, or who received an annual salary of at least £50 per year. While very few black men had either the property or salary to meet these requirements, there was no formal racial restriction in the Cape franchise.

feudal hierarchy with the Governor-General in Council at its apex. This division of the polity into two separate spheres reflected the fundamentally colonial character of South African legal culture in which 'professed legalism with its accompanying rhetoric of justice', coexisted with the 'racist abuse of power by the state'.[6]

The creation of 'differential spheres of citizenship for 'European' and 'Native' populations within one territory'[7] was reflected in section 147 of the South Africa Act of 1909. While the bulk of the South Africa Act dealt with the powers of a government, to be essentially representative of white male adults,[8] section 147 stated that '[t]he control and administration of native affairs . . . throughout the Union shall vest in the Governor-General in Council'. The connection between the exercise of authority over 'natives' and land was also made explicit by section 147, which stated that the executive (the Governor-General in Council):

> shall exercise all special powers in regard to native administration hitherto vested in the Governors of the Colonies or exercised by them as Supreme chiefs, and any lands vested in the Governor . . . for the purposes of reserves, for native locations shall vest in the Governor-General in Council, who shall exercise all special powers in relation to such reserves as may hitherto have been exercisable by any such Governor.

In essence, then, the constitutional order created by the South Africa Act—and replicated in every constitutional reform until the end of apartheid—was an essentially colonial order 'of a special type' in which the 'white' state was simultaneously a pseudo-democratic system based on a Westminster-style parliamentary system and also an authoritarian order in which the majority of the country's inhabitants lived under a classical system of colonial 'indirect rule' and the exercise of autocratic administrative authority by 'colonial authorities' in the form initially of the Governor-General in Council and later, under the Republic of South Africa Constitution Act of 1961, the State President.

---

[6] M Chanock, *South African Legal Culture 1902–1936: Fear, Favour and Prejudice* (Cambridge, Cambridge University Press, 2001) 22.

[7] Ashforth *The Politics of Official Discourse*, above n 4, 37.

[8] See South Africa Act 1909 (9 Edw 7, c 9) s 34(i), in which the quota of representatives from each province is to be 'obtained by dividing the total number of European male adults in the Union . . . by the total number of members'.

ii. Parliamentary Sovereignty

By 1806, when the British occupied and imposed their public law on the Cape, the principle of parliamentary sovereignty—that Parliament could 'do everything that is not naturally impossible'—had come to dominate English law.[9] Although the notion that judicial review over Parliament's legislative authority—mandated by some fundamental law of reason and justice—was not unknown in English jurisprudence,[10] by the time self-government was granted to the Cape and Natal, legislative supremacy was the defining feature of British parliamentarianism.[11] Despite the dominance of English constitutionalism in the Cape and Natal, the Boer Republics established in the mid-nineteenth century sought alternative sources of constitutionalism. Drafters of the Orange Free State Constitution of 1854, for example, turned to the Constitution of the United States of America, amongst other sources, and adopted rigid rules of amendment and guaranteed rights of peaceful assembly, petition, property and equality before the law.[12] Although the 1854 Constitution did not explicitly provide for judicial review or a Supreme Court, a court was established by legislation in 1876 and its power of judicial review was 'accepted as an inherent feature of the Constitution'.[13]

Despite the formal recognition of constitutional review in the Orange Free State, judicial review of legislation was applied in only one case. In this case, *Cassim and Solomon v The State*,[14] the High Court of the Orange Free State reviewed a law of 1890, which prohibited 'Asians' from settling in the State without the permission of the president.[15] Challenged on the grounds that it violated the constitutional guarantee of equality before the law, the court upheld the legislation, arguing that the constitutional guarantee had to be 'read in accordance with the *mores* of the Voortrekkers'.[16]

---

[9] Blackstone's *Commentaries in the Laws of England*, 4th edn (London, 1876) vol 1 p 129.

[10] See decision of Sir Edward Coke in *Dr Bonham's* case, 8 Co Rep 113b, 77 ER 646 (CP 1610); and R Pound, *The Development of Constitutional Guarantees of Liberty* (New Haven, Yale University Press, 1957).

[11] See J Dugard, *Human Rights and the South African Legal Order* (Princeton, NJ, Princeton University Press, 1978) 14–18.

[12] See HR Hahlo and E Kahn, *The Union of South Africa: The Development of its Laws and Constitution* (London, Stevens, 1960) 72–83 and Dugard, *Human Rights* 18–19.

[13] Dugard, *Human Rights*, above n 11, 19.

[14] *Cassim and Solomon v The State* (1892) 9 *Cape Law Journal* 58.

[15] Hahlo and Kahn, *The Union of South Africa*, above n 12, 108–09.

[16] Dugard, *Human Rights*, above n 11, 19.

Thus, even this early experiment with constitutionalism was tainted with the distinctions of racial citizenship that came to dominate later constitutional law and practice.

The attempt in 1892, by Chief Justice JG Kotze in the High Court of the South African Republic, to review the constitutionality of legislation was grounded in the Constitution's formulation of legislative power being granted by the people.[17] With repeated references to the United States Supreme Court's reasoning in *Marbury v Madison,* Chief Justice Kotze argued that as sovereignty vested in the people of the Republic and not the legislature (*Volksraad*), it was the court's duty to strike down legislation incompatible with the fundamental law of the Constitution (*Grondwet*).[18] This attempt to exercise the power of constitutional review in *Brown v Leyds NO*,[19] however, threw the state into crisis as President Kruger secured an emergency resolution of the legislature declaring that 'the judges had not and never had had the testing right'.[20] As the crisis deepened, President Kruger dismissed the Chief Justice. At the swearing-in ceremony of the new Chief Justice, he warned the judges not to follow the devil's way, as 'the testing right is a principle of the devil', which the devil had introduced into paradise to test God's word.[21]

Although the Union Constitution of 1909 followed the English tradition of adopting parliamentary sovereignty, the legislature was not completely free of external restraints. Until passage of the Statute of Westminster by the British Parliament in 1931, the Colonial Laws Validity Act of 1865 continued in theory to restrict the sovereignty of the Union Parliament. Even after the Dominium Parliaments received their independence from Britain, the South African Parliament remained bound, at least procedurally, by the entrenched clauses of the 1910 Union Constitution. While the significance of entrenchment was weakened by the removal of African voters from the common voters roll in 1936,[22] it was the constitutional struggle over the removal of 'coloured' voters that

[17] See Hahlo and Kahn, *The Union of South Africa*, above n 12, 91

[18] Dugard, *Human Rights*, above n 11, 21. See *Brown v Leyds NO* (1897) 4 Off Rep 17.

[19] *Brown v Leyds NO*, above n 17.

[20] Hahlo and Kahn, *The Union of South Africa*, above n 12, 108–09.

[21] Dugard, *Human Rights*, above n 11, 24.

[22] Native Representation Act 12 of 1936. While the Act was challenged in *Ndlwana v Hofmeyr NO & others*, 1937 AD 229, the courts refused to intervene.

secured Parliament's dominance over the Constitution.[23] The survival of
the entrenched language clause, guaranteeing the equality of English and
Afrikaans, was more a symbolic restraint than an effective constitutional
entrenchment. In effect, equal language rights relied more on a political
consensus among whites.

The rise of parliamentary sovereignty, over even the limited entrenchment of the Cape franchise, was finally secured with the adoption of the
1961 Republican Constitution.[24] From the passage of the South Africa
Amendment Act in 1958,[25] which provided that '[n]o court of law shall be
competent to enquire into or to pronounce upon the validity of any law
passed by Parliament' other than those effecting the surviving language
clause, government was determined to secure the primacy of parliamentary sovereignty. Prime Minister Verwoerd rejected calls for the adoption
of an entrenched bill of rights by the Natal Provincial Council, stating that
it would be unthinkable as 'no suggestion was made as to how rights
could be effectively guaranteed without sacrificing the sovereignty of
Parliament'.[26] Section 59 of the 1961 Republican Constitution specifically incorporated the language of the South Africa Amendment Act, thus
constitutionalising the courts' exclusion from substantive review and
explicitly limiting any judicial review over substantive legislative enact-
ments to those effecting the language clause guaranteeing the equality of
English and Afrikaans. As if to emphasise this ascendance, s 59(1) stated
that 'Parliament shall be the sovereign legislative authority in and over the
Republic, and shall have full power to make laws for the peace, order and
good government of the Republic'.

Despite these obviously substantive criteria for the passage of legitimate laws and their earlier resistance, the courts recognised that the will
of a racially exclusive Parliament was to be paramount. The crude logic of
this unrestrained conception of parliamentary sovereignty is summed up
in an earlier decision of the Appellate Division in *Sachs v Minister of Justice;
Diamond v Minister of Justice*, in which Acting Chief Justice Stratford stated
that

[23] The Separate Representation of Voters Act 46 of 1951, was challenged in
Minister of the Interior v Harris 1952 (4) SA 769 (A). See also Dugard, *Human Rights*,
above n 10, 30–31.

[24] Republic of South Africa Constitution Act 32 of 1961.

[25] South Africa Act Amendment Act 1 of 1958.

[26] E Kahn, *The New Constitution*, being a supplement to The Union of South Africa,
above n 12, (London, Stevens, 1962) 2.

arguments are sometimes advanced which do seem to me to ignore the plain principle that Parliament may make any encroachment it chooses upon the life, liberty or property of any individual subject to its sway, and that it is the function of the courts of law to enforce its will.[27]

This doctrine's impact on human rights and its 'debasement of the South African legal system' are now part of the history of apartheid.[28]

iii. Reformed Apartheid's 1983 'Tricameral' Constitution

In the face of increasing internal resistance and international isolation, the South African government looked in the late 1970s to the political reincorporation of the Indian and coloured communities as a means of broadening its social base. The outcome of this policy shift was the adoption of the 1983 Constitution, which extended the franchise to 'Indians' and 'coloureds' in a tricameral legislature with its jurisdiction distributed according to a vague distinction between 'own' and 'general' affairs. Two mechanisms ensured, however, that power remained safely in the hands of the dominant white party. First, the running of government was effectively centralised under an executive state president with extraordinary powers in both the executive and legislative arenas. Second, all significant decisions within the legislature—such as the election of the president—would be automatically resolved by the 4:2:1 ratio of white, coloured and Indian representatives, which ensured that even if the 'Indian' and 'coloured' Houses of Parliament voted in unison, the will of the 'white' House would prevail. The exclusion of the African majority from this scheme and resistance from within the targeted Indian and coloured communities meant that the 1983 Constitution was practically stillborn. The escalation of resistance and rebellion that began in late 1984 and led to the imposition of repeated states of emergency from mid-1985 sealed its fate.

B. Legal Continuity and Historical Legacies

The origins of the 1996 Constitution are embedded in South Africa's political transition. When political negotiations began in public in early

---

[27] *Sachs v Minister of Justice* 1934 AD 11, 37.
[28] See Dugard, *Human Rights*, above n 11, 36.

1990 the different political parties and movements in South Africa held different assumptions about how to create and structure a post-apartheid state. On the one hand, the apartheid government was committed to remaining in control of the transition to democracy. It continued for some time to argue that the future political dispensation should protect the interests of minorities—conceived in ethnic and racial terms—by means of guaranteed participation at all levels of government with the necessary powers, including veto rights, to protect their perceived interests. On the other hand, the ANC and its allies in the liberation movement demanded the establishment of an interim government and insisted that a future Constitution be the product of a democratically elected Constituent Assembly. Other parties and sectors within the society made different claims, including an editorial in the main Sunday newspaper, the *Sunday Times*, which called for a slightly modified replica of the US Constitution and the demand by the Inkatha Freedom Party (IFP) that a new Constitution be produced by an 'independent' panel of experts and adopted by a simple majority in a national referendum. In pursuing their various objectives the parties offered different rationales, which drew on both philosophical and historical arguments and were influenced by—or attempted to align with—the emerging post-Cold War international political culture of democratic constitutionalism.

The resolution of these debates was embedded in the politics of struggle and violent confrontation that continued throughout the first phase of South Africa's political transition. In addition, key elements of these debates had a profound impact on the process, structure and content of the 1996 Constitution. Perhaps most significantly, the debate over legal continuity on the one hand, and the need to address the historical legacies of colonialism and apartheid on the other hand, had a profound influence on the final product. Implicit in the Harare Declaration—the document adopted by the liberation committee of the Organisation of African Unity in 1988 as the basic preconditions for South Africa's re-admittance into the international community—was the assumption that there would be a radical break with the old regime. This process was similar to other negotiated processes of decolonisation, where an interim government would take power and supervise the emergence of a post-apartheid democratic government. This, after all, was what had happened in the transition to democracy in Zimbabwe. There the British sent Lord Soames to assume control of the government in Harare, from the Ian Smith/Abel Muzorewa regime, and to prepare the country for democratic elections.

The leadership of the ANC, supported by street demonstrations and other forms of mass action, continued to demand that an interim government be created as the first step in a democratic transition. Yet a number of lawyers and activists in the ANC began to question whether an interim government—with Mandela at the helm but with little power to address the legacies of apartheid and no clear date set for democratic elections—would not, in fact, allow the old regime, through its effective control of state institutions, to continue to control the pace and form of the transition to democracy.

The idea of legal continuity played an understated yet significant role in this debate. While liberation movement politicians and the general population saw no difficulty in making a clean break with the past, the lawyers (even within the liberation movement) soon grasped the significance of the regime's demand that there be legal continuity within the existing legal framework. This was a clear attempt to assert control over the transition by arguing that any new legal dispensation would have to be legally adopted by the existing institutions of the apartheid state, including the tricameral constitution that had been soundly rejected by the majority of South Africans since its adoption in 1983. On the other hand, it was clear to the lawyers that economic and political stability during the transition required some recognition of existing legal rights and duties. Thus, they recognised the need for some form of legal continuity in the democratic transition. In fact, on closer examination, it is clear that despite popular notions that the act of decolonisation involved a legal break with the past, the formal transfer of power on decolonisation often included agreements to recognise all existing law until such time as the new government made the requisite statutory amendments that would change the law. Exceptions to this include those countries in which there was a genuine revolutionary overthrow of the ancien regime, such as the 1917 Revolution in Russia, or the assumption of power by the Front for the Liberation of Mozambique (FRELIMO) in neighbouring Mozambique in 1974. Legal continuity could not be avoided; however, the implications of this principle and agreement on how it should be implemented remained an important aspect of the ongoing negotiations.

Two different aspects of the transition highlight the nature of the debate over legal continuity. First, there was the question of how a future Constitution would be created and adopted, a problem often framed in debates over Constitution-making as a distinction between 'constituted power' (*pouvoir constitué*) and 'constituent power' (*pouvoir constituant*).

Second, many activists and lawyers in the liberation movement began to argue that the need for legal continuity could not be used to set the legacies of apartheid in stone, particularly the existing allocation of land rights, which had been racially determined by law since the enactment of the 1913 Land Act, and which had resulted in the forcible dispossession of millions of black landholders. It was the need to resolve these tensions that led to the parties eventually embracing a two-stage democratic transition. This solution involved the adoption of a negotiated interim Constitution, which would itself provide for both a democratically elected government and a process through which a legitimate constituent body would produce a final Constitution.

While the outcome of negotiations produced a path for the opposing parties to preserve legal continuity and to begin to address the legacies of apartheid, any history of the negotiations must reflect both the ongoing violent confrontations that characterised this period as well as the various attempts by different parties to force through their own interpretations of agreements or even to override the negotiations and impose their own outcomes. The parties agreed in principle at the first formal negotiations for a new political dispensation, the Convention for a Democratic South Africa (CODESA) in December 1991, that there would be a united South Africa. However, they continued to hold diametrically opposed visions of the implications of this principle right up to the weeks prior to the first democratic elections in April 1994. For the apartheid regime and its various allies, those areas of South Africa that had been granted 'independence' as part of the 'homeland' policy, would have to agree to become part of the new South Africa. The ANC and its allies noted, however, that these entities had never achieved international recognition and that the right to self-determination belonged to all South Africans within the internationally recognised boundaries of the Union of South Africa that had been formed in 1910.

In a similar fashion, the debate over the legacy of apartheid became focused, in this early period, on one major issue: the question of land. The struggle against forced removals had in the last years of apartheid evolved into a return-to-the-land movement in which communities not only resisted their forcible removal from their lands but also began to claim rights of return. This struggle was characterised by active community resistance and the use of law and negotiations by progressive lawyers aligned with these communities. Sensitive to increasing global condemnation, the regime declared a moratorium on further forced removals in the late 1980s, yet continued to try to force communities to agree to reset-tlement. In the early 1990s this policy evolved into an attempt by the regime to 'resolve' the land question before a democratic government could take office. In 1991, the regime formally repealed the 1913 Land Acts and attempted to provide limited compensation or alternative land as a means to settle ongoing conflicts that threatened to undermine its claim that any new legal order must guarantee the existing rights of all property holders. Legal continuity here threatened to consolidate the unjust distributions of colonialism and apartheid and thus provided the grounds upon which the very notion of legal continuity could be chal-lenged. It was only with the acceptance of the principle of restitution of lands that had been lost due to racially discriminatory law, by all sides in the negotiations, that it became possible to accept that there could be both legal continuity and some redress of the legacies of apartheid. Restitution of land, limited to land lost in the period between 1913 and 1994, was a major compromise for the liberation movement, but also pro-vided the avenue through which a legally legitimate demand for redress could continue to be made in the ongoing Constitution-making process.

III. POLITICAL CONTEXT

While historical context is key to understanding the legal and social land-scape into which the new Constitution was born, it is also important to outline the political context that gave rise to the new constitutional dis-pensation. Despite an extraordinary history of early state-building among indigenous and colonial communities—from the rise of the Zulu Kingdom in the nineteenth century to the formation of a secession of Griqua and Boer states in which excluded and Creole communities within colonial society formed their own political communities beyond the authority of the dominant colonising power—the history of twentieth-century South Africa presents a relatively stable set of significant political groupings. From the creation of the Union of South Africa in 1910, in which the newly defeated Boer Republics of the Free State and the South African Republic or Transvaal and the two former British colonies of Natal and the Cape were brought together under a Constitution passed by the British Parliament, only a few political parties and movements have dominated the political arena. Although each of these represents a fairly complex political history of it own, the main political forces that engaged in the protracted conflict that shaped South Africa in the twentieth century represented a few distinct social forces: African nationalism, Afrikaner nationalism and parties who to a greater or lesser extent represented capital and labour.

The oldest African nationalist party on the continent is the ANC, formed as the South African Native National Congress in 1912 to unite Africans and oppose both the racially discriminatory clauses of the 1910 Union Constitution as well as the impending restrictions on land ownership contained in what would become the 1913 Land Act. While the ANC would in its early years send delegations to London and petition for inclusion in the political system, it was slowly transformed into an active opposition, making increasing demands for democratic rights and then adopting tactics of passive resistance to government policies in the 1950s. After the government banned the ANC and the breakaway Pan Africanist Congress in 1960, the liberation movements took up arms and organised in exile to challenge the government's apartheid policies. Although the arrest and imprisonment of Nelson Mandela and the leaders of the ANC's armed wing, Umkhonto we Sizwe, disrupted the armed campaign, the ANC was able to recover and to lead the struggle against apartheid in a close alliance with the South African Communist Party. Taking advantage of the Soweto student uprising in 1976, the ANC was reinvigorated by thousands of youth who had grown up in the Black Consciousness movement of the early 1970s, and as a result, the ANC emerged as the dominant force of black opposition to the apartheid regime.

Adopting tactics of mass mobilisation and ungovernability in the 1980s, the ANC brought increasing pressure on the government and, despite growing violence, initiated negotiations with business and government as the Cold War drew to an end. The release of Nelson Mandela and the repeal of the banning of the ANC, among other black political groups in February 1990, marked the beginning of South Africa's political transition from apartheid. Since its victory in the 1994 election, the ANC has been the dominant political force in South Africa, winning increasingly large percentages in each democratic election despite increasing internal tensions within its alliance with the Communist Party and the Congress of South African Trade Unions. The victory of Jacob Zuma over President Thabo Mbeki at the ANC's national conference in December 2007—and the subsequent removal of Mbeki from office— led to a struggle for the soul of the ANC and a dramatic split in the waning months of 2008. While the new split-away party, named the Congress of the People (COPE), is competing for the historic legacy of the ANC, the ANC's control of government and status as the party of liberation seems to guarantee its electoral advantage into the 2009 national elections and beyond. However, this fracturing of the ANC might reduce the party's overwhelming dominance of post-apartheid politics and provide space for the emergence of a more dynamic democracy in South Africa.

The second major political force in South Africa's twentieth-century history was Afrikaner nationalism, which became embodied in the emergence and political dominance of the National Party over the state in the period between 1948 and 1994. While the antecedents of Afrikaner nationalism may be traced to the Boer Republics and the construction of a racially based alliance between white labour and organised agricultural interests, the key issue of the 1948 election was the so-called 'colour question'. Jan Smut's ruling United Party 'fought the 1948 election on the mildly reformist but ambiguous proposals of the Native Laws Commission . . . for the "parallel" development of white and black interests',[29] a policy that sought to control black labour but recognised the inevitability of African urbanisation. In contrast, the National Party advocated for 'apartheid', promising to expel Africans from the cities and to ensure that black labour 'be admitted to the urban areas only as temporary employees obliged to return to their homes after the expiry of their employment'.[30] While the National Party did not win a majority of votes, the electoral systems weighting in favour of rural votes—by as much as 30 per cent—as a result of a constitutional compromise in the 1910 Union Constitution, gave the nationalist alliance, the National Party and the Afrikaner Party, a slim majority in Parliament. Founded in 1914, the National Party first ruled South Africa as part of a 'pact' government with the Labour Party from 1924–34. However, the reconstructed National Party of 1948 was imbued with a new ideological vision that brought together a redefined Afrikaner nationalism in the form of 'Christian-nationalism', with an explicitly racist vision of 'apartheid' and a commitment to 'anti-communism' that drew on the mounting tensions of the Cold War.

While the Apartheid regime was forced over time to modify its initial vision of apartheid, including adoption of the idea of 'separate

---

[29] D O'Meara, *Forty Lost Years: The Apartheid State and the Politics of the National Party, 1948–1994* (Randburg, South Africa, Ravan Press; Athens: Ohio University Press, 1996) 32.

[30] Sauer Report, quoted in O'Meara, *Forty Lost Years* 35.

development' in response to decolonisation across Africa, the fundamental premise of apartheid—that power should be used to secure the future of the Afrikaner nation—remained intact until the end. As it struggled to implement its vision, the apartheid regime embraced both racial and ethnic categories and attempted to balkanise the country through the creation of ten tribal 'homelands', four of which were granted 'independence'. At the same time, the apartheid regime constructed a system of laws that dictated, on the basis of race, every aspect of the lives of South Africa's inhabitants. The effect was to exclude the vast majority of people from living productive lives. The individual, communal and social consequences of the apartheid system would lead in time to its recognition as a crime against humanity. Despite begin forced into negotiations that led to the demise of the apartheid system, the National Party continued to deny that its policies were intended to cause the harm that apartheid inflicted on its victims. And while support for the party dissolved in the new South Africa, its leadership remained committed to retaining some access to political power. With the collapse of its vision of a consociational dispensation in which groups would retain a political veto over issues affecting them, the National Party accepted the idea of a Government of National Unity (GNU) in which they expected to retain significant political power. When Mandela's government failed to accord former President FW de Klerk the authority he expected as Deputy President, the National Party withdrew from the GNU. After losing even more support at the polls in 2004 and then failing in its attempt to form an anti-ANC alliance, the National Party negotiated for its leadership to be integrated into the government; the party formally joined the ANC and dissolved itself in 2007.

No other political parties achieved the same levels of public support and power as the ANC and the National Party in twentieth-century South Africa. However, a number of smaller parties have played significant public roles, including the small, white parliamentary opposition; the Communist Party; right-wing splits from the National Party; and finally the IFP, which emerged out of Inkatha YaKwaZulu, a Zulu cultural movement that was first formed in the 1920s and revived by Chief Gatsha Buthelezi as head of the KwaZulu 'homeland' administration in 1975. When it was first revived, using the colours and uniform of the passive resistance or 'Defiance Campaign' volunteers of the ANC in the 1950s, there was an assumption that Chief Buthelezi's refusal to accept 'independence' for the KwaZulu 'homeland' and the revival of Inkatha indicated some relationship with the banned ANC. Although there was some contact between Gatsha Buthelezi and Oliver Tambo, the leader of the ANC in exile, strategic differences over the armed struggle, economic sanctions and the emergence of the United Democratic Front—a legal front for the anti-apartheid movement formed in opposition to the 1983 'tricameral' Constitution—led to increasingly violent conflict between the IFP and UDF/ANC supporters. While this conflict was most brutal in the rural areas and towns of Natal, leaving more than 15,000 dead from the early 1980s until after the 1994 election, the inclusion of Buthelezi in the GNU and the acceptance by the ANC that the IFP would form the first post-apartheid administration in the province of KwaZulu-Natal brought an end to the violence. With an ANC electoral victory in KwaZulu-Natal in 2004 the IFP faced increasing internal fragmentation, leaving it now, more than ever, a regional party.

IV. CONCLUSION: CONTEXT, CONTINUITY AND THE PROBLEM OF PATH DEPENDENCY

A contextual understanding of South Africa's Constitution must be rooted in a perspective that recognises the impact of history as well as the effect of present conditions on the building of a constitutional democracy since 1994. While the history of colonialism, apartheid and exploitation have left a legacy of social and economic depravity, the experience of resistance, democratic struggle and institutional state capacity provided grounds for hope as the society came together in the aftermath and glow of the 1994 elections. The South African context is thus laden with inherent contradictions and alternate sources of hope and pessimism. Legal continuity provided a sense of institutional stability and a source of continuing tension as the new society inherited the distribution of accumulated legal rights and injustices. South African law, in particular, represents both the old and the new in this process of transformation. Just as the 1996 Constitution contains the hopes and aspirations of the majority of South Africans, the embrace of constitutionalism and the rule of law means that the processes for fulfilling these dreams will be shaped by the encrusted processes and encumbered resources that make up the South African legal tradition.

Already there is a debate over whether the democratic transition was in some way determined by a path dependency rooted in the depth of legal tradition in the country.[31] Notions of legal continuity and theories of path dependency—as well as the practices and traditions of the legal profession—may account, in part, for the role of law in South African society. Yet it is important to understand the law and the Constitution as parts of a broader historical and social context. Although the prevalence of lawyers in senior political positions may explain some of those leaders' trust in legal solutions, it is important that our understanding of the role of law does not ignore the extraordinary history of social and political struggle, both domestic and global, that led to and forced through the dramatic social and political changes that characterise the democratic transition in South Africa. It is precisely these social realities that continue to provide the context for the South African Constitution.

FURTHER READING

Chanock, Martin, *The Making of South African Legal Culture 1902–1936: Fear, Favour and Prejudice* (Cambridge, Cambridge University Press, 2001)

Dugard, John, *Human Rights and the South African Legal Order* (Princeton, NJ, Princeton University Press, 1978)

O'Meara, Dan, *Forty Lost Years: The Apartheid State and the Politics of the National Party, 1948–1994* (Randburg, South Africa, Ravan Press; Athens: Ohio University Press, 1996)

Ross, R, *A Concise History of South Africa* (Cambridge, Cambridge University Press, 1999)

Sparks, Allister, *The Mind of South Africa* (London, Mandarin Paperbacks, 1991)

---

[31] See generally, J Meierhenrich, *The Legacies of Law: Long-Run Consequences of Legal Development in South Africa, 1652–2000* (Cambridge, Cambridge University Press, 2008).

2

Democratic Transition

———❦———

Introduction – Negotiating the 1993 Interim Constitution – The Role
of Law in the Democratic Transition – The Practice of Transitional
Law – Conclusion: Transitional Law, Democratisation and Justice

I. INTRODUCTION

SOUTH AFRICA ACHIEVED democratic transition via a
two-stage process of Constitution-making. The first stage, from
approximately February 1990 to April 1994, was buffeted by ongoing violence and protests, yet the process remained ultimately under the
control of the main negotiating parties.[1] In contrast, the second stage,
from the time of the elections until the adoption of the final Constitution
at the end of 1996, was formally constrained by a complex set of constitutional principles contained in the interim Constitution.[2] This stage was
driven by an elected Constitutional Assembly made up of a joint-sitting of
the National Assembly and the Senate of South Africa's first democratic
Parliament.[3] While South Africa's first national elections in April 1994
marked the end of apartheid and the coming into force of the 1993
interim Constitution, it took another five years before the 1999 elections
swept away the last transitional arrangements at the local level, replacing

[1] See H Klug, 'Participating in Constitution-making: South African Aspirations and
Realities' in P Andrews and S Ellmann (eds), *The Post-Apartheid Constitutions: Perspectives
on South Africa's Basic Law* (Johannesburg, University of the Witwatersrand Press;
Athens, Ohio University Press, 2001). See also H Klug, *Constituting Democracy: Law,
Globalism and South Africa's Political Reconstruction* (Cambridge, Cambridge University
Press, 2000).
[2] See Constitutional Principles, Schedule 4, Constitution of the Republic of South
Africa Act 200 of 1993 [hereinafter 1993 interim Constitution].
[3] 1993 interim Constitution s 68.

them with the first democratically elected local governments under the final 1996 Constitution. The 1999 election also marked the setting of the Sunset Clauses, which had provided numerous guarantees to the old order—including a five-year government of national unity and job security for apartheid-era government officials—and facilitated the democratic transition. Even then, the transition effectively took another three years before the amnesty process, initiated by the Promotion of National Unity and Reconciliation Act, formally concluded in March 2002.

Before focusing on the constitutional products of this historical process it is useful to reflect for a moment on the specific political history of the years immediately before the parties reached agreement on the process to hold a democratic election and adopt a Constitution. These years—from the unbanning of the ANC until the agreement on an election date and an interim Constitution—were dominated by uncertainty and violence. From the moment State President F W de Klerk announced the repeal of the ban on the ANC and other political parties on 2 February 1990, the negotiations process was torn between conflicting demands. The liberation movements demanded the levelling of the political playing field, while the National Party government refused to dismantle the apartheid 'bantustans' (the 10 political enclaves created by the apartheid regime in an attempt to provide separate 'homelands' for the African majority) and insisted on remaining in control of the transition process. Even while negotiations continued, the armed wing of the Pan Africanist Congress launched a series of terror attacks on white civilians including a church in Cape Town and a golf course clubhouse in the Eastern Cape. And violence between Inkatha Freedom Party (IFP) supporters and ANC members continued unabated in parts of the country.

In the early stage of the negotiations, the ANC relied upon the Harare Declaration, an internationally adopted statement that required the apartheid regime to release all political prisoners; unban political organisations; remove military personnel from the black townships; cease political executions; end the state of emergency and repeal all legislation designed to circumscribe political activity. In a series of talks, beginning with the Groote Schuur meeting in May 1990, the ANC engaged in direct negotiations with the government to secure the implementation of the Harare preconditions. These agreements enabled the ANC to begin to re-establish a legal presence in the country as part of the process towards the normalisation of political activity. However, by December 1990—when the ANC held its first legal consultative conference in South Africa in more than 30 years—its fast-expanding legal membership reacted sharply to the rising violence directed by clandestine government forces and IFP hostel dwellers against black township communities.

At first, it seemed that the ANC leadership would respond to the pressure from its membership and demand an end to the violence as an added precondition to negotiations. It soon became clear from the pattern of violence that coincided with ANC initiatives that if an end to violence were an additional precondition to negotiations, the apartheid state would be in a stronger position to exert control over the transition. As a result, the ANC decided to take the initiative. It advanced its own plan for the transition to democracy. This plan included calling for an all-party conference; the establishment of an interim government; and holding elections for a constituent assembly to draw up a new Constitution. This plan envisaged a separate election for a democratic government once a new Constitution was adopted. At the same time, debate over the nature of the transition began to take place within the ANC. Some members began to ask whether the ANC wanted to see Nelson Mandela and other senior ANC leaders made responsible for administering the apartheid state with no ability to make substantive changes, while negotiations continued without a clear timetable or end point. In response, the National Party government argued that legal continuity was essential and that any negotiated agreements had to be legally adopted by the undemocratic tricameral Parliament as required by the existing 1983 Constitution.

With the convening of multi-party talks, at the Convention for a Democratic South Africa (CODESA) in late 1991, it seemed as if the transition process was well underway. In fact, opinions converged on a number of fundamental issues. The ANC and the government agreed on the need to establish a multi-party democracy in a united South Africa with an entrenched Bill of Rights to be adjudicated by a special constitutional tribunal. Substantive negotiations began in February 1992 with the convening of CODESA's five working groups. The working groups set out to discuss the following issues: the reincorporation of the four 'bantustans' given independence under apartheid, Transkei, Bophuthatswana, Ciskei and Venda; the creation of a transitional government to lead the country to democracy; the establishment of a set of constitutional principles; a method for drafting and adopting a new Constitution and the creation of a climate guaranteeing free political activity.

However, it soon became clear that the convergence in language masked deep differences and a clear strategy by the government to retain control of the process of transition and thus to project the power of the ruling National Party and its allies into the future through constitutional gerrymandering. Although CODESA's founding declaration included a commitment to a united South Africa, the government soon interpreted this to mean merely maintaining South Africa's internationally recognised 1910 borders. As a prerequisite to agreement on the nature of a future Constitution-making body, the government began to insist there be prior agreement that any future Constitution be premised on a strictly federal system of government based on the balkanisation of the country into a number of all-but-independent regions. It was this insistence on 'federalism' as a precondition to the creation of a democratically elected constituent assembly —and the demand that a new Constitution be adopted by 75 per cent of the proportionally elected Constitution-making body, as well as 75 per cent of the regionally elected delegates—that led to the failure of the second plenary session of CODESA in May 1992.

The response of the ANC, its allies in the labour movement and the South African Communist Party was to mobilise supporters in a campaign of mass action to demand a democratically elected constituent assembly. However, as had occurred so many times before, the ANC initiative was met with an upsurge of violent attacks on communities, culminating in the Boipatong massacre. In response, the ANC announced a formal suspension of multi-party negotiations and demanded that the government take action to halt the escalating violence. For example, the ANC noted that the government was still holding more than 300 political prisoners, in contravention of earlier agreements, and had made no effort to ban the carrying of lethal weapons by its allied parties. Inkatha, in particular, insisted that its members had a right to carry 'traditional' Zulu weapons even though its supporters were regularly implicated in attacks on ANC-supporting communities, including the Boipatong killings.

After the two-day general strike in early August 1992, it seemed that the state was ready to make concessions in order to encourage the ANC to reopen negotiations, including accepting international observers and expanding the Peace Accord structures, which were designed to address violent conflict within individual communities. Despite these concessions, the government still refused to accept a democratically controlled Constitution-making body. As evidence emerged of the government's role in political assassinations, it demanded a general amnesty, without the need to document or accept specific responsibility for particular acts. The ANC rejected the government's response and intensified its mass-action campaign to ensure free political activity in those areas—bantustans and right-wing white towns—where local administrations continued to suppress ANC organisation. This situation revealed two continuing sources of opposition to the negotiated settlement internal to the main negotiating parties. First, it revealed the government's duplicity in insisting that apartheid had been abolished while continuing to sustain apartheid's bantustan system and denying responsibility for the lack of free political activity in the areas controlled by its allies. Second, within the ANC, an element emerged comprised of people who believed that free political activity would create conditions for a more direct revolution, modelled on the popular demonstrations that had brought down the government in East Germany—termed the Leipzig option.

The ANC mass-action campaign gained momentum. Its participants demanded the adoption of an amendment to the 1983 Constitution, in the form of a proposed 'Transition to Democracy Act', which presented a detailed scheme to establish an interim government and a democratically elected Constitution-making body. More than four million workers participated in a two-day general strike in early August 1992. This action encouraged the ANC to focus on those areas of the country where bantustan administrations—the puppet regimes established by the South African government as part of its apartheid policy—engaged in widespread repression of ANC organisation. Designed to ensure free political activity, this part of the campaign focused first on the military administration in the nominally independent Ciskei bantustan. On 7 September 1992, more than 20,000 ANC members marched into the deadly machine-gun fire of the Ciskei security forces, leaving 28 dead and nearly 200 injured. The massacre of ANC demonstrators at Bisho was the final nail in the coffin of the first round of multi-party negotiations. However, the international response made it clear that the government could no longer deny responsibility for the violence its allies wrought. And within the ANC, the voices that suggested mass action could lead to a non-violent insurrection and takeover—like the one that brought down the Berlin wall—went silent.

With the negotiations on the brink of collapse yet again, the ANC and National Party government were pushed to reach agreement in the Record of Understanding on 26 September 1992, setting the scene for the creation of a new negotiating process. The key elements of this agreement were the National Party's concession regarding an elected constituent assembly and the ANC's acceptance of a government of national unity under a transitional Constitution. By accepting a democratic Constitution-making process, the National Party made it possible for the ANC to agree to the adoption of a negotiated interim Constitution, which would entrench a government of national unity for five years and ensure the legal continuity the National Party government required. The architecture of this agreement, reflecting continuity and change, allowed the multi-party negotiations—which eventually became known as the Multi-Party Negotiating Forum—to resume at the World Trade Centre outside Johannesburg in early 1993. The assassination of ANC and Communist Party leader Chris Hani by a white right-winger in April 1993 put the country again on the edge of the abyss and in many ways marked the moment when de Klerk's government realised it could no longer assert control over the transition and needed to build a working relationship with Nelson Mandela and the ANC.

The process of negotiations that followed led to the adoption in December 1993 of an interim Constitution, which came into force with the country's first democratic election in April 1994. This interim Constitution provided for the creation of a final Constitution within two years from the first sitting of the newly elected National Assembly. These provisions required that at least two-thirds of all the members of the Constitutional Assembly vote for the new Constitution. In addition, sections of a final Constitution that dealt with the boundaries, powers and functions of the provinces had to be adopted by two-thirds of all the members of the regionally constituted Senate. Once the new legislature, with both houses sitting together as a Constitutional Assembly, agreed on a draft it would have to submit it to a proposed Constitutional Court for certification. This process required the Constitutional Court to certify that the provisions of the final Constitution were substantially in accordance with the constitutional principles agreed upon during the multi-party negotiations and enshrined in Schedule Four of the interim Constitution. Only then would the final Constitution be promulgated as law. In fact, at first, the Constitutional Court declined to certify the text of the draft Constitution; it was only certified once the Constitutional Assembly amended the draft. The interim Constitution had made elaborate provision, through a series of deadlock-breaking devices, for the possibility that the Constitutional Assembly would fail to achieve sufficient consensus to reach the required two-thirds vote. However, the threat these provisions contained—in terms of delay and an eventual reduction of the threshold from two-thirds to 60 per cent—helped ensure that a spirit of eventual compromise endured.

II. NEGOTIATING THE 1993 INTERIM CONSTITUTION

Faced with the consequences—social upheaval, mass action and escalating violence—of a failed CODESA, the negotiating parties entered into a series of bilateral negotiations, which came together again to form a multi-party negotiating forum. This body thrashed out the interim Constitution that came into effect on 27 April 1994, as South Africans took part in their first-ever exercise of non-racial democracy. The assassination of Chris Hani—and the resultant mass outpouring of grief and anger—galvanised the negotiating process, providing a glimpse of the consequences that might flow from a failure to reach agreement. Having agreed to reopen multi-party negotiations at a multi-party planning conference on 5 and 6 March 1993, the parties refused to allow the right-wing assassins to achieve their aim of shattering the already-brittle negotiations process. Instead, they appealed in the name of Hani for heightened efforts to achieve a settlement.[4]

Unlike the failed CODESA talks—where negotiations were conducted between party representatives in the different working groups—the new process provided for a Negotiating Council to discuss and decide upon reports from technical committees, which would clarify and present alternatives and issues for negotiation. In addition, a 10-person planning committee was responsible for keeping the process on track by structuring the debates and dealing with grievances. Dominated by academics and lawyers, the technical committees facilitated the emergence of clear alternatives. However, a range of participants and parties from within and outside the multi-party talks remained suspicious of the 'professionalisation' of an essentially political process. Nevertheless, the process, focused as it was on the production of written proposals, gained in momentum, despite often-severe criticism of the technical committees' initial proposals and active intervention through the Negotiating Council and public debate. Although they were sent back to be reworked to reconsider their 'technical' inputs, the series of reports that flowed from the committees slowly crystallised the position of the Negotiating Council.

While the decision-making within the process remained tied to the 'sufficient consensus' formula of CODESA, even the parties who had

---

[4] See, A Sparks, *Tomorrow Is Another Country: The Inside Story of South Africa's Negotiated Revolution* (Sandton, Struik Book Distributors, 1994) 187–90.

resisted participation in CODESA (the Pan Africanist Congress and the Conservative Party) now recognised that there was no longer any alternative to a negotiated solution. Thus, the process stayed on track. The emergence of the Concerned South Africans Group (COSAG) and its subsequent transformation into the Freedom Alliance in October 1993 created a third 'rejectionist' power bloc—to rival the National Party and the ANC. Despite some awkward moments (for example, when white neo-fascist Afrikaner Weerstandsbeweging (AWB) members, who opposed the transition from apartheid, stormed the negotiating venue and assaulted a number of Inkatha delegates, among others) this alliance managed to threaten the election process and obtained a series of concessions from the major parties, the ANC and the National Party government, which went some way towards accepting the need to address ethnic concerns.

In the process of negotiating the 1993 Constitution there were significant changes in the positions of the major players as well as important continuities, which were cobbled together in the interim Constitution. Most fundamentally, the ANC's initial demand for a unitary state came to be interpreted to mean national sovereignty over the 1910 boundaries of South Africa rather than the initial concept of a central government with pre-emptive power over regional authorities. With this new emphasis, the issue of federalism—initially rejected by the ANC because of a fear that a federal structure would emasculate the central government, which needed to address the legacies of apartheid—became a central feature of the constitutional debate. By the time the Constitution was adopted by Parliament, the IFP and the white right-wing parties of the Freedom Alliance had walked out of the multi-party talks. The IFP was particularly concerned about the failure of the ANC and government sides to concede anything but concurrent legislative powers to the provinces. The attempt to address these concerns led to the amendment of the interim Constitution to grant regional legislatures powers of pre-emption over national legislation. It was only after the interim Constitution was amended a second time, however, entrenching the constitutional status of the Zulu King in KwaZulu-Natal, that the IFP agreed—within days of the polls' opening—to enter the electoral process.[5]

[5] See D Atkinson, 'Brokering a Miracle? The Multiparty Negotiating Forum' in S Friedman and D Atkinson (eds), *The Small Miracle: South Africa's Negotiated Settlement*, South African Review 7 (Johannesburg, Ravan Press, 1994) 13–43.

The consequences of this negotiated process were evident in the interim Constitution. In some instances this process led to the inclusion of rights unique to the South African transition, such as the right to economic activity and employers' rights to lock out workers in the context of collective bargaining. In other aspects, it led to a generous extension of rights and clarity of substantive issues: For example, it prohibited discrimination on the basis of sexual orientation; it contained a specific provision guaranteeing affirmative action programmes designed to enable full and equal enjoyment of rights; and it provided the right to restitution of dispossessed land rights. Other consequences included the incorporation of conflicting elements and conceptions of the constitutional structure being established. On the one hand, a tension existed between the guarantee of open and accountable government and the guarantee of existing civil service positions of bureaucrats whose training and professional culture had been opposed to openness and accountability. Other provisions empowered regions to establish their own Constitutions subject to the terms of the Constitution, while consociationalism was enforced at the local level. In addition, a *Volkstaat* Council was created whose constitutional mandate it was to consider the establishment of a 'white homeland' or *Volkstaat,* which its proponents would understand to be constitutionally autonomous from government at both the national and regional level. Furthermore, confusion about the comparative meaning of particular constitutional terms led, for example, to the inclusion of a standard of permissible expropriation—public purpose—less empowering of government action than what was intended. The technical committee had incorrectly reported that the public-purpose standard gave government more expansive powers of expropriation than the public-interest standard.[6] The outcome of this negotiated process was an interim Constitution that spliced together the different political and constitutional understandings of at least the three major power blocs engaged in the process. The effect was a Constitution that embraced competing constitutional traditions and principles.[7] While this process set the stage for vigorous debate over the true nature of the Constitution, these same tensions were extended into the next round of

[6] See M Chaskalson, 'Stumbling towards Section 28: Negotiations over Property Rights at the Multiparty Talks'(1995) 11 *South African Journal of Human Rights* 222, 237–38.

[7] See H Klug, 'Constitutional Law: Towards a New Constitutional Order' in (1993) *Annual Survey of South African Law* (Johannesburg, University of Witwatersrand) 19–28.

Constitution-making through the adoption of the Constitutional Principles set out in Schedule 4 to the interim Constitution, which guided the Constitutional Assembly in the writing of the final Constitution. Recognition of the importance of the Constitutional Principles deflected some of the different parties' concerns with the interim Constitution as they pressed to get their version of the future into Schedule 4.

III. THE ROLE OF LAW IN THE DEMOCRATIC TRANSITION

During a democratic transition, in addition to debates over a future constitutional system and how it is to be achieved, a more immediate set of problems arises concerning the way to create conditions for a democratic election. It is important to recognise that holding an election is both a necessary step towards the creation of a legitimate Constitution-making process as well as a determination of the relative support of the different parties. An election tends to ossify the demands of those who feel that they have a democratic right to their particular vision of the future or those who feel that they will lose all significant influence over the future dispensation when democratic institutions take power. Thus, the period of most negotiating flexibility is probably the period before the vote is cast; however, it is also the period in which the legitimacy of the whole process is most likely to be determined. As a result, the founders need to create a level political playing field to ensure free and fair elections and a means to assure the potential losers that they will earn a legitimate and sustainable place in the future democracy through their participation in the process. While various interim or transitional mechanisms may be adopted to serve the first of these goals, it is the creation and mutual acceptance of a set of common principles that paves the way towards the overall legitimacy needed to sustain a newly emergent democracy.

In the case of South Africa, there were two distinct levels to the first stage of the transition. First, the country adopted a number of transitional mechanisms—such as the Independent Electoral Commission and the Transitional Executive Council—that were geared to create a level political playing field for holding the first democratic elections. Second, there was an agreement to adopt an interim Constitution under which a government of national unity would rule the country while a final Constitution was negotiated and democracy extended through the reorganisation of regional government and the democratisation of local government. Even then, the final Constitution, produced by the democratically elected parliament sitting in joint session as a Constitutional Assembly, would have to conform to a set of constitutional principles agreed upon in the pre-election negotiations. Agreement on the principles and the terms of the transition was achieved in turn by adopting the notion of 'sufficient consensus', which meant that hold-out positions by smaller parties were overcome by agreement among the major opposing parties—in this case, the apartheid government and the ANC.

The legal adoption and institutional embodiment of each of these agreements and mechanisms provided the stepping stones towards each point in the process of democratisation as well as a sense of security among the participants. On the one hand, the majority was assured that the transition to democracy was becoming irreversible, while those who felt they were losing power began to recognise that the emerging legal framework was designed to guarantee the fundamental rights of all; therefore they held out the hope that they could sustain their own visions for achieving viable communal and individual goals. Crowning this process was agreement on an interim Constitution at the negotiating forum, which led to the adoption of the Constitution of the Republic of South Africa Act 200 of 1993 on 22 December 1993. The interim Constitution came into effect at one minute past midnight on Election Day, 27 April 1994, after being amended in March and again in April 1994, to guarantee the inclusion of the Inkatha Freedom Party. Although it was intended to be an interim Constitution with a life span of only five years, it effectively secured the final demise of the apartheid legal order and provided the basis for South Africa's first democratic elections.

A. Transitional Law

The legal transition was initiated by the adoption of four pieces of legislation establishing transitional institutions to guarantee a level political playing field. These statutes were initially approved by the Negotiating Council, and enacted by a special sitting of the existing tricameral Parliament in October 1993, thus guaranteeing the legal continuity the old regime demanded. The unravelling of the apartheid constitutional framework had begun with the abolition of the President's Council[8] (which had given the apartheid president effective legislative authority)

---

[8] In terms of the Constitution Amendment Act 82 of 1993.

and the amendment of the Self-Governing Territories Constitution Act[9] (which provided for the balkanisation of the country into ethnic 'home-lands'). Yet the formal shifting of legal authority away from the apartheid government only began with the passage of the Transitional Executive Council Act.[10] Together with the three other statutes passed at the same time—the Independent Electoral Commission Act,[11] the Independent Media Commission Act,[12] and the Independent Broadcasting Authority Act,[13]—the Transitional Executive Council Act provided the basis for a pre-constitutional order directed towards holding a democratic election and establishing the interim Constitution.

Of these statutes, only the Independent Broadcasting Authority (IBA) Act was designed to outlive the pre-constitutional transitional period. The IBA Act provided a system, independent of government or political party domination, for allocating and controlling the distribution and use of the broadcast and telecommunications frequency spectrum. It was designed to reverse a history of government-controlled media, maintain a diversity of views and expand the participation of those historically denied access to and control over broadcasting. And the statute explicitly furthers policies of local control, cultural diversity and the promotion of South African cultural products. The Authority is to achieve these goals through its control over the assignment and renewal of licenses. It is also empowered to issue a series of orders to licensees: to desist from particular actions; to take remedial action; and even to prohibit a licensee from broadcasting for a period up to 30 days.[14] Finally, the statute further strengthens the enforcement capacity of this new institution by providing for significant civil penalties.[15]

In contrast to the Independent Broadcasting Authority Act, the Independent Media Commission (IMC) Act was a specifically transitional device. The IMC was designed to ensure equal treatment of the different political parties taking part in the first non-racial democratic elections in order

[9] Revocation and Assignment of Powers of Self-Governing Territories Act 107 of 1993 and the Self-Governing Territories Constitutional Amendment Act 152 of 1993.

[10] Transitional Executive Council (TEC) Act 151 of 1993.

[11] Independent Electoral Commission (IEC) Act 150 of 1993.

[12] Independent Media Commission (IMC) Act 148 of 1993.

[13] Independent Broadcasting Authority (IBA) Act 153 of 1993.

[14] IBA Act, above n 13, s 66(1).

[15] IBA Act s 67.

to promote and contribute towards the creation of a climate favourable to free political participation and a free and fair election.[16]

In order to achieve this goal the Commission was directed to monitor two forms of media, the state-licensed or controlled broadcasting services and state-financed publications and information services. Appointed by the State President on the advice of the Transitional Executive Council,[17] the Commission was required to hear and adjudicate on complaints by political parties against any broadcasting licensee, publisher of a state-financed publication or state information service. After adjudicating a complaint the Commission had the power to order a specific response—including the broadcast of a particular political advertisement or party election broadcast or alternative version of a contentious programme—as well as the power to fine or suspend a broadcasting licensee. Unlike the Independent Broadcasting Authority, the commission had a limited life and dissolved at the completion and certification of the 'founding' election.

Although the National Party government rejected the ANC's demand for an interim government, the agreement to establish a Transitional Executive Council (TEC) constituted recognition of the fact that the government could not retain sole control over the transitional process. Providing for formal power-sharing over specific areas of governmental activity and outright authority over issues affecting the transition to a democratic order, the Transitional Executive Council Act allowed the negotiating parties access to the governing process without making them responsible for apartheid policies and programmes that were beyond their power to change. The TEC was constituted, in terms of section 4 of the Transitional Executive Council (TEC) Act, of all participants—governments, administrations and political groupings—in the multi-party negotiating process who wished to be represented. The TEC was directed to facilitate and promote the transition to democracy through the achievement of two primary goals: the creation and promotion of a climate of free political participation and the creation and promotion of conditions conducive to the holding of free and fair elections. Reflecting the significant contribution and success of women in the negotiating process, the Act specifically directed the TEC to have as one of its objects to

---

[16] IMC Act, above n 12, s 3.
[17] IMC Act, above n 12, s 4(2)(a).

ensure the full participation of women in the transitional and electoral structures and processes.[18]

The TEC mirrored, through its seven sub-councils, the most important government ministries and functions, thus enabling it to formally
monitor and intervene to the extent of its mandate in all the vital aspects
of governance. Among the TEC's specific powers and duties was the
power to order any government or administration under its jurisdiction
not to proceed with proposed legislation if it determined that such legislation would have an adverse effect on the TEC's objectives. This power
to issue 'desist orders' extended to any decision or action of any government, administration, political party or organisation that was a party to
the TEC. Although the IFP refused to take part in the TEC, section 21(1)
of the TEC Act made the Act applicable to all self-governing territories
regardless of the Self-Governing Territories Constitution Act 21 of 1971.
Thus, KwaZulu formally became subject to TEC oversight, despite the
KwaZulu administration's and the IFP's rejection of the TEC. In addition
to its monitoring and overseeing functions, the TEC was granted specific
powers to achieve particular transitional objectives. Section 16(10)(a)
empowered the TEC to establish and maintain a National Peacekeeping
Force. Envisioned as the nucleus of a future integrated defence force,
the National Peacekeeping Force was to bring together elements of all the
military formations under the control of the parties participating in the
TEC, with the purpose of furthering peace and public order in South
Africa. Furthermore, section 23 of the Act provided that any dispute
between the TEC or one of its sub-councils and any government, administration, political party or organisation was to be referred to the Special
Electoral Court, whose findings were final and binding and not subject to
further appeal.[19]

B. Preparing for Democratic Elections

Apart from the power-sharing devices designed to achieve a level
playing field in the political process leading up to the elections, the pre-
constitutional framework centred on two laws designed to manage the
election itself. The first of these was the Independent Electoral

[18] TEC Act, above n 10, 3(a)(iv).
[19] TEC Act s 23(5).

Commission (IEC) Act, which sought to remove the electoral process and authority for the verification of the elections from the sitting government. This approach was developed in response to the fear, among those who had been historically excluded from the vote, that government officials might attempt to interfere with the democratic process, or that government control of the process might bring suspicion upon its veracity.

The second facet of the framework, the Electoral Act 202 of 1993, dealt with the conduct of the electoral process and the technical minutiae of the election, including the form of the ballot paper, the identification of voters, the procedures at the polling stations, and the exact formula for counting the ballots and calculating the proportional distribution of legislative seats among the parties. The most significant departure from past electoral law—apart from the adoption of a universal franchise—was the move away from a constituency-based electoral system to the adoption of proportional representation in accordance with Schedule 2 of the 1993 interim Constitution. The Electoral Act proceeded to establish an Independent Electoral Commission (IEC) with responsibility for ensuring a fair electoral process and verifying the result as 'substantially free and fair'. The IEC was appointed by the State President on the advice of the TEC and was to be comprised of 'impartial, respected and suitably qualified men and women' representing a cross-section of the population.[20] Provision was also made for the inclusion of five non-South Africans drawn 'from the international community'. The Commission as a whole was to be 'independent and separate' from all existing bearers of political authority or power. It was to continue in existence until, in terms of section 9 of the Act, it was dissolved upon the completion of its mandate.

In addition to having complete responsibility and control over the electoral process,[21] the IEC was to be responsible for voter education and was required to

> take such measures as it may consider necessary for the prevention of intimidation of voters, candidates and parties.

Administratively, the IEC consisted of three branches: the Election Administration Directorate, which administered the electoral process; an Election Monitoring Directorate, which coordinated and administered the oversight process, including monitoring by the IEC itself and the coordination of local and foreign election observers; and an Election

---

[20]   IEC Act, above n 11, s 5(1).
[21]   IEC Act s 13(2)(a).

Adjudication Secretariat, which provided the necessary support and coordination for the handling of complaints and challenges to the electoral process through the Election Tribunals, Electoral Appeal Tribunals and the Special Electoral Court established in terms of sections 28 to 33 of the Act.

Established in terms of section 32 of the Independent Electoral Commission Act, the Special Electoral Court (SEC) held a unique position in the pre-constitutional transitional process in that it was empowered to act for a limited period as a court standing above the existing judicial system. Appointed by the TEC in terms of section 32(2) of the IEC Act, the SEC consisted of a chairperson, a judge of the Appellate Division of the Supreme Court; two judges of the Supreme Court designated by the Chief Justice; one member chosen from among the ranks of attorneys, advocates, magistrates or academic lawyers; and one person who may or may not be legally qualified or experienced. The court's powers over the transitional process included the power to review any decision of the IEC; to hear complaints and appeals against decisions of the IEC or the Electoral Appeal Tribunals established to adjudicate and decide on alleged electoral irregularities and infringements of the Electoral Code of Conduct; and to resolve conflicts between the state and other parties or organisations arising out of the functioning of the TEC.

IV. THE PRACTICE OF TRANSITIONAL LAW

While it would be foolhardy to argue that these transitional laws functioned in an orderly and mechanistic way, it would be equally unrealistic to ignore the vital role these laws and the institutions they created played at key moments in the democratic transition. In fact, there were two specific moments of the transition in which these transitional mechanisms made the difference in managing crises that could very well have derailed the transition to democracy and led to the escalation of violent conflict—if not to a complete reversal of the whole process. The first of these moments came when Lucas Mangope, President of the Bophuthatswana 'homeland' that had been given nominal independence by the apartheid regime, announced in March 1994 that he would not participate in the upcoming election and thus the people of that region of South Africa would not have the opportunity to vote. Another of these moments arose during the elections themselves when the process of ballot counting and verification, particularly in KwaZulu-Natal, was suspended and the outcome of the elections agreed upon through the reaching of sufficient consensus within the IEC in order to avoid damaging accusations of fraud and other conduct that undermined the claim of a free and fair election in the country. Without the existence of these transitional mechanisms it is very doubtful that the outcome of the process would have been as improbable as it was.

Both of these transitional bodies, the TEC and the IEC contributed in their own ways to the crisis that unfolded. In the case of the TEC, the body's main activity was to ensure an even political playing field by, among other things, blocking government plans to 'buy votes' through increased government expenditures on social projects in the months leading up to the elections. In one case, the TEC objected to the government's announcement of a comprehensive housing policy and only allowed the programme to proceed once the National Housing Forum, a social movement aligned with the ANC, endorsed it. At another moment in January 1994, the TEC vetoed a decision by the Development Bank of South Africa to grant a loan of R216 million to Bophuthatswana on the grounds that the regime there was not allowing free political activity, thus setting the stage for the subsequent crisis in the Bophuthatswana civil service. The IEC prepared for the elections by creating highly sophisticated and technologically advanced systems—such as the computerised results control centre at the IEC headquarters, which was supposed to 'receive and verify the vote tallies'[22]—yet through no fault of its own it had no idea how many people were eligible to vote; during the election, as many as five times and in one case eight times the number of voters expected turned up at the polls. These difficulties were only compounded by the ongoing political tensions; the last-minute agreement by the IFP to participate, requiring the addition of stickers to the already printed ballots; and finally, the fact that this body had only four months to create a new institution with more than 300,000 employees, most of whom had no electoral experience.

After Mangope announced that there would be no election in Bophuthatswana, the 'homeland's' 22,000-strong civil service went on strike demanding that their pensions and wages be paid out before 27 April, when the administration was expected to be disbanded and the

[22] S Friedman and L Stack, 'The Magic Moment: The 1994 Election' in S Friedman and D Atkinson (eds), *The Small Miracle: South Africa's Negotiated Settlement*, South African Review 7 (Johannesburg, Ravan Press, 1994) 321.

area incorporated into the new provinces under the interim Constitution. As the region dissolved into anarchy (with the looting of businesses, etc) white, right-wing paramilitaries attempted to come to Mangope's aid and through their own racist behaviour ignited a mutiny. The 'homelands" 5,000-strong army took up arms against their erstwhile 'liberators' and left Mangope holed up in his palace with no authority over the region. Since the TEC law had been enacted by the South African Parliament and Bophuthatswana was still considered an independent state by the apartheid government, it was argued that legally the TEC had no authority over this region of the country. However, in response to this crisis, the ANC felt that Mangope should be removed from office to allow the election to go ahead in that region of the country. Meanwhile, de Klerk was being pressed by conservative members of his government to use the South African Defence Force to intervene and reinstate Mangope's authority. While frantic bilateral negotiations continued between the government and the ANC in an attempt to resolve these differences, the TEC sent two representatives to evaluate the situation: Mac Maharaj, a senior member of the ANC, and Fanie van der Merwe, a senior government civil servant, who were accompanied by senior government security officers, a general, the Commissioner of Police and the director-general of foreign affairs.

A right-wing alliance—Concerned South Africans Group (COSAG)—consisting of the white Conservative Party, the Inkatha Freedom Party and the Bophuthatswana and Ciskei 'homeland' governments—opposed the democratic transition and had significant sympathy among the security forces. The conservative alliance and its forces attempted to deal directly with the generals to restore order and reinstate Mangope. However, the officially powerless TEC was able to prevent the reinstatement of Mangope and facilitate the collapse of these two holdout regimes. While it seemed at first as if the security forces would answer to the right-wing alliance, the TEC representatives insisted that the security forces had to take their orders from de Klerk, who in turn had to inform the TEC, and thus effectively negotiate with Mandela before making such a momentous decision. Once apprised of the matter, the TEC decided that the fact that government authority had broken down in the territory and that South African citizens were at risk, was sufficient cause to allow the South African Defence Force to re-establish order. It also called for the appointment of interim administrators to ensure the reincorporation of the 'homeland' and its participation in the forthcoming election. Ten days later, the civil service in the Ciskei 'homeland' took the lead from their colleagues in Bophuthatswana and went on strike demanding their pensions be paid out before the April elections. Within the day, Brigadier Oupa Gqozo, the military ruler of the Ciskei stepped down and asked the TEC to appoint an 'interim administration', thus accepting the reincorporation of his nominally independent 'homeland'. In effect, the events of the last months of minority rule demonstrated that the old regime could no longer make unilateral decisions about the future of the country and was now bound to accept a form of shared governance until the elections and coming into force of the interim Constitution on 27 April 1994.

V. CONCLUSION: TRANSITIONAL LAW, DEMOCRATIZATION AND JUSTICE

The role of law in South Africa's democratic transition has increasingly been collapsed into the notion of 'transitional justice'. However, it is important to clarify the different roles that law played in the process of democratisation in order to understand the ways in which transitional law served to provide both constraints and opportunities for the creation and subsequent implementation of the final 1996 Constitutional order. While there are extensive debates over the nature of transitional justice, particularly in the creation and practice of South Africa's Truth and Reconciliation Commission (TRC), an understanding of the role of law in the transition must reach beyond the truth-and-reconciliation paradigm. As this chapter has shown, law and legally created institutions—such as the TEC and the IEC—played significant and multiple roles in the period leading up to and beyond the first democratic elections in South Africa. The decision by the negotiating parties to adopt 'interim mechanisms', and even an interim Constitution as a means to facilitate the transition to democracy, conforms more closely to the original conception of transitional justice[23] than the more recent understandings that envision transitional justice as a means to overcome past injustices. Transitional law—which might include processes of 'transitional justice'—served, in South Africa and in many other political transitions, to facilitate the establishment of new political dispensations; however, transitional law does not necessarily produce either justice or democracy.

---

[23] See RG Teitel, *Transitional Justice* (New York, Oxford University Press, 2000).

The predominant role of law during the transition to democracy in South Africa was to create the institutional processes through which the opposing parties could seek common ground while continuing to pursue their often deeply conflicting goals. While the initial contacts and early negotiations may have been purely political in nature, as soon as the apartheid regime unbanned the ANC and other liberation movements, a series of transitional legal processes began: The government freed prisoners; enabled the return of exiles; created legal institutions to provide forms of shared control over the transition; and ultimately accepted an interim Constitution that would become the basic law of the transition to a democratic order. This interim Constitution was the epitome of a transitional law in that it was designed to have a limited life span and had at its core the provisions for achieving the creation of a democratically constituted Constitution-making body to produce a final Constitution. Three elements of the 1993 Constitution served as the basic provisions securing the transition to democracy in South Africa. First, the interim Constitution provided the legal basis for the election and empowerment of a democratic government. Second, it contained a number of provisions that ensured that there would be a process and framework for the creation of a final Constitution produced by a democratically elected Constitutional Assembly—including the 34 Constitutional Principles contained in Schedule 4. Finally, in its postamble the interim Constitution promised that a new democratic legislature would pass legislation creating a process through which amnesty would be granted in the 'pursuit of national unity' and out of a need to achieve national reconciliation.

The negotiation and adoption of these various transitional laws also framed the context that initially constructed the democratic order. The sunset clauses, which guaranteed the official positions of apartheid bureaucrats, as well as the local government law, which ensured that fully democratic local government would only come into existence after the 1999 elections, all added to the constraints that the new ANC government faced as it attempted to secure political, economic and social change at all levels of government. The subsequent passage of the Promotion of National Unity and Reconciliation Act[24] in 1995 and the establishment of the Truth and Reconciliation Commission projected the process of transition and the role of transitional law into the democratic era.[25]

---

[24] Promotion of National Unity and Reconciliation Act Act 34 of 1995.
[25] See F Du Bois and A Du Bois-Pedain (eds), *Justice and Reconciliation in Post-Apartheid South Africa* (Cambridge, Cambridge University Press, 2008).

Although the TRC sought to achieve some level of national reconciliation through its three separate branches—the victims' hearings, amnesty process and reparations committee—the TRC's focus on the political conflicts of the past produced a process of limited amnesty, account-ability and forgiveness but failed to address many of the fundamental injustices that the apartheid system produced.[26] The refusal to address the harms of apartheid policies—including forced removals and the migrant labour system—may have facilitated the political transition, but it has fundamentally undermined the legitimacy of the process in the eyes of many who recognise that the legacies of those policies continue to harm the future of millions of South African citizens. In this context, the recognition of socio-economic rights and the emphasis on restitution, employment equity and affirmative action as means to address these lega-cies gained greater political attention in the making and implementation of the final Constitution.

FURTHER READING

Atkinson, D, 'Brokering a Miracle? The Multiparty Negotiating Forum' in S Friedman and D Atkinson (eds), *The Small Miracle: South Africa's Negotiated Settlement*, South African Review 7 (Johannesburg, Ravan Press, 1994)

Du Bois, F and Du Bois-Pedain, A (eds), *Justice and Reconciliation in Post-Apartheid South Africa* (Cambridge, Cambridge University Press, 2008)

Friedman, S and Stack, L, 'The Magic Moment: The 1994 Election' in S Friedman and D Atkinson (eds), *The Small Miracle: South Africa's Negotiated Settlement*, South African Review 7 (Johannesburg, Ravan Press, 1994)

Klug, H, *Constituting Democracy: Law, Globalism and South Africa's Political Reconstruction* (Cambridge, Cambridge University Press, 2000).

Sparks, A, *Tomorrow Is Another Country: The Inside Story of South Africa's Negotiated Revolution* (Sandton, Struik Book Distributors, 1994)

---

[26] See M Mamdani, *Amnesty or Impunity? A Preliminary Critique of the Report of the Truth and Reconciliation Commission of South* Africa (TRC) (2002) 32 (3–4) *Diacritics* 33.

3

Sources of the Constitution

—————

Introduction – Constitution-Making and The Constitutional
Assembly – Legacies, Legal Traditions and the Limits of Path
Dependency – Text and Legal Interpretation – Conclusion

I. INTRODUCTION

UNLIKE UNWRITTEN CONSTITUTIONS, the South
African Constitution has a specific formal source, the document
signed into law by President Nelson Mandela as Act 108 of 1996.
This Constitution is the formal product of the Constitutional Assembly,
which met between May 1994 and December 1996. The Constitutional
Assembly included all members of both houses of Parliament elected in
South Africa's first democratic elections in April 1994. Although the
Constitutional Assembly spent many long hours debating and adopting
the different provisions of the Constitution, this document was not written on a blank slate. Similar to all other national Constitutions, the 1996
Constitution reflects a broad range of sources, including the prior interim
Constitution and legacies of the struggle against apartheid. It is also
shaped by legal continuity, which brought with it the legal and constitutional traditions of pre-democratic South Africa. All of this was overlaid
with the influences of both indigenous traditions and the international
post-Cold War consensus on human rights and political culture. These
sources all carry different degrees of coherence and legitimacy, and they
affected the final product and its implementation in multiple ways—
some of which are yet to be determined.

Constitutional Assembly chairperson Cyril Ramaphosa described
South Africa's new Constitution as the birth certificate of the new nation.

In fact, the 1996 Constitution is a classic example of an autochthonous Constitution,[1] a 'home-grown' product of negotiations among local parties who had been elected to the Constitutional Assembly. Yet, like all birth certificates, the document acknowledges its parental origins. While the birth was internationally heralded as a beacon of hope for Africa and the world, there was also a sense of recognition and a note of pride among foreign observers that revealed a familial connection. Unlike biological birth—which assumes fairly specific parentage and a beginning from which the newborn will grow to increasing independence—South Africa's new Constitution retained an umbilical connection to its many unspecified sources. Section 39, for example, explicitly directs the courts to 'promote the values that underlie an open and democratic society based on human dignity, equality and freedom' and to 'consider international law' when interpreting the Bill of Rights.[2] Furthermore, the courts are also permitted to consider foreign law.[3] While the promotion of particular values and permission to consider developments in foreign jurisdictions is hardly unique, the imperative that the courts '*must* consider international law' creates a formal and permanent link between the rights enshrined as a product of the local struggle for democracy in South Africa and the constant evolution of rights in the international environment. This imperative recognises past linkages and propels future constitutional struggles to always embrace the international, making the final Constitution as much South Africa's passport for re-admission into the international community as the birth certificate of the new nation.

II. CONSTITUTION-MAKING AND THE CONSTITUTIONAL ASSEMBLY

The explicit two-stage form of South Africa's Constitution-making process was a key aspect of this historic moment. While all post-conflict transitions have particular phases—often involving cease-fire agreements, constitutional negotiations and elections—a unique aspect of the South African process was the formal adoption of the interim Constitution. That document made provisions for the establishment of a Constitutional

[1] See Y Ghai, 'A Journey around Constitutions: Reflections on Contemporary Constitutions' (2005) 122 (4) *South African Law Journal* 804.
[2] Constitution of the Republic of South Africa Act 108 of 1996 [hereinafter 1996 Constitution] ss 39(1)(a) 39(1)(b).
[3] 1996 Constitution s 39(1)(c).

Assembly and creation of a final Constitution that would have to be certified as being consistent with a set of constitutional principles appended as Schedule 4. In order to understand how these different elements—the interim Constitution, constitutional principles and final Constitution—all serve as sources of South Africa's constitutional system, it is necessary to understand the conflicting constitutional visions advanced by the different parties to the conflict during the democratic transition. These alternative substantive visions were themselves embedded in different approaches to Constitution-making, and needed to be accommodated or subsumed in the process of creating the 1996 Constitution.

A. Different Approaches to Constitution-making

Although it is now a historical fact that the 1996 Constitution was produced by a democratically elected Constitutional Assembly, this was not a foregone conclusion to the process that was formally initiated by FW de Klerk's opening speech to the apartheid Parliament on 2 February 1990. The negotiations to end apartheid and reintegrate South Africa into the international community were initially hampered by intense differences over the process through which a new Constitution would be created. While there was a range of opinion as to how a new order was to be achieved, the key options were articulated by the three major contestants in the conflict: the African National Congress (ANC), Inkatha Freedom Party (IFP) and the National Party government that had ruled the country since 1948. The three Constitution-making options advanced by these parties spanned from the IFP's proposal that a new Constitution be written by a group of 'neutral' experts, and the National Party's plan to achieve a negotiated Constitution, to the ANC's belief that only an elected constituent assembly would have the legitimacy to produce a solution to the country's problems. However, confronted with escalating violence, endless talks-about-talks and a government committed to a lengthy transition (including some form of power-sharing in which the white minority would continue to have veto power over the black majority), the ANC launched a mass campaign demanding an interim government and a democratically elected constituent assembly.

Despite its preference for a democratically controlled constituent assembly, the ANC also recognised that the white minority would refuse to negotiate a transfer of power without some guarantees of the outcome.[4] The ANC understood the role played by the 'constitutional principles' produced by the international 'Contact Group' on Namibia in 1982. These principles were created to resolve the international conflict over South Africa's occupation of the former German colony of South West Africa. In addition, the ANC recognised the importance of achieving an internationally acceptable framework, and campaigned to promote the international adoption of its own proposals. In 1988, the ANC adopted a set of constitutional principles,[5] which it then promoted internationally as a condition for South Africa's re-admission into the global community. The international community's endorsement of the principle that South Africa should be a multi-party democracy, based on one-person-one-vote, further encouraged the ANC in its demand for an elected constituent assembly.

In stark contrast, the National Party government at first resisted calls for a democratically elected constituent assembly, envisaging instead a long transition period in which a future Constitution could be negotiated between the parties. As the holder of state power, the National Party was determined not to relinquish power before securing effective safeguards against the future exercise of governmental power by the black majority. This aim was, however, coupled with an understanding of political participation based on the relatively unrestrained exercise of executive power and the achievement of political change through the negotiation of elite interests. While ANC analysts tended to view the National Party's insistence that all 'recognised' political entities—including the political parties established in the discredited apartheid 'bantustans'—be equal participants in the negotiations as an attempt to stack the table in the regime's favour, this demand accurately reflected the National Party's notion of participation, based on its understanding of how competing political elites form a compact to govern.

From the outset, the structure of formal participation in the negotiation process was premised on a notion of consensus building among contending elites.[6] The Convention for a Democratic South Africa (CODESA),

[4] See 'Statement of the National Executive Committee of the African National Congress on the Question of Negotiations', Lusaka, 9 October 1987.

[5] African National Congress, *Constitutional Guidelines for a Democratic South Africa* (1988) reprinted in *The Road to Peace: Resource Material on Negotiations* (Marshalltown, ANC Dept. of Political Education, June 1990) 29.

[6] This was given clear, if realistic, expression in the notion of sufficient consensus—in which deadlocks in the negotiations were resolved by agreement between the National Party government and the ANC.

formed to negotiate the transition to a new constitutional order, thus reflected National Party demands for an elite pact-making process. Nevertheless, the National Party government still refused to permit CODESA to exercise legal powers, insisting that legal continuity required the approval of any new Constitution by the existing tricameral parliament, which was dominated by the National Party.[7] This assertion of the need for legal continuity carried an additional advantage for the National Party: it precluded the ANC's demand for a democratically elected Constitution-making body and required that any future Constitution be negotiated among the parties. In fact, the apartheid government argued that there could not even be a non-racial election until a new Constitution allowed a legal basis for universal adult franchise. For the National Party government, any suggestion that there should be a legal break with the apartheid past raised issues of the sovereignty of the South African state and the legitimacy of its position as a de jure government and was thus non-negotiable. As holder of state power for more than 40 years, the National Party was determined to project its power into the future. Even if it could not control the outcome, it wanted to ensure certain basic property and social interests through the insulation of private power in the post-apartheid order.[8] This project was threatened by claims to political participation by those who were formally excluded by the provisions of the existing 1983 tricameral Constitution.

The IFP adopted an even more stringent non-participatory position, viewing the very notion of a democratically elected constituent assembly as inherently undemocratic.[9] The IFP argued that since the purpose of a justiciable Constitution and a Bill of Rights is to protect minorities from the tyranny of the majority, the minorities to be protected must give their prior assent to any constitutional framework. In other words, the IFP believed it and every other minor party at the negotiating table—regardless of the extent of their political support—had to consent before a final Constitution could be adopted. Recognising the difficulties of obtaining universal consensus, the IFP called for a depoliticised process of

---

[7] Established in terms of the Republic of South Africa Constitution Act 110 of 1983.

[8] See generally, S Friedman (ed), *The Long Journey: South Africa's Quest for a Negotiated Settlement* (Johannesburg, Ravan Press, 1993) 26–27.

[9] See Inkatha Freedom Party, 'Why the Inkatha Freedom Party Objects to the Idea of the New Constitution Being Written by a Popularly Elected Assembly (Whether called "Constituent Assembly" or called by any other name)', undated submission to CODESA Working Group 2 (1992).

Constitution-making, with a group of constitutional experts retained to produce a Constitution to be adopted by all parties and endorsed in a national plebiscite.[10]

After nearly two-and-a-half years of slow progress, South Africa's democratic transition ground to a halt in mid-1992. The collapse of the CODESA negotiations marked the outer-limits of the National Party government's ability to assert a purely elite Constitution-making process. And the gunning down of ANC protesters outside Bisho highlighted the limits of the ANC's mass-action strategy to achieve an unfettered constituent assembly. Although overcoming this stalemate required concessions from both sides, the post-Cold War international consensus on the parameters of democratic transitions enabled the ANC to overcome the determination on the part of the National Party and the IFP to avoid an elected constituent assembly.

i. Constructing an Historic Compromise

ANC leader Joe Slovo's 'sunset clause' proposals, adopted by the ANC National Executive Committee in February 1993,[11] represented the epitome of an elite pact. The essential feature of the 'sunset' proposal was the offer of a constitutionally entrenched system of executive power-sharing that was to be guaranteed for five years after the first democratic election. During this period the democratically elected Parliament would be empowered to write a new Constitution, which could exclude these entrenched provisions from a future dispensation. In accepting the National Party's continued participation in government and the establishment of a set of agreed principles that each party would respect in a future constituent assembly, the proposals seemed to grant the National Party's key demands: a negotiated Constitution and future power-sharing. While initially criticised within the ANC and rejected by other parties, such as the Pan Africanist Congress, these proposals provided the linchpin that enabled the political transition to continue.

---

[10] See, Position Paper of the Inkatha Freedom Party for Submission at the CODESA meeting of 6 February 1992, reprinted in AP Blaustein and GH Flanz (eds), *Constitutions of the Countries of the World* (Dobbs Ferry, NY, Ocaeana, 1971–) South African Supplement, Release 92–2 (AP Blaustein, March 1992) 173.

[11] B Keller, 'Mandela's Group Accepts 5 Years of Power-Sharing', *New York Times* (19 February 1993) A1, col 1.

The National Party's concession of an elected constituent assembly and the ANC's acceptance of a government of national unity under a transitional Constitution provided the key elements of agreement for South Africa's democratic transition. By accepting a democratic Constitution-making process, the National Party made it possible for the ANC to agree to the adoption of a negotiated interim Constitution, which would entrench a government of national unity for five years and ensure the legal continuity the National Party government required. The architecture of this agreement reflected continuity and change as well as negotiation and participation. It allowed the multi-party negotiations to resume at the World Trade Centre outside Johannesburg, and concluded with the adoption of an interim Constitution by the South African Parliament in December 1993. This interim Constitution came into force on 27 April 1994, the eve of South Africa's first democratic elections.

B. Constitution-making in the Constitutional Assembly

Provisions for the establishment of a Constitutional Assembly were spelled out in Chapter 5 of the interim Constitution. Constituted by a joint sitting of the two houses of Parliament—the National Assembly and the Senate—the Constitutional Assembly was given two years, from the first sitting of the National Assembly, to 'pass a new Constitutional text'.[12] At its first meeting on 24 May 1994, the Constitutional Assembly, comprised of 490 members from seven political parties, elected Cyril Ramaphosa of the ANC as its chairperson and Leon Wessels of the National Party as deputy chairperson. At its second meeting in August 1994 the Constitutional Assembly established a 44-member Constitutional Committee to serve as a steering committee and created an administrative structure to manage the process of Constitution-making. The Constitutional Assembly's administrative team handled support for the Assembly and facilitated other important aspects of the process, including the following: a public participation programme that included both written and electronic submissions; a constitutional education programme; a constitutional public meetings programme; and a newsletter, *Constitutional Talk*, devoted to explaining the process. In November 1995, the administrative team

---

[12] Constitution of the Republic of South Africa Act 200 of 1993 [hereinafter 1993 interim Constitution] s 73(1).

distributed four million copies of the working draft, which was approved by the Constitutional Assembly.[13]

In addition to the Constitutional Committee, the Constitutional Assembly set up six theme committees in September 1994. These committees empowered legal and policy experts 'to collect information, ideas, views, and submissions from political parties, interest groups, and individuals on issues that would come to form the content of the constitution'.[14] The theme committees held a series of seminars and conferences that involved members of the Constitutional Assembly, interest groups, academics and non-government organisations in debates over different sections of the draft Constitution. In addition, a technical refinement team worked to ensure consistency throughout the fast-growing document and made certain it was written in plain language that ordinary citizens could read and understand. Apart from these informal mechanisms, the Constitutional Assembly was also required by the interim Constitution to appoint an independent panel of seven constitutional experts to provide advice to the Constitutional Assembly and serve as a partial deadlock-breaking mechanism if the Constitutional Assembly was unable to achieve a two-thirds majority within the required period of time.

i. Negotiating the Final Constitution

Compared to the Multi-Party negotiations at Kempton Park in 1993, Constitution-making in the Constitutional Assembly introduced a new set of imperatives and conditions. First, the relative power of the different parties had been established by their respective performances in the first democratic elections. Second, as power shifted into the new democratic institutions and the Constitution-drafting process took place in full view of the public, members of the Constitutional Assembly found themselves subject to greater pressures from their constituencies. These conditions produced several results that distinguish the drafting of the final Constitution from that of the interim Constitution.

Whereas the parties at Kempton Park had been concerned about drawing the Inkatha Freedom Party into the constitutional settlement, if this

[13] See P Bell, in (ed), *The Making of the Constitution: The Story of South Africa's Constitutional Assembly, May 1994 to December 1996* ([Cape Town?] Churchill Murray Publications, 1997).

[14] Bell, *The Making of the Constitution*, above n 13, 34.

was at all possible, there was no similar imperative in the Constitutional Assembly, where the true extent of the political support for the IFP had been laid bare by an election. When the IFP carried out its inevitable walk-out from the Constitutional Assembly, the remaining parties simply ignored it and applied themselves to the task of drafting a Constitution in its absence. Within the Constitutional Assembly there was much less incentive for the ANC to settle contentious issues on unfavourable terms than there had been at Kempton Park. Thus, the final Constitution shows fewer obvious signs of being a compromise than the interim Constitution. In respect to almost all the controversial clauses, the balance ultimately reached in the final Constitution weighed more heavily in favour of the ANC: For example, the property clause remained in the final Constitution, but it is a less-expansive clause than the one in the interim Constitution; it is offset by a comprehensive package of land rights. Under the final Constitution, the right to economic activity is even more attenuated, while the right to lockout was removed from the Constitution entirely. In addition, the right to education was reformulated to clarify that the state is under no obligation to fund culturally exclusive schools; consociationalism is no longer entrenched in local government and the provisions requiring the formation of a government of national unity were allowed to lapse, as the sunset clauses of the interim Constitution provided.[15]

The National Party briefly contemplated a confrontation with the ANC over their three key issues—property, lock-outs and cultural schools—but the dynamics of the new Constitution-drafting process left it no option but to back down. Faced with the prospect of a referendum in the event of a failure by the Constitutional Assembly to pass a new constitutional text by a two-thirds majority,[16] the National Party could not afford to make its last stand on issues in which the ANC perspective had overwhelming popular support. On 8 May 1996, 87 per cent of the members of the Constitutional Assembly voted in favour of a new constitutional text that was to form the basis of the final Constitution. The missing 13 per cent was comprised of IFP members, who steadfastly maintained their boycott of proceedings; the Vryheids-Front members,

[15] Constitutional Principle XXXIII entrenched the government of national unity until 30 April 1999. This was retained in the Final Constitution through the inclusion of the transitional provisions in Sch 6. Cl 9(2) of Sch 6 provided for the continuation of the Government of National Unity until 1999.

[16] As required by s 73(6) of the 1993 interim Constitution.

who abstained; and the two African Christian Democratic Party members, who voted against the Constitution on doctrinal grounds.

The degree of public exposure to the Constitution-drafting process was probably without historical precedent anywhere in the world. Hundreds of public meetings were held to advertise the drafting of the Constitution and to invite public participation in the process. The Constitutional Assembly published its own monthly newsletter, *Constitutional Talk*, which publicised events relating to the development of the Constitution. There was an extensive publicity campaign on television and radio, and the genesis of the Constitution from first draft to final product could be followed on a daily basis on the Internet site of the Constitutional Assembly.

ii. Creating a 'Globalised' Property Clause

The conflicts, debates and final compromise on the inclusion of a property rights clause in the Constitution provide a window through which the making of the Constitution and its interaction with global and local imperatives may be viewed. While the internationally endorsed process for the transition away from apartheid included a commitment to the rule of law and the inclusion of a justiciable bill of rights, there was no clarity on the contents of this commitment. Just prior to the beginning of substantive constitutional negotiations in early 1993, the ANC and National Party government presented dramatically disparate notions of how property should be constitutionally protected. While the ANC was willing to protect the undisturbed enjoyment of personal possessions, it wanted legislation to determine property entitlements and provisions for the restoration of land to people dispossessed under apartheid. The Government's proposals aimed at protecting all property rights and would only allow expropriation for public purposes, subject to cash compensation determined by a court of law according to the market value of the property. In response, the ANC suggested that no property clause was necessary.

As the negotiations progressed, the conflict over the property clause became focused on specific issues. The apartheid government insisted that property rights be included in the Constitution and that the measure of compensation include specific reference to the market value of the property. In response, the ANC insisted that the property clause not frustrate efforts to address land claims and that the state must have the power to regulate property without obligations to pay compensation unless there was a clear expropriation of the property. The conflict soon focused on whether provisions for land restitution should be included within the property clause or whether they should be limited to the corrective action provisions of the equality clause. The interim Constitution resolved these conflicts by providing a separate institutional basis for land restitution—which was guaranteed in the corrective action provisions of the equality clause—and by compromising on the question of compensation by including a range of factors the courts would have to consider in determining just and equitable compensation.

Despite predictions that there would be very little change in the Constitution during the second phase of the Constitution-making process—particularly on such sensitive issues as the property clause and the Bill of Rights—in fact, the property issue once again became one of the unsolvable issues and lightning rods in the Constitutional Assembly. Although the committee charged with reviewing the Bill of Rights was at first reluctant to change the formulation of the 1993 compromise, challenges centred on the question of land restitution and reform[17] once again forced open the process.[18] In this case, the impetus came from a Workshop on Land Rights and the Constitution, which was organised by one of the Constitutional Assembly's subcommittees, Theme Committee 6.3. This committee was charged with resolving issues related to specialised structures of government such as the Land Claims Commission and Court provided for in the interim Constitution. This meeting focused on the land issue and once again raised the problem of property rights in the Constitution. While some participants raised the question of whether the Constitution should offer any property protection at all, the major change from the period in which the 1993 Constitution was negotiated was that the participants in this workshop—even those representing long-established interests like the National Party and the South African Agricultural Union—now agreed on the need 'to rectify past wrongs' and the necessity of land reform. Disagreement here was over the means. The

[17] See, Constitutional Assembly, Constitutional Committee Sub-Committee: Documentation: Land Rights, 9 October 1995; Theme Committee 6.3: Specialised Structures of Government: Land Rights, Documentation 11 September 1995; and, Constitutional Assembly, Theme Committee 6.3: Specialised Structures of Government: Documentation vol 2A: Land Rights, 15 September 1995.

[18] Political agreement on the property clause was only reached at midnight on 18 April 1996. Bell, *The Making of the Constitution*, above n 13.

South African Agricultural Union, for example, continued to assert that 'it should be done in a way without jeopardising the protection of private ownership', while the National Party now embraced the World Bank's proposals, arguing that land reform should 'be accomplished within the parameters of the market and should be demand-driven'.

The outcome of this workshop and the submissions made to Theme Committee 6.3 was a report to the Constitutional Assembly that challenged the existing 1993 formulation of property rights and called for a specific land clause to provide a 'constitutional framework and protection for all land reform measures'.[19] Theme Committee 4, which was responsible for the Bill of Rights, had thus far adopted a property clause (without controversy) that merely incorporated the 1993 Constitution's restitution provisions into the property clause. However, the report on Land Rights threw the proverbial cat among the pigeons. Some objected to Theme Committee 6.3's very discussion of property rights, while others sensed an opportunity to reopen the debate on property rights and to once again question their very inclusion in the Bill of Rights. As a result, the Draft Bill of Rights published by the Constitutional Assembly on 9 October 1995 included an option that there be 'no property clause at all'.

In this context, an alternative option began to gain momentum. This option was a property clause that would include a list of specific land rights as well as a sub-clause insulating land reform from constitutional attack. A strategy to insulate land restitution and land reform from constitutional attack had been implicit from early on in the debate, including a specific sub-clause insulating state action aimed at redressing past discrimination in the ownership and distribution of land rights. This sub-clause enabled the negotiators to reach a compromise between those demanding the removal of the property clause and those, like the Democratic Party, who remained opposed to even the social democratic formulation modelled on the German Basic Law.[20] Still, the debate raged on and the draft formulations of the property clause continued to evolve. Political agreement on the property clause was only finally reached at midnight on 18 April 1996, when sub-section 28(8), the 'affirmative action' or insulation sub-clause of the property clause was modified to

[19] See, Constitutional Assembly, Constitutional Committee Subcommittee, Documentation: Land Rights, Monday 9 October 1995.

[20] See Constitutional Assembly, Constitutional Committee, Documentation: vol 2A Land Rights, Friday 15 September 1995, pp 13–41.

make it subject to section 36(1), the general limitations clause of the Constitution.[21]

The final property clause reflects the democratic origins of the Constitutional Assembly. It guarantees not only the restitution of land taken after 1913[22] and a right to legally secure tenure for those whose tenure is insecure as a result of racially discriminatory laws or practices,[23] but it also includes an obligation for the state to enable citizens to gain access to land on an equitable basis.[24] Furthermore, the state is granted a limited exemption from the protective provisions of the property clause so as to empower it to take 'legislative and other measures to achieve land, water and related reform, in order to redress the results of past racial discrimination'.[25]

Despite agreement in the Constitutional Assembly, the property clause was presented to the Constitutional Court as violating the Constitutional Principles and therefore grounds for denying certification of the Constitution. Opponents raised two major objections: First, unlike the interim Constitution, the new clause did not expressly protect the right to acquire, hold and dispose of property; second, they argued, the provisions governing expropriation and the payment of compensation were inadequate.[26] The Constitutional Court rejected both of these arguments. First, the Court noted that the test to be applied was whether the formulation of the right met the standard of a 'universally accepted fundamental right' as required by Constitutional Principle II. Second, the Court surveyed international and foreign sources and observed that

> [i]f one looks to international conventions and foreign constitutions, one is immediately struck by the wide variety of formulations adopted to protect the right to property, as well as by the fact that significant conventions and constitutions contain no protection of property at all.[27]

In conclusion, the Court argued that it could not

> uphold the argument that, because the formulation adopted is expressed in a negative and not a positive form and because it does not contain an express

---

[21] See Bell, *The Making of the Constitution*, above n 13.
[22] 1996 Constitution s 25(7).
[23] 1996 Constitution s 25(6).
[24] 1996 Constitution s 25(5).
[25] 1996 Constitution s 25(8).
[26] *Certification of the Constitution of the Republic of South Africa* 1996 CCT 23/1996 [hereinafter *First Certification* case] [70].
[27] *First Certification* case [71].

recognition of the right to acquire and dispose of property, it fails to meet the prescription of CPII [Constitutional Principle II].[28]

The second objection met the same fate with the Court, which concluded that an

> examination of international conventions and foreign constitutions suggests that a wide range of criteria for expropriation and the payment of compensation exists . . . [and thus the] approach taken in NT 25 [New Text section 25] cannot be said to flout any universally accepted approach to the question.[29]

Although it may be argued that the property clause in the final Constitution is unique to South Africa and is the product of South Africa's particular history of dispossession, it is also important to note how resolution of the property question was framed by international options. While the Constitutional Court could argue that the particular formulation of the clause was compatible with global standards—given the variety of formulations in existence—it is also true that those who advocated that there should be no property clause in the Constitution were compelled by the politics of recognition of property rights to accept its inclusion. The politics of Constitution-making, in this instance, were bounded on both sides. Two options were silenced: the option of widespread nationalisation, initially advocated by the ANC, which may have been facilitated by the exclusion of a property clause; and the conflicting demands for strict protection of property guaranteeing market-value compensation for any interference. Instead, the parties were able to use the international and foreign lexicon of treaties, Constitutions and case law to formulate a specifically South African compromise. This resolution enabled the political transition, and left open, for future fact-specific confrontations, the exact interpretation of the new Constitution's property clauses. The political conflicts over property rights were thus projected into the future where their resolution would continue to depend on local responses to—and interpretations of—global standards.

---

[28] *First Certification* case [72].
[29] *First Certification* case [73].

III. LEGACIES, LEGAL TRADITIONS AND THE LIMITS OF PATH DEPENDENCY

While the final 1996 Constitution, as a unique document, is the primary source of South Africa's Constitutional order, the rights, aspirations and ideas formulated in this document also have particular histories within the context of South Africa. Most prominent among these sources are the legacies of struggle, the notions of rights and the collective demands that made up the history of resistance to colonialism and apartheid. Another important source of understanding and tradition is the history of law and the professional training and traditions of legal practitioners and educators in South Africa.

These legacies and the complexity they impose on any simple theory of path dependency are highlighted by understanding the alternative visions the different parties had for the resolution of conflict in South Africa. It may be argued that the ANC, as the dominant political force in the country and now government for more than 15 years, has continued to pursue its original vision of political and economic transformation. Yet it is also important to note that this vision—which includes policies of affirmative action, black economic empowerment and land reform—consists of policies that are not required by the Constitution but are among many policy alternatives that may be validly pursued under the Constitution. Understanding these alternative visions and the extent to which they are either facilitated or precluded by the Constitution is important for evaluating different options for governance in South Africa that are possible within the democratic space opened by the Constitution. As much as theories of path dependency emphasise that prior choices and events do not simply determine the future but might rather constrain future institutional and policy choices in particular ways, the constitutional product of the democratic transition in South Africa does not guarantee a transformed society but rather facilitates and hinders particular options within the realm of democratic contestation.

A. Legacies of Struggle and Legal Tradition

Advocacy of human rights and demands for political and social rights kept the notion of inalienable rights alive within the anti-apartheid movement and social movements inside South Africa. Two documents stand out as the products of these claims. First is the ANC's African Claims in South Africa, which reformulated the Atlantic Charter's principles of freedom and democracy from the perspective of Africans in South Africa. Adopted by the ANC on 16 December 1945, this

> Bill of Rights . . . made the revolutionary claim of one man one vote, of equal justice in the courts, freedom of land ownership, or residence and of movement . . . claimed freedom of the press, and demanded equal opportunity in training and in work.[30]

The Freedom Charter, adopted on 26 June 1955 by the Congress of the People at Kliptown, is the second expression of the aspiration of South Africans for a charter of rights.[31] The Congress Alliance launched the Congress of the People in 1954. It was not a single event but a series of discussions culminating in the adoption of the Freedom Charter. Professor ZK Mathews, who proposed the Congress of the People, called for 'a gathering to which ordinary people will come, sent there by the people. Their task will be to draw up a blueprint for the free South Africa of the future'.[32] While the Freedom Charter, with its guarantee of individual and collective rights was to remain the blueprint of the ANC vision for a post-apartheid South Africa, it in no way contradicted the organisation's view or understanding of democratic authority and even legislative supremacy. The assertion of both political and socio-economic rights in the Freedom Charter represented the claims of the people against the apartheid government and the promises of a future ANC government, not the justiciable rights of individuals or groups.

The ANC's publication of the *Constitutional Guidelines for a Democratic South Africa* in mid-1988 marked a dramatic shift away from unrestrained democratic authority in the South African debate. By publicly committing itself to the adoption of a Bill of Rights enforceable through the courts, the ANC assured fellow South Africans and the world of its commitment to constitutionalism and to the introduction of judicial review.[33] But the ANC had

---

[30] M Benson, *The African Patriots: The Story of the African National Congress of South Africa* (London, Faber, 1963) 117.

[31] See R Suttner and J Cronin, *30 Years of the Freedom Charter* (Johannesburg, Ravan Press, 1986).

[32] R Suttner, *The Freedom Charter: The People's Charter in the Nineteen-Eighties* ([Cape Town], University of Cape Town, 1984) 1.

[33] African National Congress, *Constitutional Guidelines for a Democratic South Africa* (1988), above n 5. See also A Sachs, *Protecting Human Rights in a New South Africa* (Cape Town, Oxford University Press, 1990).

yet to embrace the notion of constitutional supremacy. Judicial review in this conception would be limited to the protection of rights and did not imply a system of constitutional supremacy in which the courts would be able to measure all government action against the provisions and structural implications of the Constitution. The initial consequence of this initiative was the adoption of the Harare Declaration by the Organisation of African Unity (OAU) in August 1989.[34] This document used the *Constitutional Guidelines* as a basis for outlining the minimum principles of a post-apartheid Constitution acceptable to the international community, and was later adopted by the Non-Aligned Movement and the United Nations General Assembly.[35] Finally, the ANC proposed its own Bill of Rights for a New South Africa in 1990, with further amendments in 1991 and 1992.[36]

While it may be pointed out that many of the participants in the political leadership on both sides of the conflict in South Africa had legal training and experience, it is a bold claim to say that this commonality determined the course of the negotiated solution. Such a strong claim for path dependency must confront not only the clearly different experiences and notions of law held by participants such as Nelson Mandela, Oliver Tambo and FW de Klerk, but also the fact that their common experience—in legal education and practice—was steeped in the legal positivism so ingrained in South African legal culture. There is some validity to the notion that these political leaders, given their legal backgrounds, might have been more comfortable with the role of lawyers (such as Cyril Ramaphosa, Arthur Chaskalson and Roelf Meyer) in the negotiations and Constitution-making process. However, compared to politicians who may not have had this background, it would be a very strong claim for path dependency to say that this common legal background determined the embrace of constitutionalism. Instead, we might look to the alternative ideas of political and social transformation articulated by the parties and

[34] See, I Phillips, 'The Political Role of the Freedom Charter' in N Steytler (ed), *The Freedom Charter and Beyond: Founding Principles for a Democratic South African Legal Order* (Cape Town, Wyvern, 1991) 78.

[35] United Nations Centre Against Apartheid, 'Declaration on the Question of South Africa by the Ad Hoc Committee on Southern Africa of the Organization of African Unity', Harare, 21 August 1989, *Notes and Documents* 7/89 (October 1989).

[36] See ANC Constitutional Committee, *A Bill of Rights for a New South Africa* (Bellville, Cape Province, Centre for Development Studies, 1990) and 'ANC Draft Bill of Rights: A Preliminary Revised Text' (May 1992) in A Sachs, *Advancing Human Rights in South Africa* (Cape Town, Oxford University Press, 1992) at Appendix 1. 25 [hereinafter ANC Draft].

how a constitutional framework provided a means to meld these visions into a basic agreement on governance.

B. Alternative Strategies to Confront the Past and Frame the Future

The clearest way to understand the alternative visions held by the liberation movement and the apartheid government at the beginning of the democratic transition is to review the two disparate positions articulated at that time on a future Bill of Rights for South Africa: one, by the South African Law Commission; and the other put forth by the ANC Constitutional Committee. While not all aspects of these alternative visions are conceivable within the parameters of the 1996 final Constitution, the continuing co-existence of many of these possibilities and the inherent tensions they represent were important sources of the Constitution.

The South African Law Commission's draft, published in August 1991, weighed strongly in favour of the protection of existing rights against future state action. This emphasis was evident in the focus of the first article of the draft, which asserted that all the

> rights set forth in this Bill are fundamental rights to which every individual and, where applicable, also every juristic person in South Africa is entitled in relation to legislative and government bodies, and save as otherwise provided in this Bill those rights shall not be circumscribed, limited, suspended or infringed by any legislative or executive or administrative act of any nature.[37]

Leaving aside the difficulties of constitutional interpretation that may arise from the description of all rights as fundamental and the reality of often conflicting-rights,[38] the Commission's primary emphasis on limiting the scope of state action had profound implications for programmes designed to address the vast inequalities a democratic government would inherit from apartheid. For example, the Law Commission's draft made no attempt to reach beyond the strictly formal notion of 'equality before the law'. The draft framed the right to equality before the law as a negative restriction on the activities of the state rather than as a positive right of each citizen to equal treatment or equal protection of the law. Although

[37] South African Law Commission, Project 58: Group and Human Rights: Interim Report, August 1991 [hereinafter Law Commission Draft] Art 1, p 686.

[38] See generally, 'Methods of Constitutional Interpretation' in JH Garvey and TA Aleinikoff (eds), *Modern Constitutional Theory*, 2nd edn (St Paul, MN, West Publishing, 1991) 26–113.

this negative interpretation was not cited as the exclusive meaning of the article,[39] nothing in the draft stressed the need to address the historic exclusion of the black majority by working towards equal participation in the society or even the lesser standard of equal opportunity.

The narrowness of the Commission's approach to equal opportunity was confirmed in its handling of the problem of private discrimination. The Commission simply asserted that

> no legislation or executive or administrative act shall directly or indirectly make available to an individual who or a group which merely on the ground[s] of race or colour refuses to associate with any other individual group, any public or state funds to foster the creation or maintenance of such discrimination or exclusion.[40]

Under this formulation, the state could not fund discriminatory action; however, at the same time the Commission proceeded to assert that the state could not 'compel individuals or groups to associate with other individuals or groups'.[41] This approach elevated, to constitutional status, a negative interpretation of the right to association—a right to disassociation—over the right to equality. Thus, while the state would be prohibited from funding discriminatory organisations and activities, it would also be prohibited from outlawing or restraining private organisations that sought to limit their membership to certain groups, even if these limits were on grounds that were widely viewed as unacceptable, such as race and gender.

By assuming that a Bill of Rights should apply only to the relationship between the state and its citizens—and by specifically excluding schools from receiving any state support if attendance was limited on racial grounds—the Law Commission's draft implied that it would be constitutionally acceptable to maintain racial exclusivity or private apartheid in the educational arena, so long as it was not supported by the state. However, given South Africa's history of racist exclusion and economic inequalities, a constitutional principle of equality unable to pierce the shield of a purported 'right of disassociation' would have protected private racial discrimination.

---

[39] Law Commission Draft Art 3(a) does precede this explanation of the right to equality before the law with the statement that the right 'means, *inter alia*, . . .; which leaves scope for other meanings.

[40] South African Law Commission, Summary of Interim Report, Group and Human Rights (August 1991) [hereinafter Law Commission Summary] 23 para k. See also, Law Commission Draft, above n 37, Art 17(c).

[41] Law Commission Draft, above n 37, Art 17(b).

Confronted with demands for corrective measures that would require the state to address racial and economic inequalities, the Commission characterised affirmative action as usually linked to 'the recognition of socio-economic rights as fundamental rights'[42] and argued for the inclusion of a restricted form of affirmative action, 'because idealism and enthusiasm for our new South Africa should not be dampened'[43]. The Commission's vision for constitutional provisions addressing apartheid's legacy was, however, limited to enabling the legislature to voluntarily adopt 'special programmes to guarantee that all members of society are afforded equal opportunities of realising their potential . . . [and] involves the application of funds to give all citizens an equal position at the starting line as far as possible'.[44] The Commission's draft granted the highest legislative body the power, through the passage of

> legislation of general force and effect [to] introduce such programmes of affirmative action and vote such funds therefore as may reasonably be necessary to ensure that through education and training, financing programmes and employment all citizens have equal opportunities of developing and realising their natural talents and potential to the full.[45]

Thus, the Commission incorporated a restricted form of affirmative action, as an exception to its guarantee of equality before the law. By restricting affirmative action to the adoption and implementation of legislative programmes 'of upliftment', the Commission effectively collapsed two different concepts—affirmative action and good government—into one. No distinction was made between legislative programmes to address issues of homelessness, educational reform, job creation etc—which are the normal responsibilities of a democratic government—and the Commission's notion of affirmative action. This lack of distinction was based on the Commission's unarticulated assumption that any government programme to aid the poor or to improve social conditions in a particular area would amount to an unequal distribution of benefits to another racial group—on the presumption that poverty would remain racially segregated. For the Commission, such programmes would be a violation of equal treatment and therefore need to be validated by an affirmative action exception to the constitutional guarantee of equal treatment. As the Law Commission noted

---

[42] Law Commission Summary, above n 40, p 15, para 1.51.
[43] Law Commission Summary, above n 40, p 15, para 1.54.
[44] Law Commission Draft, above n 37, p 303, para 7.97.
[45] Law Commission Draft, above n 37, p 303, para 7.98. See Art 3(b) of the Draft.

in its Report: 'this may mean that more funds have to be expended per capita on black education and training, black housing etc'.[46]

The ANC's proposed Bill of Rights, on the other hand, introduced a constitutional vision of collective action to overcome South Africa's legacy of racial domination and inequality. This vision assumed a wider interpretation of the notion of equality and created and incorporated a strategy for realising a constitutional duty—originally proposed in the ANC *Constitutional Guidelines*—to actively eradicate 'the economic and social inequalities produced by racial discrimination'.[47] Central to this vision was the guarantee of formal equality, asserting—in contradiction of the essence of all prior South African Constitutions—that 'all South Africans are born free and equal in dignity and rights'.[48] Article 1 guaranteed that 'no individual or group shall receive privileges or be subjected to discrimination, domination or abuse on the grounds of race'.[49] Herein lay the clue to the ANC's wider conception of equality. If this were to be interpreted in isolation from the draft's other provisions as guaranteeing simply equal treatment, the proposal would fail to confront apartheid's imposed inequalities. However, when read in the spirit of the entire draft, it becomes clear that the conception of equality in the draft envisaged a process through which equal opportunity would be attained by addressing past discrimination and maintained through the guarantee of non-discrimination and 'equal protection under the law'.[50]

The ANC's strategy for attaining equal opportunity rested on five prongs. First, the draft Bill of Rights guaranteed formal equality. Taken together with the guarantee of political rights[51]—including the entrenchment of multi-party democracy to be ensured through 'regular, free and fair' elections[52]—the promise of formal equality made it clear that legislative power would rest in the hands of the country's majority, which had thus far been excluded from political participation. And although this power would be bounded by individual and collective rights guaranteed in a justiciable Bill of Rights, a democratically elected government would clearly have the power to introduce legislation

---

[46] Law Commission Draft, above n 37, p 303, para 7.97.
[47] ANC *Constitutional Guidelines*, above n 5, para I.
[48] ANC Draft, above n 36, Art.1(1).
[49] ANC Draft, above n 36, Art 1(2).
[50] ANC Draft, above n 36, Art 1(3).
[51] See ANC Draft, above n 36, Art 3.
[52] ANC Draft, above n 36, Art 3(4).

and pass laws to improve the lot of the now-enfranchised victims of apartheid.

Second, the ANC draft proposed an explicit, constitutionally mandated and protected process of affirmative action. Based on the principle of redressing past discrimination, Article 14 would have facilitated the creation of programmes to 'procure the advancement and the opening up of opportunities'[53] by both public and private bodies. The second clause of this article revealed the drafters' textured understanding of the notion of equality. In stating that 'any action taken in terms of the above [Art. 14] shall not be deemed to contradict the principle of equal rights for all South Africans as set out in Article 1',[54] the draft makes it clear that the notion of equal treatment guaranteed by Article 1(2)—and reiterated in the anti-discrimination provision in the section protecting children's rights[55]—incorporated the prerequisite of equal opportunity. Article 14's protection of affirmative action was designed to guarantee a process that would, over time, confront accumulated and structured patterns of inequality, while making it clear that the formal equality guaranteed by Article 1 was not a barrier to energetic action to redress apartheid's legacy.

Third, there was the adoption of a type of enhanced affirmative action principle in Article 15's mandate of 'positive measures'.[56] This section of the ANC draft moved from a general assertion of the state's duty to promote both racial and gender equality to the inclusion of very specific mandates to transform the racial composition of the public service—including the 'defence and police forces and the prison service'.[57] It also made explicit the legislature's powers to enact laws to require 'nongovernmental organisations and private bodies to conduct themselves in

---

[53]   ANC Draft, above n 36, Art 14(1).

[54]   ANC Draft, above n 36, Art 13(2). It is interesting to note that Art 14(2) was completely rewritten after it was pointed out that the wording of the earlier version, which stated that 'no provision of the Bill of Rights shall be construed as derogating from or limiting in any way the general provisions of this article', [ANC 1990 Draft, at Art 13(2)] was vague and subject to broad interpretation. As the note to the new clause acknowledges, it 'was interpreted to mean that the principle of affirmative action would be so powerful as to override all personal rights and freedoms' [ANC Draft, Note to Art 14(2), p 15]. This clarification makes it clear that the function of the affirmative action clause 'is to supplement and strengthen the equality clause, not to override other provisions of the Bill of Rights' [ibid].

[55]   ANC Draft, above n 36, Art 10(3).

[56]   ANC Draft, above n 36, Art 15.

[57]   ANC Draft, above n 36, Art 15(6).

accordance with the [articles'] principles'.[58] Provision was thus made for
a constitutional mandate of positive obligations or enhanced affirmative
action to be applied to private non-state action.

The fourth prong in the ANC draft confronted apartheid's enforced
inequalities by including a duty to work towards achieving social and economic rights, implicit in the adoption of mandatory provisions requiring
the state to take action to guarantee a 'progressively expanding floor of
enforceable minimum rights'.[59] Although the inclusion of these socio-
economic rights was understood as essential for confronting South
Africa's vast inequalities, this section of the ANC's draft also promised
that the new constitutional order would continue to be responsive to the
rights and needs of the disadvantaged and less powerful, beyond the necessary period of affirmative action. Finally, Article 11(4) of the ANC draft
provided an explicit power to divert resources from the richer to the
poorer regions of the country. Although this power was obviously related
to the extension of a minimum floor of socio-economic rights, it had a distinct impact of its own in that it provided for the distribution of resources
away from the so-called 'first-world' parts of South Africa to the underdeveloped bantustan regions that were the stepchildren of apartheid.

The different drafts that emerged in the context of the negotiations
towards a democratic transition revealed the underlying conceptions the
two sides had of the role of a Bill of Rights and constitutionalism in a
post-apartheid South Africa. On the one hand, the government-
sponsored South African Law Commission conceived of a Bill of Rights
as a means to protect existing interests and social relations from future
state interference. Adopting a classical eighteenth-century conception of
the relationship between the state and civil society, the Law Commission
strove to protect individual citizens by imposing significant restraints on
state action, particularly through its guarantees of civil and political rights.
This was a welcome development in a context where state lawlessness
had been the hallmark of government domination of the disenfranchised
black majority. However, the only concession the Commission made to
demands for a post-apartheid state to be constitutionally committed to
addressing the legacy of apartheid was its reluctant acceptance of the
state's duty to provide for the education of its citizens.

One of the most confusing aspects of the Law Commission's draft
was its characterisation of all rights as fundamental while simultaneously

---

[58] ANC Draft, above n 36, Art 15(9).
[59] ANC Draft, above n 36, Art 11(2).

limiting their application to legislative and executive acts. Under this approach, the Bill of Rights could not be applied to challenge existing common law or customary law rules that discriminated or violated any of its other provisions. It was this restricted notion of constitutionalism that revealed the essence of the Law Commission's approach. Instead of an embodiment of human rights, the Bill of Rights proposed by the law Commission would have built a wall between public and private action. In doing so, it would have restricted constitutional rights to the protection of individuals and shielded private interests from state interference. The consequence of this approach in South Africa would have been to preserve areas of private activity from the impact of the Bill of Rights; in effect, protecting private apartheid.

In a diametrically opposite approach, the Constitutional Committee of the ANC understood constitutionalism as a means to enshrine rights and to direct state activity towards the achievement of the popular aspirations that infused the struggle against apartheid. While protecting individual autonomy from state interference by building protections against state lawlessness into its draft proposals, the ANC draft promised the creation of a constitutional framework dedicated to the eradication of apartheid by exposing both public and private discrimination to legal attack. In its most innovative sections, the ANC draft reached beyond the mere assertion of social and economic rights and attempted to frame so-called second- and third-generation rights in a 'negative' way so as to make them justiciable in the same way as so-called first-generation, or civil and political rights. The ANC draft embraced an innovative constitutionalism that attempted to empower the state and place duties on the legislature to confront the legacy of apartheid.

Significantly, it was only in the areas of property and economic rights in the Law Commission's draft—and in the area of worker's rights in the ANC draft—that emphasis was placed on the recognition of individual and collective entitlements. Whether designed to restrain or empower, both drafts retained a fundamentally statist approach to constitutionalism. Even the commitment to open government reflected in the ANC draft, which included a right to information, was framed in limiting language, entitling recipients of the right only to 'all the information necessary to enable them to effective use of their rights'.[60]

---

[60] ANC Draft, above n 36, Art 4(3).

Finally, the incompatibility of these opposing approaches to constitutionalism reflected both the conscious and unconscious goals of their authors. The Law Commission was attempting to prevent the future Constitution and Bill of Rights from enforcing a fundamental restructuring of the South African legal system. By restricting the role of a Bill of Rights to the creation of a protective wall between the state and private activity, the Law Commission's proposals would have protected existing entitlements and deflected the impact of the shift in political power that was the consequence of the transition to democracy. In contrast, the ANC draft empowered a future state to confront the inequalities created by the apartheid system. By requiring all South Africans—in both their public and private activities —to confront apartheid's separation and inequalities, such a Bill of Rights would provide the constitutional basis for building a future South African citizenry with a common sense of belonging.[61] According to this view, it was only by confronting the legacy of apartheid that South Africa would be able to move towards the creation of a single but diverse nation. It was with these alternative visions that the main parties entered the Constitution-making process.

C. The 1993 Interim Constitution

While neither of these alternative strategies to address South Africa's racial conflict and historic inequalities unequivocally triumphed over the other in the democratic transition, the influences of these contested alternatives serve in many ways as sources of continuing constitutional tensions and meaning. The first phase of the democratic transition was buffeted by popular participation and strengthened by elements of internal participation within the ANC alliance, yet it remained ultimately under the negotiating parties' control. In contrast, an elected Constitutional Assembly (constituted by a joint sitting of the National Assembly and the Senate of South Africa's first democratic Parliament) drove the second phase.[62] Yet the process was also formally constrained by a complex set of constitutional principles contained in the interim Constitution.[63]

---

[61] See generally KL Karst, *Belonging to America: Equal Citizenship and the Constitution* (New Haven, Yale University Press, 1989).

[62] 1993 interim Constitution s 68.

[63] See 1993 interim Constitution Sch 4.

Furthermore, the provisions of the interim Constitution that addressed the creation of a final Constitution clearly influenced the distribution of power in the Constitutional Assembly. While requiring that a new Constitution be passed within two years from the first sitting of the National Assembly,[64] Chapter 5 of the interim Constitution required that at least two-thirds of all the members of the Constitutional Assembly vote for the new Constitution.[65] In addition, sections of a final Constitution dealing with the boundaries, powers and functions of the provinces had to be adopted by two-thirds of all the members of the regionally constituted Senate, giving the provinces established under the interim Constitution an important lever of influence in the Constitutional Assembly.[66]

Given the possibility that the Constitutional Assembly could fail to obtain the necessary two-thirds agreement on either a new Constitution or on the provincial arrangements, the interim Constitution provided elaborate deadlock-breaking mechanisms. First, a panel of constitutional experts[67] appointed by two-thirds of the Constitutional Assembly (or alternatively, by each party holding 40 seats in the Constitutional Assembly)[68] was required to seek amendments to resolve deadlocks within 30 days.[69] Second, if the draft text unanimously agreed upon by the panel of experts was not adopted by a two-thirds majority, the Constitutional Assembly could approve any draft text by a simple majority of its members.[70] However, in this latter case, the new text would have to be first certified by the Constitutional Court, then submitted to a national referendum, requiring ratification by at least 60 per cent of all votes cast.[71] Failure to obtain a 60-per-cent ratification would force the president to dissolve Parliament and call a general election for a new Constitutional Assembly.[72] The new Constitutional Assembly would

[64]   1993 interim Constitution s 73(1).

[65]   1993 interim Constitution s 73(2). The acceptance of a two-thirds threshold involved an important shift in position for the National Party which had attempted to require a seventy-five percent majority to pass a new constitution within the constitution-making body. This demand led to the collapse of negotiations within the CODESA framework. See Friedman, *The Long Journey*, above n 8, 31.

[66]   Friedman, *The Long Journey*, above n 8, 31.

[67]   1993 interim Constitution s 72(2).

[68]   1993 interim Constitution s 72(3).

[69]   1993 interim Constitution s 73(3) and (4).

[70]   1993 interim Constitution s 73(5).

[71]   1993 interim Constitution s 73(6)–(8).

[72]   1993 interim Constitution s 73(9).

then have one year to pass a new Constitution;[73] however, the majority required for passage of the Constitution would be reduced from two-thirds (66.6 per cent) to 60 per cent.[74]

The interim Constitution allowed many of these requirements to be amended by a two-thirds majority of a joint sitting of the National Assembly and Senate.[75] However, section 74 prohibited the repeal or amendment of the Constitutional Principles contained in Schedule 4 of the 1993 Constitution and required the Constitutional Court to certify that the new constitutional text complied with those principles. The possibility of amending the Constitution-making procedures thus effectively reduced the interim Constitution's framework for producing the new Constitution to three key elements. First, any amendment of the Constitution-making procedures required a two-thirds majority of all the members of the National Assembly and Senate, requiring agreement between at least the ANC and the National Party or IFP. Second, under all circumstances, the Constitutional Assembly was bound by the Constitutional Principles agreed to by the parties at the multi-party talks and included in Schedule 4 of the interim Constitution. And third, the Constitutional Court had to declare that the new constitutional text complied with the Constitutional Principles.

The tension between adherence to constitutional principles and the unfettered powers of a democratic Constitution-making body was explicitly addressed in the negotiations and was reflected in the interim Constitution. Invoking the need for legal continuity and minority guarantees, the National Party government always insisted on entrenching basic constitutional principles agreed upon through negotiations.[76] Although this stance was at odds with the ANC's demand for a democratic constituent assembly with unlimited freedom to draft the final Constitution, the ANC nevertheless accepted the need to provide certain assurances regarding the future constitutional framework. To this end, the ANC had published its own *Constitutional Guidelines* in 1988 and had lobbied for their international endorsement. Conversely, while the National Party government eventually accepted that a new Constitution would fail to gain popular acceptance unless an elected Constitution-making body adopted it, it attempted to ensure that the Constitutional Assembly would

---

[73] 1993 interim Constitution s 73(10).

[74] 1993 interim Constitution s 73(11).

[75] 1993 interim Constitution s 62(1).

[76] See, Friedman, *The Long Journey*, above n 8, 62.

be bound to produce a Constitution within a framework acceptable to the National Party.

IV. TEXT AND LEGAL INTERPRETATION

The main features of the 1996 Constitution include its founding provisions, the Bill of Rights and the chapter on co-operative government, which structures the relationship among the national, provincial and local spheres of government. In addition, the Constitution—similar to other post-Cold War Constitutions—includes specific chapters on public administration, the security services and finance. More unique are the chapters on 'State Institutions Supporting Constitutional Democracy' and on 'Traditional Leaders'. While the founding provisions define the nature of the post-apartheid state—emphasising principles of democracy, human rights and equality—a key feature is the specific provision that this 'Constitution is the supreme law of the Republic' and that any 'law or conduct inconsistent with it is invalid'. The provisions in the chapter on 'State Institutions Supporting Constitutional Democracy' reflect this commitment to constitutional democracy. The provisions establish a series of independent constitutional bodies including the following: Public Protector; Human Rights Commission; Auditor General; and Electoral Commission. They also establish a Commission for the Promotion of the Rights of Cultural, Religious and Linguistic communities and a Commission for Gender Equality. In contrast to these, the chapter on traditional leaders as well as the general provisions guaranteeing self-determination and the option of adopting additional charters of rights 'in order to deepen the culture of democracy', reflect the specific concerns flowing from South Africa's own negotiated transition rather than the global constitutional paradigm of the late twentieth century and beyond.

A. Interpretation as a Source of the Constitution

Justice Kentridge offered the following admonishments in *S v Zuma*—one of the Constitutional Court's very early cases: 'the Constitution does not mean whatever we might wish it to mean', and '[i]f the language used by the lawgiver is ignored in favour of a general resort to "values" the result is not interpretation but divination'. Despite these warnings, he nevertheless recognised that a Constitution 'embodying fundamental principles should *as far as its language permits* be given a broad construction'.[77] This emphasis on the ordinary meaning of the language of the Constitution has raised some concern that the inherent positivism of South African lawyers may restrict or serve as a drag on the interpretative project so central to the transformative potential of the Constitution.[78] However, this concern is counterbalanced by the Constitutional Court's own assertion in the very next case that 'whilst paying due regard to the language that has been used', the process of interpretation should be both generous and purposive, so as to give 'expression to the underlying values of the Constitution'.[79] It is this broader approach to constitutional interpretation that has marked the jurisprudence of the Constitutional Court thus far.

i. Constitution as Statute

While the Constitutional Court, from its earliest judgments, has rejected a purely textual approach to interpretation, there remains a tendency both on and off the bench to continue to assert the importance of the ordinary or plain meaning of the text as the primary source of constitutional rules.[80] Writing the Court's opinion in *S v Zuma*,[81] the Court's very first judgment, Acting Justice Kentridge emphasised the importance of the text, arguing that '[w]hile we must always be conscious of the values underlying the Constitution, it is nonetheless our task to interpret a written instrument'. He proceeded to cite Lord Wilberforce, warning that 'even a constitution is a legal instrument, the language of which must be respected'.[82] The Constitution itself provides statute-like definitions for three particular terms and lays out a specific scheme for interpreting the Bill of Rights. In the first instance, section 239 defines the document's use of three terms: national legislation, provincial legislation and organ of state. However, this section contains an internal caveat, to the effect that

---

[77] *S v Zuma* 1995 (2) SA 642 (CC) [17].

[78] See D Davis, *Democracy and Deliberation* (Kenwyn, Juta, 1999) 24–30.

[79] *Makwanyane* 1995 (3) SA 391 (CC) [9].

[80] See A Fagan, 'In Defence of the Obvious: Ordinary Language and the Identification of Constitutional Rules' (1995) 11 *South African Journal on Human Rights* 545.

[81] *S v Zuma*, above n 77.

[82] *S v Zuma*, above n 77, [17].

these meanings apply 'unless the context [in the Constitution] indicates otherwise'.[83] In the second instance, the Constitution lays down a set of interpretative rules that the courts, tribunals or other fora must apply when interpreting the Bill of Rights. [84] These specify the source of values[85] as well as particular sources of law that the court either must or may consider when interpreting the Bill of Rights.[86] This section also indicates that the Bill of Rights is not exhaustive, and that other rights or freedoms may be recognised, from common law, customary law or statute, so long as they do not conflict with the rights guaranteed in the Bill of Rights.[87]

ii. Legislative History

Historically, South African courts had refused to give much weight to legislative history. However, evidence that capital punishment was subject to extensive debate in negotiations before and during the Constitution-making process presented the Court, in *S v Makwanyane*, with two problems. First, the Court had to clarify its own relationship to the Constitution-making process, indicating what weight the views of the framers were due in interpreting the Constitution. Second, adducing evidence of the intent of the framers—despite their presence in society and even among members of the Court—required the Court to reconsider the status of legislative history in the interpretative process. While South African courts have traditionally limited the use of legislative history to evidence on the 'purpose and background of the legislation in question',[88] the Constitutional Court noted that courts in England, Australia and New Zealand had subsequently relaxed the exclusionary rule.[89] Furthermore, the Court noted that in

> countries in which the constitution is similarly the supreme law, it is not unusual for the courts to have regard to the circumstances existing at the time the constitution was adopted, including the debates and writings which formed part of the process.[90]

---

[83] 1996 Constitution s 239.
[84] 1996 Constitution s 39.
[85] 1996 Constitution s 39(a).
[86] 1996 Constitution s 39 (b) and (c).
[87] 1996 Constitution s 39 (3).
[88] *Makwanyane*, above n 79, [13].
[89] *Makwanyane*, above n 79, [14] and [15].
[90] *Makwanyane*, above n 79, [16].

Following these developments, the Court accepted the reports of the technical committees to the multi-party negotiating process as 'equivalent to the *travaux préparatoires* relied upon by the international tribunals', to provide evidence of context for the interpretation of the Constitution.[91] The Court, however, limited the scope of reliance on these materials to the specific context of *Makwanyane* and similarly situated cases 'where the background material is clear, is not in dispute, and is relevant to showing why particular provisions were or were not included in the Constitution'.[92]

Although the founders of South Africa's new constitutional order are still living, the Constitutional Court has recognised that any attempt to ascertain their intent—or to base interpretation of the Constitution on their original intent—is confounded by the Constitution-making process itself. While accepting the usefulness of background evidence provided by the record of the negotiations, the Court cautions against reliance on the comments of individual participants in the Constitution-making process 'no matter how prominent a role they might have played', as the Constitution is the 'product of a multiplicity of persons'.[93] The Court thus recognised from its inception the problem most constitutional theories of original intent fail to take cognisance of: the collective nature of the Constitution-making exercise. Legislative history may provide a context for understanding why various issues, such as the restitution clauses, were included or excluded as products of political compromises and exchanges between the negotiating partners. Yet the Court has recognised that rules of aggregation, in fact, provide a completely separate source of delegation to future generations of the need to decide on particular meanings or issues.

Having accepted the salience of legislative history, the Court argued that the 'clear failure to deal specifically in the Constitution with this issue [the death penalty] was not accidental'.[94] Support for this conclusion, the Court argued, is found in the 'Solomonic solution' proposed by the South African Law Commission in its Interim Report on Group and Human Rights in 1991, under which 'a Constitutional Court would be required to decide whether a right to life expressed in unqualified terms could be

[91] *Makwanyane*, above n 79, [17].
[92] *Makwanyane*, above n 79, [19].
[93] *Makwanyane*, above n 79, [18].
[94] *Makwanyane*, above n 79, [20].

circumscribed by a limitations clause contained in a bill of rights'.[95] Thus the Court concluded that the failure of the founders to resolve this issue left to the Constitutional Court the duty to decide whether the 'provisions of the pre-constitutional law making the death penalty a competent sentence for murder and other crimes', were consistent with the fundamental rights enshrined in the Constitution.[96]

iii. Public Opinion and Constitutional Values

Recognition that public opinion seemed to favour the retention of the death penalty posed a separate and distinct problem for the fledgling Constitutional Court as it set out to establish its place and legitimacy as a new and unique institution in the South African legal order. Asserting its role as the protector of the Constitution and human rights in a post-apartheid South Africa, the Court chose this opportunity to make a clear declaration that it would 'not allow itself to be diverted from its duty to act as an independent arbiter of the Constitution'.[97] Discounting the significance of public opinion, the Court argued that public opinion in itself is 'no substitute for the duty vested in the Courts to interpret the Constitution and to uphold its provisions without fear or favour'.[98] If public opinion were to be decisive, Justice Chaskalson declared, 'there would be no need for constitutional adjudication'.[99]

The Constitutional Court's blunt dismissal of public opinion was, however, mediated by a second line of argument, which appeared in a number of the concurring opinions. Here the Court justified its rejection of the death penalty, despite opposing public opinion, as based on the recognition of a national will to transcend the past and to uphold the standards of a 'civilised democratic' society.[100] Society's will to break with the past and to establish a community built on values antithetical to the maintenance of capital punishment was evident, the Court argued, in the decision to adopt a new Constitution and Bill of Rights. As Justice O'Regan argued in her concurring opinion, the 'new Constitution stands as a monument to this society's commitment to a future in which all

---

[95] *Makwanyane*, above n 79, [22].
[96] *Makwanyane*, above n 79, [25].
[97] *Makwanyane*, above n 79, [89].
[98] *Makwanyane*, above n 79, [88].
[99] *Makwanyane*, above n 79, [88].
[100] *Makwanyane*, above n 79, [199].

human beings will be accorded equal dignity and respect'.[101] In these arguments the Court seemed to embrace the legal fiction of the 1993 Constitution's Preamble which—despite its negotiated status and formal adoption by the unrepresentative tricameral Parliament—announced that 'We, the people of South Africa declare that . . . [and] therefore [adopt] the following provisions . . . as the Constitution of the Republic of South Africa'.[102]

For his part, Justice Didcott rejected the undue influence of public opinion, embracing instead the 'altruistic and humanitarian philosophy which animates the Constitution enjoyed by us nowadays' as reflecting the true aspirations of the South African people. In his concurring opinion Justice Didcott first repeated Justice Chaskalson's citation[103] of the classic statements by Justices Powell and Jackson of the United States Supreme Court, who argued, respectively, that the 'assessment of popular opinion is essentially a legislative, not a judicial, function', and that 'the very purpose of a bill of rights is to withdraw certain subjects from the vicissitudes of political controversy, to place them beyond the reach of majorities'. Second, Justice Didcott went on to argue that the decision to abolish or retain capital punishment is a constitutional question, the determination of which is the duty of the Court and not of representative institutions.[104]

Justice Kentridge repeated this concurrent rejection of public opinion and embrace of national values. Arguing that public opinion, 'even if expressed in Acts of Parliament, cannot be decisive',[105] he suggests that while clear public opinion 'could not be entirely ignored', the Court 'would be abdicating [its] . . . constitutional function' if it simply deferred to public opinion.[106] Justice Kentridge proceeded to discount evidence of public opinion on the grounds that there had been no referendum or recent legislation.[107] He suggested, instead, that the reduction in executions after 1990 and the official executive moratorium on the death penalty, 'while not evidence of general opinion, do cast serious doubt on the acceptability of capital punishment in South Africa'.[108]

[101] *Makwanyane*, above n 79, [344].
[102] 1993 interim Constitution, Preamble.
[103] *Makwanyane*, above n 79, [89].
[104] *Makwanyane*, above n 79, [188].
[105] *Makwanyane*, above n 79, [200].
[106] *Makwanyane*, above n 79, [200].
[107] *Makwanyane*, above n 79, [201].
[108] Ibid.

These countermajoritarian concerns regarding the 'appeal to public opinion',[109] were overshadowed in the Court's arguments by a reliance on the 'evolving standards of civilization',[110] which the court inferred were incorporated into South African jurisprudence by the country's aspiration to be a free and democratic society.[111] It is this national ambition, contained in the constitutional commitment 'to promote the values which underlie an open and democratic society based on freedom and equality'[112] that the Court presented as the source of social mores underlying the new constitutional dispensation. In this context, Justice Kentridge concluded that the 'deliberate execution of a human, however depraved and criminal his conduct, must degrade the new society which is coming into being'.[113] A similar reliance on the Constitution's inherent morality as a source of a public or national will that supersedes simple public opinion can be found in Justice Langa's argument that 'implicit in the provisions and tone of the Constitution are values of a more mature society, which relies on moral persuasion rather than force; on example rather than coercion'.[114]

B. International and Comparative Sources

The provisions of section 39 of the Constitution, which require courts and other interpreters of the Bill of Rights to consider international law and explicitly allow them to consider foreign law, are a fairly unique aspect of South Africa's interpretative project. These provisions call for interpreters to draw upon a vast range of external sources for interpretive and constitutional values. The provision in section 35 of the 1993 Constitution that admonishes the Courts to 'have regard to public international law applicable to the protection of the rights entrenched' was, in fact, strengthened in the second round of Constitution-making. In *S v Makwanyane,* the Constitutional Court emphasised that section 35(1) of the 1993 Constitution did not require,[115] but rather permitted, the

---

[109] Ibid.
[110] *Makwanyane*, above n 79, [199].
[111] *Makwanyane*, above n 79, [198] and [199].
[112] 1993 interim Constitution s 35.
[113] *Makwanyane*, above n 79, [199].
[114] *Makwanyane*, above n 79, [222].
[115] *Makwanyane*, above n 79, [39]. *Cf,* s 39(1)(b) of the 1996 Constitution which states that the court's 'must consider international law'.

Courts to 'have regard to'[116] public international law as 'guidance as to the correct interpretation of particular provisions'.[117] However, section 39 of the 1996 Constitution now states that when interpreting the Bill of Rights the Court 'must consider international law'.[118] Thus, it is now mandatory for the Court to address the interpretation of rights given in international documents and by international fora.

The reference to foreign law remains less positive, however. While the reference to foreign law in section 39 is permissive, the Constitutional Court has urged caution in respect to the use of comparative Bill of Rights jurisprudence and foreign case law. The Court noted in *Makwanyane* that these sources 'will no doubt be of importance, particularly in the early stages of the transition when there is no developed indigenous jurisprudence in this branch of the law', but 'will not necessarily offer a safe guide to the interpretation' of the Bill of Rights.[119] The Court has since noted that the Constitution requires the Court to give attention to international experience 'with a view to finding principles rather than to extracting rigid formulae, and to look for rationales rather than rules'.[120] Even with the recognition of the need to draw on foreign materials, until South Africa produces its own body of constitutional jurisprudence as a source of interpretation, the Court's use of both international materials and comparative law in the *Makwanyane* case is revealing. Instead of relying on the international and foreign materials for legal precedent, the Court used these materials primarily as a means to distinguish the South African case. The only case quoted with unqualified approval, as equivalent and possibly a source of the Court's decision, was the decision of the Hungarian Constitutional Court.[121] Instead, the Court tended to use the international and comparative materials as sources for specific lines of argument and justification and, in a more general sense, for supporting the general role of the court and judicial review in particular.[122]

While the use of foreign case law has since leached into South Africa's constitutional jurisprudence beyond the interpretation of the Bill of Rights permitted in section 39 of the Constitution, early predictions and

---

[116] *Makwanyane*, above n 79, [37].

[117] *Makwanyane*, above n 79, [35].

[118] 1996 Constitution s 39(1)(b).

[119] *Makwanyane*, above n 79, [37].

[120] *Coetzee v Government of the Republic of South Africa* 1995 (4) SA 631 (CC) [57].

[121] *Makwanyane*, above n 79, [38].

[122] See, eg, *Makwanyane*, above n 79, [14], [15], [17], [18] and [89].

fears that the Constitutional Court might uncritically follow foreign jurisprudence—particularly that of the United States Supreme Court—have proven unfounded. Even in cases dealing with the interpretation of the Bill of Rights, the Constitutional Court has urged caution when using foreign case law. In *Sanderson v Attorney-General, Eastern Cape*,[123] a case dealing with the right of an accused to be tried within a reasonable time, the Constitutional Court argued that '[c]omparative research is generally valuable, and is all the more so when dealing with problems new to our jurisprudence but well developed in mature constitutional democracies'. But, the court noted, 'the use of foreign precedent requires circumspection and acknowledgement that transplants require careful management', and therefore it is not a question of merely adopting one or another test from US jurisprudence "without recognising that our society and our criminal justice system differ from those in North America'.[124] This is particularly the case, the Court argued, if one adopts

> the assertion of right requirement of *Barker* [a US case] without making allowance for the fact that the vast majority of South African accused are unrepresented and have no conception of a right to a speedy trial. To deny them relief . . . because they did not assert their rights would be to strike a pen through the right as far as the most vulnerable members of our society are concerned.[125]

This circumspection is even more evident in non-Bill-of-Rights cases. In such cases, the Constitutional Court has been quick to point to differences in 'constitutional language and structure, as well as history and culture' as reasons for the Court to be fairly circumspect.[126] For example, the Constitutional Court drew heavily on Australian and Canadian jurisprudence in one of the first cases that dealt with the distribution of powers between the national and regional governments. The case involved a dispute over the National Education Policy Bill that was then before the National Assembly, and the Court explicitly warned off the relevance of the federal experience in the United States. In this case, brought as a case of abstract review (in which a law's constitutionality may be challenged on its face by particular constitutionally defined litigants,

---

[123]   *Sanderson v Attorney-General, Eastern Cape,* 1998 (2) SA 38 (CC).

[124]   *Sanderson,* above n 124, [26].

[125]   *Sanderson,* above n 124, [26].

[126]   See, Richard C Blake, *The Frequent Irrelevance of US Judicial Decisions in South Africa,* (1999) 15 *South African Journal on Human Rights* 192, 197.

such as the president or premier of a Province, before a specific cause of
action arises), the petitioners focused on the claim that the 'Bill imposed
national education policy on the provinces'[127] and thereby 'encroached
upon the autonomy of the provinces and their executive authority'.[128]
They also claimed the 'Bill could have no application in KwaZulu-Natal
because it [the province] was in a position to formulate and regulate its
own policies'.[129] While all parties accepted that education was defined as
a concurrent legislative function under the interim Constitution, the contending parties imagined that different consequences should flow from
the determination that a subject matter is concurrently assigned by the
Constitution to both provincial and national government.

KwaZulu-Natal and the Inkatha Freedom Party, which held the majority of seats in the regional legislature at that time, assumed a form of US-
style pre-emption doctrine in which the National Assembly and national
government would be precluded from acting in an area of concurrent
jurisdiction so long as the province was capable of formulating and regulating its own policies. In rejecting this argument, the Constitutional
Court avoided the notion of pre-emption altogether and instead argued
that the 'legislative competences of the provinces and Parliament to make
laws in respect of schedule 6 [concurrent] matters do not depend upon
section 126(3)', which, the Court argued, only comes into operation if it is
necessary to resolve a conflict between inconsistent national and provincial laws.[130] The Court thus rejected the notion of pre-emption as a valid
interpretation of the relationship between national and regional powers
and instead argued that cooperative governance allowed for coexistence
and even some dissonance in the exercise of concurrent jurisdiction, so
long as there is not an irreconcilable conflict. Even if there is irreconcilable conflict and the 'conflict is resolved in favour of either the provincial
or national law the other is not invalidated' it is merely 'subordinated and
to the extent of the conflict rendered inoperative'.[131] Supported by the
comparative jurisprudence of Canada and Australia, the Court was able
to make a distinction between 'laws that are inconsistent with each other

---

[127] *Ex parte Speaker of the National Assembly: Re Dispute Concerning the Constitutionality
of Certain Provisions of the National Education Policy Bill 83 of 1995,* 1996 (3) SA 289 [here-
inafter *National Education Bill* case] [8].

[128] *National Education Bill* case [8].

[129] *National Education Bill* case [8].

[130] *National Education Bill* case [16].

[131] *National Education Bill* case [16].

and laws that are inconsistent with the Constitution'[132] and thereby argue that 'even if the National Education Policy Bill deals with matters in respect of which provincial laws would have paramountcy, it could not for that reason alone be declared unconstitutional'.[133]

The Constitutional Court's approach clearly aimed to reduce the tensions inherent in the continuing conflict between provincial and national governments, particularly in relation to the continuing violent tensions in KwaZulu-Natal. It also took the opportunity to explicitly preclude an alternative interpretation. Focusing on arguments before the Court that relied upon the United States Supreme Court's decision in *New York v United States*,[134] the Court made the point that '[u]nlike their counterparts in the United States of America, the provinces in South Africa are not sovereign states'.[135] Furthermore, the Court warned that '[d]ecisions of the courts of the United States dealing with state rights are not a safe guide as to how our courts should address problems that may arise in relation to the rights of provinces under our Constitution'.[136] It is no surprise that as time has passed, the Constitutional Court has turned increasingly to its own jurisprudence as a source of precedent and for legal arguments. Despite this natural inward shift for sources of jurisprudential argument, the Constitutional Court has continued to view its rights jurisprudence in global terms. Today, however, the South African Constitutional Court is as likely to be cited in rights cases before courts in other countries as it is to quote from foreign or international sources.

V. CONCLUSION

While the written Constitution is the primary source of constitutional law in post-apartheid South Africa, the task of interpreting and implementing the Constitution requires us to understand the deeper legal traditions as well as the social and political legacies that are the embedded sources of this document. At the most basic level, the core principles of the Constitution were first reflected in the negotiated principles included in Schedule 4 of the interim Constitution. The Constitutional Court was

---

[132]   *National Education Bill* case [16].
[133]   *National Education Bill* case [20].
[134]   *New York v United States* 505 US 144 (1992).
[135]   *National Education Bill* case [23].
[136]   *National Education Bill* case [23].

called upon to apply these principles to certify that the Constitutional Assembly had remained true to the agreements reached by the parties who negotiated the terms for establishing a democratic South Africa. Many of these principles, however, were specifically tailored to address the direct concerns of various parties in the negotiations. The fundamental sources of the Constitution arose from the particular history and traditions of South Africa's political struggles, legal practices and culture. At the same time, the Constitution points beyond South Africa's borders and calls upon the courts to take international law and foreign jurisprudence into consideration when interpreting the rights guaranteed by the Constitution. The diversity of legitimate sources provides wide scope for an interpretative practice that must recognise that the Constitution is a living tree whose meaning and application will grow as South African society moves away from its multiple legacies of colonialism, apartheid, deprivation and violence. Yet for the promise of the Constitution and democratic transition to be fulfilled, those undertaking this interpretative task will have to remain loyal to the fundamental vision of a new society that remains at the heart of the final 1996 Constitution.

FURTHER READING

Asmal, K, with Chidester, D and Lubisi, C (eds), *Legacy of Freedom: The ANC's Human Rights Tradition* (Johannesburg, Jonathan Ball, 2005)

Ebrahim, H, *Soul of a Nation: Constitution-Making in South Africa* (Cape Town and Oxford, Oxford University Press, 1998)

Friedman, S (ed), *The Long Journey: South Africa's Quest for a Negotiated Settlement* (Johannesburg, Ravan Press, 1993)

Ghai, Y, 'A Journey around Constitutions: Reflections on Contemporary Constitutions' (2005) 122 (4) *South African Law Journal* 804

4

Constitutional Principles

———◦•◦———

Introduction – Constitutional Principles – Constitutional Principles in the Constitutional Court – Constitutional Principles in Practice – Founding Principles, Basic Structure and the Future – Conclusion

I. INTRODUCTION

T HE CONCEPT OF constitutional principles has a very specific meaning in the South African context. While the principles that underlie the British Constitution are of great significance to current practice and interpretation of that Constitution,[1] reference to constitutional principles in South Africa is understood to mean the 34 Constitutional Principles that made up Schedule 4 of the 1993 interim Constitution. These Constitutional Principles were the key to South Africa's two-stage Constitution-making process. From the perspective of the different political parties that negotiated the democratic transition, these principles guaranteed that their primary objectives would be secured in the final outcome. For this reason, Schedule 4 and the requirement that the Constitutional Court certify that the Constitutional Assembly abide by these principles in producing the final Constitution, were the only parts of the interim Constitution that could not be amended by a two-thirds majority; in fact, these provisions could not be amended or repealed and were set in stone as the core of the negotiated agreement. Before exploring the specific Constitutional Principles contained in Schedule 4 and their role in relation to the 1996 Constitution, it is necessary to take a more general

---

[1] See, P Leyland, *The Constitution of the United Kingdom*, (Oxford, Hart Publishing, 2007) 35.

look at the nature and role of constitutional principles, particularly in the context of post-colonial Constitution-building.

II. CONSTITUTIONAL PRINCIPLES

While principles of democracy, human rights and the rule of law are considered central to legitimate processes of state reconstruction, there is neither universal agreement on the content of these principles nor on the practical implications for institution building. These principles include a variety of forms of government, a range of different individual and even group rights as well as quite different notions of what the balance should be between judicial authority and democratically elected or responsible institutions at different levels of government. Adopting a list of constitutional principles does not guarantee the future, but it does provide a process and a framework within which areas of commonality may be defined and questions of difference may be located. Providing an institutional mechanism through which these principles may be brought to bear on the debate over constitutional provisions—or a means to evaluate the final product adopted by a democratically elected Constitution-making body—provides a zone of comfort for those who do not feel that their central concerns are likely to be adequately reflected in the democratic process, whether they are past elites or excluded minorities.

Another important role that the debate over constitutional principles plays is that it postpones or mediates the necessity of making hard or immediate decisions on what might be effectively non-negotiable issues. Adopting a broad principle allows the conflicting parties to put aside an issue for further debate while working on issues over which there might be greater agreement. This postponement, with continuing engagement between the parties, is an important element in building the basic elements of trust between opposing groups. And it is central to the ultimate success of a democracy-building project. Constitutional principles are rarely definitive and contain, in most cases, a degree of constructive ambiguity that enables all parties to feel they might be able to live with the outcome of the process. At times, the different parties in South Africa held diametrically opposite understandings of the meanings of particular principles, but this often acknowledged ambiguity was precisely what allowed the process to go forward.

One of the effects of the process of negotiating constitutional principles is to slowly entrap the constitutional conflict in a process of argumentation and alternative legal propositions. This process precludes some outcomes and mediates the differences between what might be considered acceptable alternatives. It is often influenced as much by international understandings as it is affected by the particular historical and material parameters of the local conflict. Finally, the commitment to constitutional principles promotes constitutional engagement over exit and the ever-present threat of violence this implies.

A focus on constitutional principles and the need to frame a democratic transition within the realm of a broadly agreed-upon set of principles thus provides a potential means of entrapping non-negotiable conflicts into ongoing but manageable constitutional struggles. The key element in this process—drawing participants in and enabling them to sustain their own visions of a viable alternative to the present situation—is the practice of constitutional imagination, in which the different concepts and options are invested with meanings more or less in accord with the hopes and aspirations of the different parties. Despite often divergent understandings and deliberately opened-ended agreements over meaning, I argue that the framing of constitutional principles in the South African case facilitated the progress of the transition to democracy and provided the means of incorporating often inconsistent and conflicting ideas about the parameters of the future—whether in the form of explicit guarantees or institutional arrangements. It was this principled ambiguity that allowed the conflict to be 'civilised', despite continuing violence and vociferous, if not fundamental, disagreement.

A. Sources and History of Constitutional Principles

The constitutional principles that have framed post-Cold War transitions to democracy stem from a range of sources, including local constitutional histories and the evolving international standards reflected in the post-World War II human rights agreements, the Helsinki process and the experience of decolonisation. For Southern Africa, the first explicit articulation of constitutional principles as a basis for negotiating a democratic transition emerged in the form of the 1982 Principles produced by the Western Contact Group for Namibia. Given the legal status of Namibia (a former German colony, League of Nations mandate and finally illegally occupied territory, after the United Nations withdrawal of the mandate was recognised as binding by the International Court of Justice), it was often assumed that the idea of constitutional principles would be unique to that conflict. The implementation of Security Council Resolution 435 led to these principles being adopted as the guiding principles of the Namibian Constitutional Assembly, which drew up Namibia's Constitution after the 1990 elections. And the idea of constitutional principles as a means of framing a democratic transition would become key to South Africa's surprisingly successful transition to democracy.

It is possible to claim that the idea of constitutional principles was foreshadowed in South Africa by the ANC's 1944 presentation of the African Claims document—demands framed around the promises of the Atlantic Charter—or presaged by the ANC's adoption of the Freedom Charter in 1955. However, neither of these documents offered binding promises or institutional assurances to opponents of the ANC. It was only with the publication of the ANC's *Constitutional Guidelines* in 1988 that there was an attempt to offer a broad outline of a future system of governance and rights. It was the internationalisation of the principles expressed in the *Guidelines* through the Harare Declaration of the OAU's liberation sub-committee and in the UN General Assembly's Declaration Against Apartheid in 1989, that a clear set of parameters was established. Within this structure, the process of building a democratic South Africa could begin to be negotiated.

Even then the debate over constitutional principles had only begun. The parties failed to agree on the Declaration of Intent, a minimal set of principles adopted at their first formal meeting—the Convention for a Democratic South Africa, in December 1991. The debate over principles that began at that time would become central to the negotiations in the Multi-Party Negotiating Forum that convened in early 1993 and led to the adoption of the '1993 Interim Constitution' under which South Africa held its first democratic elections and elected Nelson Mandela as president. Even then the role of constitutional principles was not exhausted, as an even larger number of constitutional principles had been included in an appendix to the 1993 Constitution for the purpose of providing a framework for the work of the newly elected bicameral legislature, which served in joint sitting as a Constitutional Assembly with the mandate to produce a final Constitution within two years. In the end, the Constitutional Court was called upon to apply the principles to determine whether the final Constitution could be certified and adopted as the last formal act of the democratic transition. Building South Africa's democracy is, however, an ongoing project.

B. The 34 Constitutional Principles in Schedule 4

The Constitutional Principles incorporated into Schedule 4 of the interim Constitution contained an amalgam of broad democratic principles consistent with the new international post-Cold War consensus on constitutionalism and a mass of detail specific to the needs of the South African negotiating parties. Once the parties had agreed in the Multi-Party Negotiating Forum to a 'two-phased transitional process', attention shifted to establishing a set of broad constitutional principles that could be agreed upon as the basis for a deal. To this end, the parties agreed in July 1993 to adopt 26 Constitutional Principles as a guide for the future. As the parties recognised the significance of these principles, the emphasis of the negotiations shifted: The parties become more focused on ensuring that their concerns were addressed in the Constitutional Principles than on delaying the negotiations on the interim Constitution, which would only control the elections—set for 27 April 1994—and the first five years of a Government of National Unity. As a result, the number of Constitutional Principles expanded from 26 to 34; the final addition was a principle that recognised the status of a traditional monarch,[2] which was incorporated through an amendment to the interim Constitution, promulgated the day before the first democratic elections.

Among the general principles the parties adopted were those guaranteeing a common citizenship and a 'democratic system of government committed to achieving equality between men and women and people of all races',[3] as well as the enjoyment of 'all universally accepted fundamental rights',[4] the separation of powers[5] and the supremacy of the Constitution.[6] In addition to principles protecting the political role of minority political parties[7] and special procedures and majorities for future constitutional

---

[2] Constitution of the Republic of South Africa Act 200 of 1993 [hereinafter 1993 interim Constitution] Sch 4, Constitutional Principle [hereinafter CP] XIII(2).

[3] 1993 interim Constitution Sch 4 CP I.

[4] 1993 interim Constitution Sch 4 CP II.

[5] 1993 interim Constitution Sch 4 CP VI.

[6] 1993 interim Constitution Sch 4 CP IV.

[7] 1993 interim Constitution Sch 4 CP XIV.

amendments,[8] a large number of principles provided extraordinary detail on the structure of government, particularly on the definition and division of powers among national, regional and local levels of government.[9] Concern over the allocation of powers between the national and regional levels of government led to the inclusion of an elaborate set of criteria for determining the allocation of powers between these spheres of government.[10] Finally, a set of principles ensured the establishment of a Government of National Unity for five years and provided assurances to the civil service, police and military that these institutions would be non-partisan and that members of the public service would be 'entitled to a fair pension'.[11]

Most dramatic of the specific provisions were those requiring the recognition of 'traditional leadership, according to indigenous law'[12] and 'collective rights of self-determination'.[13] In addition, recognition of the Zulu King and the provision of a *Volkstaat* Council were added by amendment to the main body of the Constitution just prior to the April 1994 elections as a way to include parts of the Freedom Alliance, particularly the Inkatha Freedom Party (IFP) and the Afrikaner right-wing led by ex-South African Defence Force General Constant Viljoen. Finally, the parties amended the Constitutional Principles to provide that provincial recognition of a traditional monarch would be protected in a final Constitution[14] and that any territorial entity established through the assertion of a right to self-determination by 'any community sharing a common culture and language heritage'[15] would be entrenched in the new Constitution.[16]

This inclusion of a plethora of constitutional principles and provisions served to enable the elections to go forward and the democratic transition to proceed, but they also served to defer a range of substantive issues into the next phase of Constitution-making. Although the individual constitutional principles were open to differing interpretations, the interaction of the different principles would later revive many of the conflicts their

---

8   1993 interim Constitution Sch 4 CP XV.
9   1993 interim Constitution Sch 4 CPP XVI–XX.
10   1993 interim Constitution Sch 4 CP XXI.
11   1993 interim Constitution Sch 4 CPP XXIX–XXXIII.
12   1993 interim Constitution Sch 4 CP XIII.
13   1993 interim Constitution Sch 4 CP XII.
14   1993 interim Constitution Sch 4 CP XIII(2).
15   1993 interim Constitution Sch 4 CP XXXIV(1).
16   1993 interim Constitution Sch 4 CP XXXIV(3).

inclusion was designed to lay to rest. A significant difference, however, is that these conflicts were now transferred to a completely different arena. In effect, the shift to a democratically elected Constitutional Assembly changed the terms of these debates and led to the inclusion of a range of new issues. Despite this change, there continued to be different interpretations of the Constitutional Principles—both within the different political parties within the Constitutional Assembly and later before the Constitutional Court. These different understandings are still drawn upon in political discourse and in legal debates over the meaning of specific constitutional provisions, as well as in specific cases before the Constitutional Court.

C. The Role of Constitutional Principles

The Constitutional Principles negotiated by the South African parties represented a vast and often contradictory range of possibilities, and the very process of negotiating and providing justification for their inclusion changed the parameters of constitutional imagination in South Africa. Some believed the Constitutional Principles provided the basis for continued sectarian claims by particular ethnic minorities or traditionalists that embraced values that were seemingly in conflict with the broader democratic thrust of the process. Yet, the international frame within which they were located gave weight to those who insisted on a democratic interpretation of the overall framework. Yet it is important to note that the constitutional principles played very different roles at different moments in South Africa's process of democratisation. In this sense, the idea of constitutional principles clearly embraces an important temporal element, in addition to the broader substantive implications of the principles.

The publication of the ANC *Constitutional Guidelines* in 1988 can be seen as an opening gambit in the process of negotiations and an intervention designed to preclude internal options that the apartheid government was then considering. To ANC activists and supporters, the 1988 principles served as a signal of the possibility of a negotiated transition; they also functioned as a promise of democratic intentions to those South Africans who feared the possibility of a future ANC government. In this way, the 1988 principles initiated the process in which the concept of constitutional principles became central to enabling the transition to democracy.

The Harare Declaration, which began the process of internationalising the ANC's 1988 Principles, took a step further: It outlined an internationally acceptable process of democratisation, including the establishment of an interim government to oversee the transition. This latter demand failed to recognise that the apartheid government would not agree to relinquish political power until there were some guarantees regarding the shape of a future South Africa. This problem pushed the question of the Constitution-making process to the top of the political agenda, but provided no means to resolve the different visions of who should participate in what form of process to create a new Constitution. It did, however, make it clear that any resolution of the conflict would need to meet minimum international standards if South Africa was to be accepted back into the world community.

The effect of combining the debate over constitutional principles with the requirement that any future constitutional dispensation meet minimum international standards as defined by international human rights principles framed the parameters of acceptable options. This framing had a powerful impact on the shape of the debate over different constitutional options and the available alternatives: It precluded the demand for nationalising the land and key national industries, and it also precluded demands for ethnic self-determination and empowered the cross-party coalition of women demanding that claims of tradition should not override gender equality. Here, too, there were distinctly temporal and geographic elements to the framing of these principles. Take, for example, the idea that national self-determination meant that all the people living within the historic colonial boundaries of the Union of South Africa should vote together to determine the future of the country. This was the prevailing understanding in 1991 and was accepted as consistent with the international law of self-determination that had evolved in the context of decolonisation. Yet within a few years, the Bosnian War and the Dayton Accords that ended that war would have opened up a debate over the right of ethnic minorities to claim self-determination and might have provided a basis for the claims of those in South Africa claiming the recognition of ethnic groups, such as the advocates of an 'Afrikaner' homeland or ethnic 'vetoes' in South Africa.

While agreeing on a list of 34 Constitutional Principles and including them in Schedule 4 of the interim Constitution was less difficult then first predicted, the key issue remained: how would the parties resolve the dual problems of process and substance? Although it could be argued that the principles provided clear substantive criteria to Constitution-makers, it was less clear how they would serve to bind the process. It was the decision to require a new Constitutional Court to certify that the final Constitution adhered to the requirements of the Constitutional Principles that created the degree of confidence necessary for the democratic transition to go forward. While this was by no means the only issue, its importance for creating the atmosphere of trust so important to political transitions cannot be overestimated.

III. CONSTITUTIONAL PRINCIPLES IN THE CONSTITUTIONAL COURT

Following its adoption by the Constitutional Assembly, the new constitutional text was submitted to the Constitutional Court for certification that it complied with the Constitutional Principles as required by section 71 of the interim Constitution. Apart from the ANC and the Pan Africanist Congress, all the other political parties represented in the Constitutional Assembly filed objections to certification before the Constitutional Court. While a total of 84 private parties filed objections, only the political parties and 27 private parties were granted permission to advance oral arguments to the Court in proceedings that continued for nine days before the Constitutional Court.[17]

A. The Certification Judgments

The Constitutional Court delivered its judgment on 6 September 1996, refusing to certify that the text of the final Constitution adopted by the Constitutional Assembly on 8 May 1996 met the conditions required by the Constitutional Principles. This was an extraordinary display of the power of judicial review, given that 86 per cent of the democratically elected Constitutional Assembly had adopted the text, after last minute political compromises. But this view must be balanced by understanding the way in which the Constitutional Court carefully pointed out, in its unanimous, unattributed, opinion, that 'in general and in respect of

---

[17] *Ex parte Chairperson of the Constitutional Assembly: In re Certification of the Constitution of the Republic of South Africa, 1996'* 1996 (4) SA 744 (CC) [24]–[25]. [hereinafter *First Certification* case].

the overwhelming majority of its provisions', the Constitutional Assembly had met the predetermined requirements of the Constitutional Principles. As a consequence, the reaction of the main political parties was to embrace the Court's decision and to reject attempts by others to use the denial of certification as a tool to reopen settled debates. Instead, the Constitutional Assembly focused solely on the issues raised by the Constitutional Court and within two months passed an Amended Text.

While the Constitutional Court identified specific aspects of the text that failed to comply with particular constitutional principles, all the concerns expressed by the Constitutional Court fell into two broad categories: that the text fulfil the guarantee that the Constitution be the supreme law of the land, protecting the integrity and independence of constitutional institutions; and, that the text provide an adequate framework for the distribution of power among different levels of government. In its opinion the Court identified six ways in which the Court felt the text failed to meet these two broader constitutional goals of constitutional supremacy and institutional independence. First, and most significantly for the future of constitutional supremacy, the Court believed the text failed to provide adequate procedures for constitutional amendment. Even though the text provided that a two-thirds majority of the National Assembly had to pass any future constitutional amendments, the Constitutional Court held that the Constitutional Principles required both procedural guarantees as well as special majorities for the enactment of valid constitutional amendments.[18] Furthermore, the Court argued that the failure to provide a higher degree of protection against amendment of the Bill of Rights as compared to other sections of the Constitution was inconsistent with Principle II, which required an entrenched Bill of Rights.[19]

Second, the judgment identified two areas of law that had been key to the negotiated solution and which the Constitutional Assembly had attempted to preclude from future challenges by placing them beyond constitutional scrutiny: the Labour Relations Act[20] and the Promotion of National Unity and Reconciliation Act.[21] In both cases, the Constitutional Court found that the attempt to insulate these laws from constitutional scrutiny violated

[18]   *First Certification* case [152]–[156].
[19]   *First Certification* case [157]–[159].
[20]   Labour Relations Act 66 of 1995.
[21]   Promotion of National Unity and Reconciliation Act 34 of 1995.

the constitutional principle guaranteeing constitutional supremacy.[22] Third, and also related to the negotiations over labour rights, was the provision granting employer associations but not individual employers the right to engage in collective bargaining. The Constitutional Court here argued that Constitutional Principle XXVIII guaranteed that individual employers should also have the right to engage in constitutionally protected collective bargaining.[23]

Fourth, the Court identified two areas in which the independence of constitutionally created offices or institutions was not adequately protected. The Court argued that the provisions for the removal of the Public Protector and the Auditor General by Parliament—on the grounds of misconduct, incapacity or incompetence—were inadequate to protect the independence of these officials.[24] Reviewing the general provisions for the creation of a Public Service Commission, the Constitutional Court also argued that the failure to specify its functions and powers in the text meant that it was not possible for the Court to either certify that it would be independent and impartial nor ensure that its powers would not be so limited as to ensure it would not have a detrimental effect on the guarantee of provincial autonomy.[25]

Fifth, the Constitutional Court's concern over the allocation of power among different levels of government was reflected in the Court's argument that the provisions for local government were inadequate and the debate over whether the powers and functions allocated to the provinces were substantially less than in the interim Constitution. In the first instance, the Court noted that the text provided no framework for local government or formal procedures for the exercise of legislative powers at the local government level. At the same time, the Court argued that the text's guarantee of an entrenched power of local government to collect excise tax was inappropriate and violated the guarantee that the Constitution provide 'appropriate fiscal powers and functions for different categories of local government'.[26]

Finally, the Constitutional Court held that on balance the powers and functions given to the provinces were substantially less than or inferior to those the provinces enjoyed under the interim Constitution, and thus

---

[22] *First Certification* case [149]–[50].
[23] *First Certification* case [69].
[24] *First Certification* case [163]–[165].
[25] *First Certification* case [176]–[177].
[26] *First Certification* case [303]–[305].

failed to satisfy Constitutional Principle XVIII(2).[27] However, the Court went on to argue that although there was a reduction in provincial powers in the areas of policing, education, local government and traditional leadership, when

> [s]een in the context of the totality of provincial power, the curtailment of these four aspects of the Interim Constitution schedule 6 powers would not ... be sufficient in themselves to lead to the conclusion that the powers of the provinces taken as a whole are substantially less than or substantially inferior to the powers vested in them under the Interim Constitution.[28]

It was only when this reduction of power over specific matters was combined with the greater scope for national legislation to override conflicting provincial legislation that the overall reduction of provincial powers reached a level that violated the Constitutional Principles. This was particularly so where the text created a presumption that national legislation passed by the National Council of Provinces automatically prevailed over conflicting provincial legislation.[29]

The *First Certification* case turned on a number of specific instances where the Constitutional Assembly had failed to meet the requirements of the Constitutional Principles, such as the collective bargaining provision or the failure to provide an adequate framework for local government. Other issues flagged by the Constitutional Court all involved aspects of the text that to some degree affected the capacity or integrity of institutions or constitutional provisions designed to secure the country's new commitment to constitutional democracy. Although it has been argued that many of these issues could have been decided in favour of certification,[30] the result reflected the Constitutional Court's assertion of the centrality of constitutional democracy in the Constitutional Principles and also the broader acceptance of constitutionalism among all political parties in the Constitutional Assembly. Recognition of the status of the Constitutional Court and the commitment of the political parties to the process was confirmed when on 11 October 1997 the Constitutional Assembly adopted an Amended Text, which had been carefully redrafted

----

[27]   *First Certification* case [306]–[481].

[28]   *First Certification* case [479].

[29]   *First Certification* case [480].

[30]   See, M Chaskalson and D Davis, 'Constitutionalism, the Rule of Law and the *First Certification* Judgment: *Ex parte Chairperson of the Constitutional Assembly: In re Certification of the Constitution of the Republic of South Africa, 1996* 1996 (4) SA 744 (CC)' (1997) 13 *South African Journal on Human Rights* 430.

to meet the requirements of the Court's certification decision. The Constitutional Court made quick work of the process of certification and certified the Amended Text on 4 December 1997.

B. The Constitutional Court's Approach to Certification

The legitimacy of the certification judgments is to a large extent the product of the Constitutional Court's handling of its own role in the process. Instead of trumpeting its constitutional duty to review the work of the Constitutional Assembly, the Court was careful to point out that the Constitutional Assembly had a large degree of latitude in its interpretation of the Principles and that the Court's role was judicial and not political. While this may be dismissed as merely hiding behind legalism, this deference to the democratic Constitution-making process shaped the Court's approach to its task. In defining its mode of review, the Court specifically identified two separate questions. First, the Court would examine whether the 'basic structures and premises of the NT [[New Text] was in] . . . accordance with those contemplated in the CPs'. By conducting this inquiry, the Court established a minimum threshold the Constitutional Assembly had to meet and found that the New Text satisfied those standards. The significance of this approach is that despite arguments that the certification judgments are unique, under the final Constitution, the Court is granted the authority to determine the constitutionality of any future Constitutional Amendments.[31] Significantly, at least two justices of the Constitutional Court have referred to the notion of the basic structure of the Constitution used by the Indian Supreme Court in its jurisprudence striking down validly enacted Constitutional Amendments. To this extent, the Constitutional Assembly and the Court have left open the future of the Court's role in the formal Constitution-making or amending process under the final Constitution.

Second, the Court's methodology held that only once the Court decided that the New Text accorded with the basic structure and premises, it would turn to an analysis of whether the details of the New Text complied with the Constitutional Principles. By turning to a detailed analysis of the content of the New Text, the Court asserted its power and duty to ensure compliance by testing the text against the Constitutional

---

[31] Constitution of the Republic of South Africa Act 108 of 1996 [hereinafter the 1996 Constitution] s 167(4)(d).

Principles; however, the Court was also careful to limit the scope of this review. It accomplished this limiting strategy by asserting the formal legal distinction between politics and law.[32] The Court noted that it 'has a judicial and not a political mandate' and that this 'judicial function, a legal exercise' meant that the Court had 'no power, no mandate and no right to express any view on the political choices made by the CA [Constitutional Assembly] in drafting the NT [New Text]'.[33] The Court asserted that its interpretation of the Constitutional Principles was consistent with its jurisprudential commitment to a 'purposive and teleological application which gives expression to the commitment to "create a new order" based on a "sovereign and democratic constitutional state"' in which 'all citizens' are 'able to enjoy and exercise their fundamental rights and freedoms'.[34] It also asserted that the Court was not concerned with the merits of the Constitutional Assembly's choices. In fact, the Court emphasised the scope of the Constitutional Assembly's latitude by arguing that while the New Text

> may not transgress the fundamental discipline of the CPs . . . within the space created by those CPs interpreted purposively, the issue as to which of several permissible models should be adopted is not an issue for adjudication by this Court. That is a matter for the political judgment of the CA, and therefore properly falling within its discretion.[35]

In contrast, however, the Court took a robust view of its judicial role of establishing legal precedent. Faced with the dilemma of alternative constructions in which one interpretation could be held to be in violation of the Constitutional Principles, the Court adopted the traditional judicial strategy of upholding that interpretation which would avoid a declaration of unconstitutionality. This raised the spectre of a future Court revisiting the issue and adopting an interpretation that would be in violation of the

---

[32] This strategy of judicial deference is interesting in a context where the Constitutional Assembly had, in its drafting of the new text, gone so far as to incorporate the precise language of Constitutional Court opinions where the Court had expressly addressed a constitutional question—for example, in the Constitutional Assembly's reformulation of the limitations clause so as to exclude the notion of the essential content of the right. Furthermore, despite popular political pressure to rescind the Court's holding against the death penalty, the Constitutional Assembly merely retained the previous formulation of the rights relied upon by the Court in that case.

[33] *First Certification* case, above n 17, [27].

[34] *First Certification* case [34]–[35].

[35] *First Certification* case [39].

Constitutional Principles. In this 'judicial' context, the Court claimed the power to bind the future, holding that a 'future court should approach the meaning of the relevant provision of the NT on the basis that the meaning assigned . . . in the certification process . . . should not be departed from save in the most compelling circumstances'.[36]

The Court took a similarly robust attitude to its judicial role in its second certification judgment when it certified the final Constitution.[37] In this case, political parties and other interested groups attempted to reopen issues that had not been identified as the basis for the Court's refusal to certify in the first round of certification. While accepting these challenges, the Court noted the

> sound jurisprudential basis for the policy that a court should adhere to its previous decisions unless they are clearly wrong . . . [and that] having regard to the need for finality in the certification process and in view of the virtual identical composition of the Court that considered the questions barely three months ago, that policy is all the more desirable here.[38]

As a result, the Court made it clear that a party wishing to extend the Court's review beyond those aspects identified in the first certification judgment would face a 'formidable task'. Through this reliance on a classic judicial strategy of deference to past decisions, the Court was able to significantly limit the scope of its role in the final certification judgment. It was this change in posture towards the certification process—combined with the fact that the Constitutional Assembly fully addressed all but one of the Court's concerns—that ensured a swift certification when the Constitution was submitted to the Court a second time. Significantly, the Court relied less on the specifics of the Constitutional Principles and instead emphasised the fundamental elements of constitutionalism contained in the text: 'founding values which include human dignity, the achievement of equality, the recognition and advancement of human rights and freedoms, the supremacy of the Constitution and the rule of law'.[39] While the Court still had to recognise that the powers and functions of the provinces—the most contentious issue in the whole Constitution-making process—remained in dispute between the parties,

---

[36] *First Certification* case [43].

[37] *Ex parte Chairperson of the Constitutional Assembly: In re Certification of the Amended Text of the Constitution of the Republic of South Africa, 1996* 1997 (2) SA 97 (CC) [hereinafter *Second Certification* case].

[38] *Second Certification* case [8].

[39] *Second Certification* case [25].

the Court held, in essence, that the removal of the presumption of constitutional validity of bills passed by the National Council of Provinces (NCOP) had tipped the balance.[40] Thus, despite the recognition that provincial powers and functions in the Amended Text remained less than or inferior to those accorded to the provinces in the interim Constitution, this was not substantially so[41] and therefore a basis for denying certification no longer existed.

IV. CONSTITUTIONAL PRINCIPLES IN PRACTICE

The outcome of establishing and applying constitutional principles, in the case of South Africa, was the local adoption of a globally bounded notion of democratic constitutionalism that enabled political reconstruction—or the democratic transition—to proceed. This process also tested the institutional capacity of the new system of governance to address the conflicts that arose from often irreconcilable political demands. This realm of bounded possibilities, created by the introduction of constitutionalism, was constantly infused with the incompatible constitutional imaginations of local contestants. In order to demonstrate this process, I will focus on a specific set of struggles over traditional leadership and regional autonomy that had been waged alternatively in the name of indigenous culture, Zulu tradition, federalism and limited government. These differences were most intense in KwaZulu-Natal where they had been the political source of violent conflict between the IFP and the ANC. The Constitutional Court's engagement with these two sets of political conflicts in the first years of the new democracy—and in particular through the enforced dialogue of the judicial process—demonstrates how the adoption of constitutional principles and a constitutionalist discourse made 'legitimate' rules and practices for the 'civilising' of local difference available. The result provided a means, in effect, to civilise the political conflicts that until then had tended to degenerate into violent confrontation.

In the process of negotiating the 1993 Constitution there were significant changes in the positions of the three major players as well as important continuities that became cobbled together in the interim Constitution. Most fundamentally, the ANC's initial demand for a unitary state came to be interpreted as national sovereignty over the 1910 bound-

---

[40] *Second Certification* case [153]–[157].
[41] *Second Certification* case [204(e)].

aries of South Africa rather than its initial meaning of a central government with pre-emptive power over regional authorities. Unlike the ANC, however, the IFP refused to concede its central claim to regional autonomy and, in its alliance with white pro-apartheid parties, continued to threaten to disrupt the transitional process. Although factions of the IFP seemed ready to contest the elections for the KwaZulu-Natal regional government, the party's leader Chief Gatsha Buthelezi interpreted his party's poor showing in pre-election polls as cause to promote an even more autonomous position: encouraging and supporting King Goodwill Zwelethini in his demand for the restoration of the nineteenth-century Zulu monarchy with territorial claims beyond even the borders of present-day KwaZulu-Natal.

Although the protagonists of a federal solution for South Africa had advocated a national government of limited powers, the interim Constitution reversed the traditional federal division of legislative powers by allocating enumerated powers to the provinces. This allocation of regional powers took place according to a set of criteria incorporated into the Constitutional Principles and in those sections of the Constitution dealing with the legislative powers of the provinces. The IFP rejected the allocation, however, on the grounds that the Constitution failed to guarantee the autonomy of the provinces. Despite the ANC's protestations that the provincial powers guaranteed by the Constitution could not be withdrawn, the IFP pointed to the fact that the allocated powers were only concurrent powers and that the national legislature could supersede local legislation by establishing a national legislative framework covering any subject matter. This tension between provincial autonomy and the ANC's assertion of the need to establish national frameworks guaranteeing minimum standards and certain basic equalities led to an amendment to the 1993 Constitution before the Constitution even came into force. According to the amendment, the provinces were granted exclusive powers in the following areas of legislative authority: agriculture; gambling; cultural affairs; education at all levels, except tertiary; environment; health; housing; language policy; local government; nature conservation; police; state media; public transport; regional planning and development; road traffic regulation; roads; tourism; trade and industrial promotion; traditional authorities; urban and rural development and welfare services. Difficulty arose in distinguishing the exact limits of a region's exclusive powers and the extent to which the national legislature was able to pass general laws affecting rather broad areas of governance.

Although the provinces had the power to assign executive control over these matters to the national government if they lacked administrative resources to implement particular laws, the interim Constitution provided that the provinces had executive authority over all matters over which they had legislative authority. In addition, the provinces retained authority over matters assigned to them by the transitional clauses of the Constitution or delegated by national legislation. The net effect of these provisions was continued tension between non-ANC provincial governments and the national government over the extent of regional autonomy and the exact definition of their relative powers. In this context, three particular cases arose before the Constitutional Court in 1996 in which we may trace the role of the Court in both silencing and enabling the constitutional imaginations of the contending parties. All three cases involved, among other issues, claims of autonomy or accusations of national infringement of autonomy by the province of KwaZulu-Natal. As such they represent three moments when the Court was called upon to help shape the boundary between contending claims of constitutional authority to govern, unresolved by the negotiated settlement. Two cases directly implicated actions of the KwaZulu-Natal legislature and its attempts to assert authority within the province—in one case over traditional leaders and in the other the Constitution-making powers of the province. The first case involved a dispute over the National Education Policy Bill, which was then before the National Assembly.[42]

Objections to the National Education Policy Bill focused on the claim that the 'Bill imposed national education policy on the provinces' and thereby 'encroached upon the autonomy of the provinces and their executive authority'. The IFP made the further claim that the 'Bill could have no application in KwaZulu-Natal because it [the province] was in a position to formulate and regulate its own policies.'[43] While all parties accepted that education was defined as a concurrent legislative function under the interim Constitution, the contending parties imagined that different consequences should flow from the determination that a subject matter is concurrently assigned to both provincial and national government.

KwaZulu-Natal, and the IFP in particular, assumed a form of pre-emption doctrine in which the National Assembly and national

---

[42] *Ex Parte Speaker of the National Assembly: In Re Dispute Concerning the Constitutionality of Certain Provisions of the National Education Policy Bill 83 of 1995*, 1996 (3) SA 165 (CC) [hereinafter *National Education Bill* case].

[43] *National Education Bill* case, above n 42, [8].

government would be precluded from acting in an area of concurrent jurisdiction so long as the province was capable of formulating and regulating its own policies. In rejecting this argument, the Constitutional Court avoided the notion of pre-emption altogether and instead argued that the 'legislative competences of the provinces and Parliament to make laws in respect of schedule 6 [concurrent] matters do not depend upon section 126(3)', which the Court argued only comes into operation if it is necessary to resolve a conflict between inconsistent national and provincial laws.[44] The Court's rejection of any notion of pre-emption is an interpretation of the Constitution that enables both national and provincial legislators to continue to promote and even legislate on their own imagined solutions to issues within their concurrent jurisdictions without foreclosing on their particular options until there is an irreconcilable conflict.

Having avoided siding categorically with either national or provincial authority, the Court took a further step. It argued that even if a 'conflict is resolved in favour of either the provincial or national law the other is not invalidated' it is merely 'subordinated and to the extent of the conflict rendered inoperative'.[45] Supported by the comparative jurisprudence of Canada[46] and Australia,[47] the Court was able to make a distinction between 'laws that are inconsistent with each other and laws that are inconsistent with the Constitution'.[48] It thereby argued that 'even if the National Education Policy Bill deals with matters in respect of which provincial laws would have paramountcy, it could not for that reason alone be declared unconstitutional'.[49]

The Constitutional Court's approach clearly aimed to reduce the tensions inherent in the continuing conflict between provincial and national governments, particularly in relation to the continuing violent tensions in KwaZulu-Natal. It also took the opportunity to explicitly preclude an alternative interpretation. Focusing on arguments before the Court that relied upon the United States Supreme Court's decision in *New York v United States,* the Court made the point that '[u]nlike their counterparts in the United States of America, the provinces in South Africa are not

[44] *National Education Bill* case, above n 42, [16].
[45] *National Education Bill* case, above n 42, [16].
[46] *National Education Bill* case, above n 42, [17].
[47] *National Education Bill* case, above n 42, [18].
[48] *National Education Bill* case, above n 42, [16].
[49] *National Education Bill* case, above n 42, [20].

sovereign states'.[50] Furthermore, the Court warned that '[d]ecisions of the courts of the United States dealing with state rights are not a safe guide as to how our courts should address problems that may arise in relation to the rights of provinces under our Constitution'.[51] In effect, the Court's approach was to begin to draw a boundary around the outer limits of provincial autonomy while simultaneously allowing concurrent jurisdiction to provide a space in which different legislatures could continue to imagine and assert their own, at times contradictory, solutions to legislative problems within their jurisdiction.

The scope of such a definition of concurrent jurisdiction was immediately tested in a case challenging two bills before the KwaZulu-Natal provincial legislature, which purported in part to preclude national action affecting the payment of salaries to traditional authorities in KwaZulu-Natal.[52] In this case, brought by ANC members of the KwaZulu-Natal legislature, the objectors argued that the bills were unconstitutional as they amounted to an attempt to 'frustrate the implementation of the [national] Renumeration of Traditional Leaders Act' by preventing the Ingonyama (Zulu King) and traditional leaders 'from accepting remuneration and allowances which might become payable to them in terms of the national legislation'.[53] Furthermore, the challengers argued, the object of this provincial legislation 'was to create a relationship of subservience between them [traditional leaders] and the provincial government', an object outside the scope of the province's concurrent powers with respect to traditional authorities.[54]

The Court's first response was to lament that the political conflict concerning KwaZulu-Natal had degenerated to a state in which the right to pay traditional authorities, as a means to secure influence over them, should have become an issue. Recalling that traditional leaders 'occupy positions in the community in which they can best serve the interests of their people if they are not dependent or perceived to be dependent on political parties or on the national or provincial governments', the Court

[50] *National Education Bill* case, above n 42, [23].

[51] Ibid

[52] *Ex Parte Speaker of the KwaZulu-Natal Provincial Legislature: In re KwaZulu-Natal Amakhosi and Iziphakanyiswa Amendment Bill of 1995; Ex Parte Speaker of the KwaZulu-Natal Provincial Legislature: In re Payment of Salaries, Allowances and Other Privileges to the Ingonyama Bill of 1995,* 1996 (4) SA 653 (CC) [hereinafter *KwaZulu-Natal Amakosi/Ingonyama* case].

[53] *KwaZulu-Natal Amakosi/Ingonyama* case [16].

[54] Ibid.

noted that its role is limited to deciding 'whether the proposed provincial legislation is inconsistent with the Constitution'.[55] Faced with continuing and seemingly intractable political conflict between the IFP and ANC in KwaZulu-Natal, however, the Court reasserted its duty to interpret legislation narrowly in order to avoid constitutional conflicts. Taking this approach it upheld the legislative competence of the KwaZulu-Natal legislature and the constitutionality of the two Bills. In effect, the Court allowed the KwaZulu-Natal legislature to continue to imagine its own authority in this area, merely postponing clear questions of conflict between the national and provincial legislation to a later date.

The outer limit of the Court's tolerance for alternative constitutional visions was, however, reached in the third case, in which the Court was asked to certify the Constitution of the Province of KwaZulu-Natal.[56] Although the provincial legislature had unanimously adopted the KwaZulu-Natal draft Constitution, the Constitutional Court held that there were 'fundamental respects in which the provincial Constitution is fatally flawed',[57] and therefore declined to certify it. The Court considered these flaws under three headings. Two sets of problems were essentially procedural in nature and involved attempts by the KwaZulu-Natal legislature: (1) to avoid the Constitutional Court's determination of the text's inconsistency with the interim Constitution;[58] and (2) to suspend the certification process itself until particular sections could be tested against the final Constitution.[59] While the Court rejected these devices as being in conflict with the certification process and as attempting to circumvent the process, the most significant problem with the text was the KwaZulu-Natal legislature's usurpation of national powers.

Referring to the Court's decision in *The National Education Policy Bill* case, in which it made a 'distinction between the history, structure and language of the United States Constitution which brought together several sovereign states . . . and that of our interim Constitution',[60] the Court held that parts of the proposed KwaZulu-Natal Constitution appeared to have 'been passed by the KZN Legislature under a misapprehension that it

[55] *KwaZulu-Natal Amakosi/Ingonyama* case [18].

[56] *Ex Parte Speaker of the KwaZulu-Natal Provincial Legislature: In re Certification of the Constitution of the Province of KwaZulu-Natal, 1996*, 1996 (4) SA 1098 (CC) [hereinafter *KwaZulu-Natal Constitution Certification* case].

[57] *KwaZulu-Natal Constitution Certification* case [13].

[58] See *KwaZulu-Natal Constitution Certification* case [36]–[38].

[59] See *KwaZulu-Natal Constitution Certification* case [39]–[46].

[60] *KwaZulu-Natal Constitution Certification* case [14].

enjoyed a relationship of co-supremacy with the national Legislature and even the Constitutional Assembly'.[61] Drawing a clear boundary around the permissible constitutional aspirations of the IFP in KwaZulu-Natal, the Court rejected the draft text's attempt to 'confer' legislative and executive authority upon the province[62] and to 'recognize' the authority of the government and 'competence' of the national Parliament in other respects.[63] While it recognised the right of the IFP-dominated KwaZulu-Natal legislature to exercise its powers to draft a provincial Constitution— and possibly to include its own bill of rights—the Court clearly rejected the IFP's attempt to assert its vision of regional autonomy beyond the core meaning of the negotiated compromise represented by the 1993 Constitution. Furthermore, the Court clearly silenced the extreme option of provincial sovereignty, stating that the assertions of recognition were 'inconsistent with the interim Constitution because KZN is not a sovereign state and it simply has no power or authority to grant constitutional "recognition" to what the national Government may or may not do'.[64]

Although the IFP had walked out of the negotiations at which the interim Constitution was drafted and refused to participate in the Constitutional Assembly during the making of the 1996 Constitution, it nevertheless proceeded to produce its own provincial Constitution and submitted it to the Constitutional Court in terms of the 1993 interim Constitution. Even as its vision of regional autonomy became increasingly isolated, the IFP still imagined that it could be achieved within the parameters of the interim Constitution. The Constitutional Court silenced this particular attempt, but did not foreclose on the IFP's vision of greater regional autonomy. Instead of suffering complete defeat, the IFP was able to take solace: On that same day, the Court refused to certify the draft of the final Constitution, in particular because it believed the draft had failed to grant provinces the degree of autonomy they were guaranteed in the Constitutional Principles.[65] However, when the Constitutional Court finally certified the 1996 Constitution,[66] the IFP remained dissatisfied over the limited degree of provincial autonomy recognised in the Constitution. By that time however, the IFP, as the

---

[61]   *KwaZulu-Natal Constitution Certification* case [15].
[62]   *KwaZulu-Natal Constitution Certification* case [32].
[63]   *KwaZulu-Natal Constitution Certification* case [34].
[64]   Ibid
[65]   See *First Certification* case, above n 17.
[66]   See *Second Certification* case, above n 37.

governing party in KwaZulu-Natal, was not about to exit the system; instead, it joined the other opposition parties in saying it would take the opportunity in the following year's legislative session to review the Constitution,[67] thus keeping its vision alive.

V. FOUNDING PRINCIPLES, BASIC STRUCTURE AND THE FUTURE

The Constitutional Principles contained in Schedule 4 of the interim Constitution formed an integral part of the supreme law of the Constitution during the transitional period. However, the adoption of the final Constitution and its certification by the Constitutional Court terminated the legally significant role of those principles. Despite some attempts to argue that since they served as the basis for the creation and certification of the 1996 Constitution they should remain at the core of the Constitution, the express inclusion of a set of founding provisions in Chapter 1 of the Constitution provides the most explicit source of the principles underlying the final Constitution. This chapter begins with a description of the Republic of South Africa as 'one, sovereign, democratic state founded' on a particular set of values. These founding values include the following:

> human dignity, the achievement of equality and the advancement of human rights and freedoms; non-racialism and non-sexism; supremacy of the constitution and the rule of law; as well as the basic principles of an electoral democracy, universal adult suffrage, a national common voters role, regular elections and a multi-party system of democratic government to ensure accountability, responsiveness and openness.[68]

The status of these founding provisions is further enhanced by the requirement that any amendment to section 1 of the Constitution, which contains these constitutional values, may only be achieved with a 75 per cent majority in the National Assembly and the support of six of the nine provinces. This is a level of constitutional entrenchment that requires a degree of electoral support that even the hugely popular ANC led by Nelson Mandela did not come close to reaching. Even at its zenith in the third democratic election, the ANC dominated the election, but only just reached a two-thirds majority.

---

[67] *Mail and Guardian* (11 Nov 1996).
[68] 1996 Constitution c 1 s 1(a)–(d).

While it is clear that a legislative or executive act or even a constitutional amendment that explicitly violates the core meanings of these founding values would be struck down as unconstitutional, it is still unclear exactly how these values may be raised by litigants and applied in litigation. The Constitutional Court has declared that although the 'values enunciated in section 1 of the Constitution are of fundamental importance', they are not the basis of justiciable rights.[69] Instead, the Court argues, they 'inform and give substance to all the provisions of the Constitution', but 'do not . . . give rise to discrete and enforceable rights in themselves'.[70] This is a significant qualification since the highly entrenched founding values are presumably not subject to the limitation clause analysis of section 36, which acknowledges that 'rights in the Bill of Rights may be limited . . . to the extent that the limitation is reasonable and justifiable in an open and democratic society based on human dignity, equality and freedom'. This tension was put to the test when the United Democratic Front (UDM), a small parliamentary opposition party, challenged a series of constitutional amendments and related legislation that allowed elected representatives to switch political parties without losing their seats. Claiming that these changes would undermine minority parties and thus adversely impact the founding values of multi-party democracy and the rule of law, the UDM argued that they should be struck down as unconstitutional and could not be justified in terms of the limitation clause analysis. The Court rejected the claim that floor crossing undermined democracy and the rule of law. And while it recognised in the UDM case that these founding values 'inform the interpretation of the Constitution and other law, and set positive standards with which all law must comply to be valid', the Court did not elevate these rights above other rights in the Bill of Rights based on their status as foundational values.[71]

Chapter 1 also includes provisions guaranteeing the supremacy of the Constitution by declaring that 'law or conduct inconsistent with [the Constitution] is invalid',[72] and stating that there 'is a common South African citizenship'.[73] However, this section does not claim to exhaust all

---

[69] *Minister of Home Affairs v National Institute for Crime Prevention and the Re-Integration of Offenders (NICRO) & Others* 2005 (3) SA 280 (CC) [hereinafter *NICRO*] [21].

[70] *NICRO* [21].

[71] See *United Democratic Movement v President of the Republic of South Africa & Others* 2003 (1) SA 678 [19] [hereinafter *UDM*].

[72] 1996 Constitution, c 1 s 2.

[73] 1996 Constitution, c 1 s 3(1).

the principles the Constitution encompasses nor are all the founding provisions in Chapter 1 equivalent in form and status to Constitutional Principles.[74] In fact, the Constitutional Court has repeatedly made reference to the Constitution as embodying an 'objective, normative value system', which is, in many ways, a broader conception of underlying constitutional principles than either the specific clauses of section 1 or the original Constitutional Principles contained in Schedule 4 of the interim Constitution. This notion of an 'objective, normative value system' has been articulated most often in relation to the interpretation of constitutional rights—and even with explicit reference to the role this notion plays in the German Constitutional system—as a 'guiding principle' for all levels of the constitutional order—the legislature, executive and judiciary.

The heightened entrenchment of the founding values in section 1 has also led to discussion about the applicability of the 'basic structure' doctrine, the idea that the courts may strike down even procedurally perfect constitutional amendments as being incompatible with the implicit framework or basic structure of the Constitution. The Constitutional Court first made reference to the 'basic structure doctrine'—which is part of Indian Supreme Court jurisprudence—in a challenge by KwaZulu-Natal to amendments made to the interim Constitution in 1995.[75] Here the Court made reference to the possibility that 'a purported amendment to the Constitution, following the formal procedures prescribed by the Constitution, but radically and fundamentally restructuring and reorganizing the fundamental premises of the Constitution, might not qualify as an "amendment" at all'.[76] Despite this statement, on the two occasions when the Court has had the opportunity to invoke the doctrine it has declined to apply it, or to even decide whether it would be applicable in the South Africa constitutional context.[77] This situation has led some commentators to argue that the idea of a 'basic structure doctrine' is clearly not 'coterminous with the special protection given to the foundational values' in section 1 of the Constitution.[78] At the same time,

[74] 1996 Constitution, c 1 s 4 (national anthem) or s 5 (national flag).

[75] *Premier KwaZulu-Natal & Others v President of the Republic of South Africa & Others* 1996 (1) SA 769 (CC).

[76] *Premier KwaZulu-Natal & Others v President of the Republic of South Africa & Others* 1996 (1) SA 769 (CC) [47].

[77] See *UDM*, above n 72, and *NICRO*, above n 69.

[78] C Roederer, 'Founding Provisions' in S Woolman et al (eds), *Constitutional Law of South Africa*, 2nd edn, (Kenwyn, Juta, 2006) ch 13, p 16.

the Constitutional Court's refusal to find the constitutional amendments at stake in the *UDM* case in tension with the founding principle of democracy has led some to conclude that 'the threshold for the deployment of the foundational values to protect the basic structure of the South African constitutional legal order is very high and that only extraordinary amendments to that order will trigger the protection afforded by' section 1 of the Constitution.[79]

VI. CONCLUSION

Although the idea and application of constitutional principles played a central role in the transition to democracy and the creation of South Africa's post-apartheid constitutional order, there is a significant difference between the 34 Constitutional Principles that guided the Constitutional Assembly in writing the 1996 Constitution and the foundational values that have become part of the final Constitution. In addition to the explicit 'foundational values' enshrined in section 1 of the Constitution, the Constitutional Court has made reference to a whole range of constitutional values that undergird the Court's view of its interpretative role. Apart from the foundational provisions of section 1, these include: those values articulated in the Preamble and implicit in the overall framework and structure of the Constitution, such as the promotion and protection of fundamental human rights;[80] the transformation of the society into one 'in which there will be human dignity, freedom and equality';[81] the idea of *ubuntu,* which former Chief Justice Langa described as placing 'some emphasis on community and on the interdependence of the members of the community' as well as regulating 'the exercise of rights by the emphasis it lays on sharing and co-responsibility and the mutual enjoyment of rights by all'.[82] Other constitutional values are explicitly included as sets of principles in different sections of the Constitution. These explicit values include the principles of co-operative government and intergovernmental relations;[83] the principles governing state institutions

---

[79]   Roederer, 'Founding Provisions', above n 78, 17.
[80]   See *Samuel Kaunda & Others v President of the Republic of South Africa* 2005 (4) SA 235 (CC) [220].
[81]   See *Soobramoney v Minister of Health (KwaZulu-Natal)* 1998 (1) SA 765 (CC) [8].
[82]   See *S v Makwanyane* 1995 (3) SA 391 (CC) [224]–[225].
[83]   1996 Constitution s 41(1).

supporting constitutional democracy;[84] the basic values and principles governing public administration;[85] and the principles governing national security in the Republic.[86] Finally, the Constitutional Court has repeatedly referred to the notion that the Constitution 'embodies . . . an objective, normative value system'[87] and reflects cosmopolitan values to the extent that the courts are required by section 39 of the Constitution to 'consider international law' when interpreting the Bill of Rights;[88] 'may consider foreign law';[89] and 'must promote the spirit, purport and objects of the Bill of Rights' when interpreting any legislation or 'when developing the common law or customary law'.[90] These broadly defined values of the Constitution are thus expected to permeate every aspect of South African law—including the decisions and actions of public officials as well as private parties—when their behaviour affects the rights of other individuals.

FURTHER READING

Chaskalson, M and D Davis, 'Constitutionalism, the Rule of Law and the First Certification Judgment: *Ex parte Chairperson of the Constitutional Assembly: In re Certification of the Constitution of the Republic of South Africa, 1996* 1996 (4) SA 744 (CC)' (1997) 13 *South African Journal on Human Rights* 430

Ex parte Chairperson of the Constitutional Assembly: 'In re Certification of the Constitution of the Republic of South Africa, 1996' 1996 (4) SA 744 (CC)

Ex parte Chairperson of the Constitutional Assembly: In re Certification of the Amended Text of the Constitution of the Republic of South Africa, 1996, 1997 (2) SA 97 (CC)

Republic of South Africa, *Interim Constitution*, Schedule 4 (1993)

Roederer, C, 'Founding Provisions' in S Woolman et al (eds), *Constitutional Law of South Africa*, 2nd edn (Kenwyn, Juta & Co, 2006)

[84] 1996 Constitution s 181(2)–(5).
[85] 1996 Constitution s 195(1)(a)–(j).
[86] 1996 Constitution s 198 (a)–(d).
[87] See *Carmichele v Minister of Safety and Security & Another* 2001 (4) SA 938 (CC) [54]; *S v Thebus & Another*, 2003 (6) SA 505 (CC) [27]–[28].
[88] 1996 Constitution s 39(1)(b).
[89] 1996 Constitution s 39(1)(c).
[90] 1996 Constitution s 39(2).

5

The Bill of Rights

<hr/>

Introduction – Constitutional Rights – Interpreting the Bill of Rights – The Bill of Rights within the Frame of Dignity, Equality and Freedom – Socio-economic Rights – Bill of Rights, Rule of Law and States of Emergency – Conclusion: Pursuing Rights in a Land of Vast Inequalities

I. INTRODUCTION

SOUTH AFRICA'S BILL of Rights is often heralded as the crowning achievement of the democratic transition and as having produced 'some of the most progressive decision-making in the world, including the prohibition of the death penalty and the legalisation of abortion'.[1] The legalisation of abortion was, in fact, a legislative act[2] and not a direct product of the Bill of Rights. However, the assumption that individual rights, including reproductive rights, have come to dominate public perception of South African law is not unfounded. For example, the late Etienne Mureinik, an eminent legal scholar, argued that the new Constitution and the Bill of Rights in particular must serve as a 'bridge away from a culture of authority' and must lead the country towards a 'culture of justification—a culture in which every exercise of power is expected to be justified'.[3] The idea of a culture of justification is, of course, one particular vision of the Bill of Rights' role within a constitutional order. Justifying the exercise of power is central to the notion of

---

[1] A Sparks, *Beyond the Miracle: Inside the New South Africa*, (Johannesburg/Cape Town, Jonathan Ball, 2003) 47.

[2] Choice on Termiantion of Pregnancy Act 92 of 1996.

[3] E Murienik, 'A Bridge to Where? Introducing the Interim Bill of Rights' (1994) 10 *South African Journal on Human Rights* 31, 32.

negative rights in which individuals are protected against the arbitrary imposition of state power. While this conception of rights might have been at the core of the Bill of Rights in the 1993 interim Constitution, the final 1996 Constitution added a new set of positive rights that placed clear duties on the state to provide access to some basic resources, which are essential to the lives of individual citizens and communities.

The Constitution explicitly states that '[t]his Bill of Rights is a corner-stone of democracy in South Africa',[4] a statement that highlights the interconnectedness of democratic participation and the guarantee of rights that was so essential to the democratic transition in South Africa. At the same time, the description of rights that introduces the Bill of Rights in the 1996 Constitution also emphasises the duty of the state to 'respect, protect, promote and fulfil the rights' while simultaneously acknowledging that the rights are themselves subject to limitations provided for in the Constitution. This careful balancing of rights within the constitutional order is a key feature of the Constitution. Despite the great attention the Constitutional Court has received for striking down the death penalty and upholding socio-economic rights, a more nuanced understanding of the role the Bill of Rights has played during its first 15 years must include a clear acknowledgement of the strategies the Constitutional Court has employed to ensure that the recognition and enforcement of rights remain deeply connected to the democratic process. These strategies are illustrated most vividly in the cases where the Court has found laws to be constitutionally inadequate but has suspended granting a remedy until Parliament has had the time to amend the offending law itself. Significantly, this strategy has been used most prominently in highly contentious cases, such as those involving striking down customary rules of intestate succession and the upholding of same-sex marriage, both on grounds of gender equality.

Another important dimension of the Bill of Rights is the depth of its expected impact on the legal system and society. While the end of apartheid heralded a public commitment to human rights and promises of social transformation, the realities of post-apartheid South Africa have been stark. Beginning with a dramatic crime wave, a rising HIV/AIDS pandemic and growing inequality, the first decade and a half of democratic rule has struggled to live up to the promise of the post-1994 election

---

[4] Constitution of the Republic of South Africa Act 108 of 1996 [hereinafter 1996 Constitution] s 7(1).

euphoria. Despite dramatic policy innovations and even a transformation of law, the legal system itself has battled to deliver on the promise of rights. Even as the Constitutional Court adopted progressive and widely acclaimed decisions upholding and extending rights, the lower courts, government officials and state institutions across the country have been mired in problems of racial transformation, capacity building and a legacy of institutional neglect. These problems include specific issues that have had an impact on the effectiveness of rights, including the shrinking of resources for non-governmental organisations; the small community of public interest lawyers; and the fact that most lawyers, government officials and the broader population have yet to make the leap between the symbolic embrace of a human rights culture in the new South Africa and the more basic attitudes of mutual respect and dignified treatment of others that form the core of a human rights culture. The Bill of Rights is being implemented against this backdrop, producing a situation in which constitutional rights are, on the one hand, condemned as impediments in the fight against crime and, on the other hand, increasingly claimed as a source of legitimacy for the demands of those who continue to feel excluded from the Bill of Rights' promise of a more secure and dignified life.

II. CONSTITUTIONAL RIGHTS

South Africa's Bill of Rights is expansive, and it covers a comprehensive range of concerns that include traditional political and civil rights as well as what have been referred to as 'subsequent generations' of rights, which include socio-economic, cultural and environmental rights. These rights incorporate not only individual claims but also communal forms of rights that might be held and exercised by groups of people including trade unions and employers' organisations[5] as well as cultural, religious and linguistic communities.[6] The Bill of Rights also attempts to open up and strengthen participation in the process of governance by guaranteeing access to information and promising administrative action by government officials that is 'lawful, reasonable and procedurally fair'.[7] Although these latter guarantees are constrained by the requirement that national

---

[5] 1996 Constitution s 23(4) and (5).

[6] 1996 Constitution s 31(1)(a) and (b).

[7] 1996 Constitution s 33(1).

legislation must give effect to these rights, the existence of these clauses has forced the post-apartheid state to publicly address these questions even as it battles to create and maintain an effective administration.

While the Bill of Rights provides for the protection of an extraordinary range of rights, it is important to recognise that given the legacies of apartheid, it is also premised upon a deep and substantive understanding of the need to achieve equality in South Africa. To this end, the Bill of Rights addresses some of the most egregious consequences of the legally imposed inequalities of the past—such as access to land ownership. It also adopts a broad definition of equality that includes provisions that protect affirmative action as a mechanism to deal with this legacy. In addition to prohibiting discrimination on the basis of race, sex, age and ethnic origin, the Bill of Rights also lists the following categories of protection: pregnancy, marital status, sexual orientation, disability and language. Furthermore, in cases of alleged discrimination on any of the listed grounds, such discrimination is assumed to be unfair, thus shifting the burden of proof onto those denying that the prima facie effect of discrimination is not the consequence of their actions. Finally, these constitutional protections are not limited to relations between the state and individuals; they are applied to both governmental and private conduct, with the Constitution mandating the legislature to enact laws to prevent or prohibit unfair private discrimination. The Promotion of Equality and Prevention of Unfair Discrimination Act enacted in February 2000 to fulfil this constitutional mandate is a wide-ranging statute that aims to eradicate social and economic inequalities, 'especially those that are systematic in nature, which are generated in our history by colonialism, apartheid and patriarchy, and which brought pain and suffering to the great majority of our people'.[8]

The state is explicitly charged with the duty to 'respect, protect, promote, and fulfil the rights in the Bill of Rights'.[9] Yet it is important to recognise that the rights guaranteed are subject to limitations, which the Bill of Rights explicitly provides. While it is commonly understood that no rights are absolute—and that one person's rights might indeed interfere with the exercise of another person's—the Constitution does not simply leave the policing of these boundaries to the courts. Instead, it follows the approach of the Canadian Charter of Rights and Freedoms as

---

[8]   Promotion of Equality and Prevention of Unfair Discrimination Act 4 of 2000, Preamble.

[9]   1996 Constitution s 7(2).

interpreted by the Supreme Court of Canada, which attempts to define the relevant criteria that must be considered when weighing the conflict between rights or between a person's rights and the government's need to exercise its power in a particular circumstance. The general limitations clause in the Bill of Rights attempts to regulate these tensions, stating that rights may only be limited by laws

> of general application to the extent . . . reasonable and justifiable in an open and democratic society based on human dignity, equality and freedom, taking into account all relevant factors including: (a) the nature of the right; (b) the importance of the purpose of the limitation; (c) the nature and extent of the limitation; (d) the relation between the limitation and its purpose; and (e) less restrictive means to achieve the purpose.[10]

In practice, the application of the limitations clause has seen the emergence of a balancing test in which the Constitutional Court effectively merges these criteria in deciding whether the limitation of the right is justified. The most significant effect of this process is to shift the burden of proof on to those who seek to justify the limitation of a right rather than those who are claiming the right. This is distinct from the traditional common law approach to rights, which carves out a space for justified interference in fundamental rights by limiting the scope of the rights themselves and requires those asserting their rights to show that their claims fall within the more limited scope of the relevant fundamental right. Furthermore, the Constitution's statement regarding 'human dignity, equality and freedom'[11] defines the type of society against which any infringement of a constitutional right must be compared. In *Hugo,* the Constitutional Court explicitly cited the Canadian Supreme Court's judgment in *Egan v Canada*, in which that court 'recognized that inherent human dignity is at the heart of individual rights in a free and democratic society' and that the right to equality 'means nothing if it does not represent a commitment to recognizing each person's equal worth as a human being, regardless of individual differences'.[12] Applying the limitation clause in *S v Makwanyane,* the Constitutional Court argued the following:

> [L]imitation of constitutional rights for a purpose that is reasonable and necessary in a democratic society involves the weighing up of competing values,

---

[10] 1996 Constitution s 36(1).

[11] ibid.

[12] 1996 Constitution s 36(1); *President of the Republic of South Africa v Hugo*, CCT 11/96, decided 18 April 1997, [41].

and ultimately an assessment based on proportionality . . . which calls for the balancing of different interests. In the balancing process, the relevant considerations will include the nature of the right that is limited, and its importance to an open and democratic society based on freedom and equality; the extent of the limitation, its efficacy and . . . whether the desired ends could reasonably be achieved through other means less damaging to the right in question.[13]

These criteria are now enshrined as relevant factors in the limitations clause of the 1996 Constitution and yet the process of applying the limitations clause essentially remains a balancing test. Describing its process of interpretation, the Constitutional Court in *S v Bhulwana* stated the following:

> [T]he Court places the purpose, effects and importance of the infringing legislation on one side of the scales and the nature and effect of the infringement caused by the legislation on the other. The more substantial the inroad into fundamental rights, the more persuasive the grounds of justification must be.[14]

In addition to various internal limitations—such as the exclusion of hate speech and propaganda for war from the right to free expression—and the more general limitation on the duty of the state to take 'reasonable legislative and other measures within its available resources, to achieve the progressive realization' of various social and economic rights, the Bill of Rights makes elaborate provisions for the derogation of rights in a State of Emergency. Significantly, however, the Bill of Rights also restricts the process of derogation by specifying a set of non-derogable rights and setting conditions that must be observed in cases where persons may be detained in the event of a State of Emergency. Finally, the Bill of Rights also lays down its own internal rules of interpretation, which require those with authority to interpret the rights to 'promote the values that underlie an open and democratic society based on human dignity, equality and freedom'; to 'consider international law'; and to explicitly allow for the consideration of foreign law.[15]

The rights protected by the Constitution are not restricted to those enumerated in the Bill of Rights. The sources of rights are defined in very broad and unlimited terms,[16] and concern that access to these rights

---

[13]   1996 Constitution s 36(1); *S v Makwanyane* 1995 (3) SA 391 (CC) [hereinafter *Makwanyane*] [104].

[14]   *S v Bhulwana*, 1996 (1) SA 388 (CC) [18].

[15]   1996 Constitution s 39(1).

[16]   See 1996 Constitution s 39(3): 'The Bill of Rights does not deny the existence of any other rights or freedoms . . . to the extent that they are consistent with the Bill.'

might be restricted by the traditionally narrow standing rules led Constitution-makers to adopt very generous provisions aimed at facilitating the enforcement of rights. Not only are victims of rights violations able to approach the courts on their own behalf, but 'anyone acting on behalf of another person who cannot act in their own name'[17] can initiate claims before the courts, as well as people acting on behalf of a group or class of persons, if they are acting in the public interest.[18] Not only are class actions guaranteed, but associations may sue on their members' behalf; although the rights of 'legal entities' or 'juristic persons' such as corporations are only guaranteed 'to the extent required by the nature of the rights and the nature of that juristic person'.[19] Even though the South African Constitution casts a wide net in its attempt to protect the human rights of all its inhabitants, it leaves to the courts the task of resolving the conflicts between rights and the limits that must inevitably be placed on rights in the process of governance. In order to facilitate this balancing the Bill of Rights contains explicit limitations clauses, mentioned above. But in the end, the application of rights will depend on the commitment of government officials who wield public power and on the members of the judiciary, who are given the ultimate task of interpreting the Bill of Rights and resolving the conflicting rights that opposing parties inevitably claim. The effectiveness of these rights, is, however, as much the product of social mobilisation and civil society engagement as it is the consequence of institutional cultures developed within the realms of the state.

III. INTERPRETING THE BILL OF RIGHTS

Justice Kentridge admonished in the Constitutional Court's first opinion, *S v Zuma,* that 'the Constitution does not mean whatever we might wish it to mean' and '[i]f the language used by the lawgiver is ignored in favour of a general resort to "values" the result is not interpretation but divination'. He nevertheless recognised that a Constitution 'embodying fundamental principles should *as far as its language permits* be given a broad construction'.[20] This emphasis on the ordinary meaning of the language of the

---

[17] 1996 Constitution s 38(b).
[18] 1996 Constitution s 38.
[19] 1996 Constitution s 8(4).
[20] *S v Zuma* 1995 (2) SA 642 (CC) [17].

Constitution raised some concern that the inherent positivism of South African lawyers would restrict or serve as a drag on the interpretative project so central to the transformative potential of the Constitution.[21] However, this concern was counterbalanced by the Constitutional Court's own assertion in its very next case that 'whilst paying due regard to the language that has been used', the process of interpretation should be both generous and purposive, in order to give 'expression to the underlying values of the Constitution'.[22] This broader approach to constitutional interpretation has marked the jurisprudence of the Constitutional Court. Despite concerns that some of the more recently appointed judges might be more executive-minded in their interpretations, the Court has thus far maintained its generous and purposive approach in its interpretation of rights.

A. Generous Interpretation

In *Zuma,* the Constitutional Court drew on the judgment of Lord Wilberforce in *Minister of Home Affairs (Bermuda) v Fisher*[23] to argue that a generous interpretation of rights is an appropriate approach to take as it 'gives to individuals the full measure of the fundamental rights and freedoms' guaranteed in the Bill of Rights.[24] The significance of this approach was made evident in another early case under the interim Constitution when petitioners, whose cases had commenced before the adoption of the Constitution, attempted to claim their rights under the Constitution. A simple response to their claim, advocated by a minority of the Justices on the Constitutional Court, was to adopt a plain-meaning approach and to deny their claims on the grounds that section 241(8) of the interim Constitution stated in clear language that 'pending cases shall be dealt with as if the Constitution had not been passed'.[25] The majority of the Court, however, rejected this approach. Justice Mohammed, for the majority, once again citing Lord Wilberforce, argued that constitutional interpretation must avoid 'the austerity of tabulated legalism' and that an

[21] See D Davis, *Democracy and Deliberation* (Kenwyn, Juta, 1999) 24–30.
[22] *Makwanyane,* above n 13, [9].
[23] *Minister of Home Affairs (Bermuda) v Fisher* [1980] AC 319 (PC).
[24] *Minister of Home Affairs (Bermuda) v Fisher* [1980] AC 319 (PC) [328]–[329].
[25] *S v Mhlungu* 1995 (3) SA 391 (CC) [78].

interpretation which withholds the rights guaranteed by [the Bill of Rights] ... from those involved in proceedings which fortuitously commenced before the operation of the Constitution would not give to [the Bill of Rights] ... a construction which is 'most beneficial to the widest amplitude' and should therefore be avoided if the language and context of the relevant sections reasonably permits such a course.[26]

This approach, which simply offered a broad interpretation of rights over a narrow interpretation, may be explained as part of the response to the previous denial of rights that characterised South African legal history. Others argue that this approach may be inherent in the two-phase analysis of rights that occurs in the context of a general limitations clause. Instead of having to restrict the scope of a right out of a concern that a broad reading will have implications beyond the circumstances of the case being decided, the Court is able, according to this argument,

to adopt a broad construction of the right in the first (interpretative) stage of the enquiry, then ... require the state or the person relying on the validity of the infringement to justify the infringement in the limitation stage of the litigation.[27]

Although the Constitutional Court continues to apply a generous interpretation[28] of rights, it also tends, when confronted with a conflict between a generous and purposive interpretation, to 'demarcate the right in terms of its purpose'.[29]

B. Purposive Interpretation

In addition to a generous interpretation, the Constitutional Court has repeatedly referred to the necessity of adopting a purposive approach to the interpretation of rights. The essence of this approach involves identifying the core values that underlie the inclusion of a particular right in the Bill of Rights and adopting an interpretation of the right that 'best supports and protects those values'.[30] This approach is also closely linked

---

[26] *Mhlungu* [9].

[27] J De Waal, I Currie and G Erasmus, *The Bill of Rights Handbook*, 4th edn (Lansdowne, South Africa, Juta, 2001) 134.

[28] See *South African National Defence Force Union v Minister of Defence* 1999 (4) SA 469 (CC) [28].

[29] De Waal, Currie and Erasmus, *The Bill of Rights Handbook*, 4th edn, above n 27, 135.

[30] De Waal, Currie and Erasmus, *The Bill of Rights Handbook*, 4th edn, above n 27, 131.

to a contextual understanding of the interpretative project. This linkage of purpose and context has, at times, made a profound impact on the scope of the right at issue and it has not always had the effect of expanding the right. For example, the Constitutional Court's development of the right to equality has clearly been enhanced by the Court's exploration of the linkages between the rights of dignity and equality—both in defining the purpose of equal treatment as the basis for individual dignity and by emphasising the contextual relationship of the rights to dignity and equality in the constitutional text; however, the effects on the concepts of freedom and certain social and economic rights, such as health and education, have been less expansive.

In the first instance, the Constitutional Court rejected an expansive reading of the right to freedom advocated by Justice Ackermann in *Ferreria v Levin*.[31] The majority of the Court in that case argued that the right to freedom in the text of the Constitution was placed alongside the rights not to be subject to detention without trial, torture or other forms of cruel, inhuman and degrading punishment, thus indicating that the core purpose of the right was to protect an individual's physical liberty. The majority relied upon this purposive interpretation to reject Justice Ackermann's definition of the right to freedom as a residual right of individuals not to have the state place obstacles in the way of their choices and activities.[32] Instead of a broad libertarian interpretation of the right, the idea of freedom became anchored to an older tradition of freedom from physical restraint that is rooted in the common law jurisprudence of liberty. Thus a combined analysis of the textual context and a purposive interpretation of the right to freedom in effect restricted the scope of the right's interpretation.

Again, while it might be possible to conceptualise rights to life or education in broad purposive terms—providing access to a dialysis machine for a patient who would likely die if access were denied, or requiring the state to provide public education in accordance with the language, cultural and even religious convictions of communities in a multi-cultural society—the Constitutional Court has relied on the interaction of purpose and context to effectively constrain claims based on such broad readings of these rights. In the *Soobramoney* case,[33] the applicant claimed a right of access to dialysis in a public hospital, but the Court rejected such

---

[31] *Ferreira v Levin NO* 1996 (1) SA 984 (CC).

[32] *Ferreira v Levin NO* 1996 (1) SA 984 (CC) [69].

[33] *Soobramoney v Minister of Health (KwaZulu-Natal)*, 1998 (1) SA 765 (CC).

a broad definition of the right to life on the grounds that the state's positive obligations to provide access to health care are contained in section 27 and therefore the Court could not interpret the right to life to impose additional obligations [on the state] that were inconsistent with section 27.[34] The right to health contained in section 27 is limited explicitly to a duty on the state to 'take reasonable legislative and other measures, within its available resources'.[35]

Justice Mahomed adopted a similar strategy when he argued in the *Gauteng School Education Policy Bill*[36] against public funding for a school to serve the needs of a particular cultural, language and religious community. He noted in that case that the interim Constitution had separate clauses guaranteeing publicly funded basic education in the language of choice where practicable, on the one hand, while another clause guaranteed freedom to establish educational institutions based on culture, language or religion. In his analysis of the right, Justice Mahomed noted both the textual context of the clause—as distinct from the clause guaranteeing funding—and argued that a purposive interpretation of the right did not require the guarantee of state resources in order for the right to serve its goal. Thus, he reached the following conclusion:

> [The right] is neither superfluous nor tautologous. It preserves an important freedom. The constitutional entrenchment of that freedom is particularly important because of our special history initiated during the fifties, in terms of the system of Bantu education. From that period the State actively discouraged and effectively prohibited private educational institutions from establishing or continuing private schools and insisted that such schools had to be established and administered subject to the control of the State. The execution of these policies constituted an invasion of the right of individuals in association with one another to establish and continue, at their own expense, their own educational institutions based on their own values. Such invasions would now be constitutionally impermissible.[37]

As a result, the Court found that the applicants had no right to publicly funded schools to serve particular cultural, language or religious needs, but instead possessed a more limited right to establish their own schools

[34] See De Waal, Currie and Erasmus, *The Bill of Rights Handbook*, 4th edn, above n 27, 139 and *Soobramoney* [15].

[35] 1996 Constitution s 27(2).

[36] *Ex parte Gauteng Provincial Legislature: in re Dispute Concerning the Constitutionality of Certain Provisions of the Gauteng School Education Policy Bill 83 of 1995* 1996 (3) SA 617 (CC).

[37] *Gauteng School Education Policy Bill*, above n 36, [8].

with their own resources. In effect then, the interpretative impact of the emphasis on context and purpose is to limit the scope of the right under consideration.

C. Positive Obligations and Accountability

Distinct from each other, but so far closely related in the Court's jurisprudence, has been the interpretation of rights as imposing not only negative but also positive obligations on the government and the Court's emphasis on the 'accountability of those exercising public power [as] . . . one of the founding values'[38] of the new constitutional order. While the negative interpretation of rights is considered quite standard, the Court's embrace of the notion that rights impose a positive obligation on the state brings it closer to the jurisprudence of the German Constitutional Court and the European Court on Human Rights, as compared to the United States Supreme Court, which has eschewed such an approach. In two cases, dealing respectively, with challenges to the Prevention of Family Violence Act and the dismissal of a civil case brought by a woman who had been assaulted by a sex-offender who was awaiting trial and had been granted bail on the advice of the police, the Constitutional Court has focused on the positive obligations imposed by constitutional rights. In *S v Baloyi,* the Court found that the statute, when read in terms of the state's constitutional duty to 'respect, protect, promote and fulfil the rights in the Bill of Rights',[39] obliged the 'State directly to protect the right of everyone to be free from private or domestic violence'.[40] Focusing on the rights to life, dignity, freedom and security of person, the Court argued in *Carmichele v Minister of Safety and Security* that in 'some circumstances there would also be a positive component which obliges the State and its organs to provide appropriate protection to everyone through laws and structures designed to afford such protection'.[41]

More recently, the Court upheld the state's positive obligation to provide protection to citizens and the requirement that government and organs of state be held accountable for their conduct. This case arose out

---

[38] *Rail Commuters Action Group et. al v Transnet Ltd t/a Metrorail et. al* CCT 56/03, decided on 26 November 2004 [hereinafter *Rail Commuters*] [74].

[39] 1996 Constitution s 7(2).

[40] *S v Baloyi,* 2000 (2) SA 425 (CC) [11].

[41] *Carmichele v Minister of Safety and Security* 2001 (4) SA 938 (CC) [44].

of the intersection of government's policy of privatisation and the escalating crime rate, which has been a feature of post-apartheid South Africa. The case, *Rail Commuters Action Group v Transnet Ltd t/a Metrorail*,[42] was brought by rail commuters in the Western Cape who argued that a publicly traded company, in which the state is the only shareholder, bore responsibility, together with the police, to protect passengers from crime on the trains. Justice O'Regan recognised that the principle of accountability 'may not always give rise to a legal duty whether in private or public law'[43] and that 'private law claims are not always the most appropriate method to enforce constitutional rights'.[44] But she nevertheless concluded that the rail company, as an organ of state, bore a positive obligation 'to ensure that reasonable measures are in place to provide for the security of rail commuters . . . regardless of who may be implementing them'.[45]

D. Internal Directives for Interpretation

Apart from particular definitional clauses and the precise requirements of the limitations clause in the Bill of Rights, a number of other specific guides to interpretation exist in the Constitution. First, there are limitations internal to specific rights in the Bill of Rights, most obviously the clauses providing that freedom of expression does not extend to propaganda for war; incitement of imminent violence; or advocacy of hatred that is based on race, ethnicity, gender or religion, and that constitutes incitement to cause harm.[46] Second, the Bill of Rights includes explicit interpretative provisions that outline the sources of values and law to be considered by the Constitutional Court in interpreting the Bill of Rights as well as the requirement that every court, tribunal or forum must, when interpreting any legislation or developing either the common law or customary law, 'promote the spirit, purpose and objects of the Bill of Rights'. Finally, the Constitution includes a number of sets of principles, including those establishing and governing state institutions supporting democracy, a fundamental prerequisite for the protection of rights.

---

[42] *Rail Commuters*, above n 38.
[43] *Rail Commuters* [78].
[44] *Rail Commuters* [80].
[45] *Rail Commuters* [84].
[46] 1996 Constitution s 16(2)(a)–(c).

E. Duty to Develop the Common Law and Customary Law

One of the central aspects of the *Carmichele* decision was the holding that 'where the common law deviates from the spirit, purport and objects of the Bill of Rights, the courts have an obligation to develop it by removing that deviation'[47] and 'that this duty upon judges arises in respect both of the civil and criminal law, whether or not the parties in any particular case request the court to develop the common law'[48] as provided for in section 39(2) of the Constitution. While some have argued that this provision has more to do with the application of the Constitution rather then its interpretation,[49] it clearly holds major implications for the Court's interpretative project and the meaning of the Bill of Rights in ordinary people's lives. This has been demonstrated most recently in cases involving the definition of marriage and the question of whether the principle of primogeniture, in the context of the customary law of succession, could be saved from constitutional invalidity.

In the first case,[50] two women approached the High Court requesting that the common law of marriage be developed—in accordance with the Constitution's enshrinement of equality on the ground of sexual orientation—to allow them to marry. When their application was dismissed they appealed to the Supreme Court of Appeal. There Justice Cameron held, in accordance with the constitutional obligation to develop the common law and the 'strides that our equality jurisprudence has taken in respect of gays and lesbians in the last ten years',[51] that the common law concept of marriage is developed to embrace same-sex partners as follows: 'Marriage is the union of two persons to the exclusion of all others for life'.[52] In the second case,[53] the Constitutional Court consolidated a group of cases in which the 'customary' law of succession had led to the exclusion

---

[47] *Carmichele*, above n 41, [33].

[48] *Carmichele* [34].

[49] De Waal, Currie and Erasmus, *The Bill of Rights Handbook*, 4th edn, above n 27, 143.

[50] *Marie Adriaana Fourie, Cecelia Johanna Bonthuys and Minister of Home Affairs, Director-General of Home Affairs and Lesbian and Gay Equality Project, Supreme Court of Appeal of South Africa*, Case no: 232/2003, decided 30 November 2004 [hereinafter *Fourie*].

[51] *Fourie* [12].

[52] *Fourie* [49].

[53] *Nonkululeko Letta Bhe et. al. v Magistrate, Khayelitsha et al,* CCT 49/03; *Charlotte Shibi v Mantabeni Freddy Sithole et al,* CCT 69/03; *South African Human Rights Commission et al v President of the Republic of South Africa et al,* CCT 50/03, decided 15 October 2004 [hereinafter, *Bhe*].

of female children, wives and sisters in the distribution of the estates of the deceased. The majority of the Court declared the 'customary' law rule of primogenitor to be a violation of the constitutional right to gender equality, and Justice Ngcobo argued that, in his view, 'the rule of male primogeniture should be developed in order to bring it in line with the rights in the Bill of Rights'.[54] Rejecting the majority's preference to have the common law-based Intestate Succession Act apply until there is legislative reform of indigenous law, Justice Ngcobo suggested that first customary law could continue to apply where the parties agreed and in the event of a dispute the Magistrates' Court, which has jurisdiction, should consider what 'the most appropriate system of law to be applied' should be. In doing so, he argued, 'the Magistrate must have regard to what is fair, just and equitable', and pay 'particular regard to the interest of the minor children and any other dependent of the deceased'.[55] While the majority declined these invitations to explicitly develop the common law, this remains a significant option for the Constitutional Court as it encounters conflicts between the rights guaranteed in the Bill of Rights and pre-existing common and customary law rules that are at odds with these rights.

IV. THE BILL OF RIGHTS WITHIN THE FRAME OF DIGNITY, EQUALITY AND FREEDOM

Dignity, equality and freedom play a foundational role in South Africa's post-apartheid Constitution. Not only are these rights individually protected and included as founding values of the Constitution but they are also reiterated as the basic criteria of any open and democratic society in which a limitation of a right would be justifiable. They are also cited as the basic principles underlying the values of a democratic society, which must be promoted through the interpretation of rights. At the same time, the Constitutional Court has recognised the inherent connectedness of these rights, both in their substantive interpretation and when used as markers of the underlying principles of the new society. However, this recognition poses a difficult challenge for the project of constitutional interpretation. On the one hand, the Court's jurisprudence has adopted the most generous interpretation of individual rights to dignity, equality and freedom. On the other hand, it recognises that the boundaries of

---

[54] *Bhe* [139].
[55] *Bhe* [240].

constitutional rights are 'limited by every other right accruing to another citizen'[56] and 'by the legitimate needs of society'.[57]

This approach has made it possible for the Court to elevate the right to dignity, particularly in the context of equality, where 'the constitutional protection of dignity requires us to acknowledge the value and worth of all individuals as members of our society.' However, the Court's jurisprudence on freedom—with the inherent tensions between an atomistic conception of individual freedom and a broader notion of individuals exercising their freedom within the context of their membership in a community[58]—has proved more complex. In this sense, a tension exists in the interpretative visions of dignity, equality and freedom that inform the Constitutional Court's jurisprudence. Sometimes these visions are asserted as independent criteria, while at other moments they are employed in combination or as a means to inform their respective or related content. This tension may be illustrated by focusing on the right to dignity, which the Court has declared to be, together with the right to life, 'the most important of all human rights, and the source of all other personal rights in the Bill of Rights'.[59]

The high status of dignity in the constitutional order is justified first by the argument that the 'Constitution asserts dignity to contradict our past . . . [i]t asserts it too to inform the future, to invest in our democracy respect for the intrinsic worth of all human beings".[60] In fact, there are no less than five specific references to human dignity in the 1996 Constitution. First, human dignity, together with 'equality and the advancement of human rights and freedoms' is one of the founding provisions contained in section 1. This section may only be amended by a 75 per cent majority of the National Assembly supported by six of the nine provinces, which makes it virtually unchangeable. Second, there are four separate references to human dignity within the Bill of Rights: It is listed as a key democratic value the state is obliged to uphold; as an explicit substantive right; and as both a non-derogable right in the event of a State of Emergency and as a factor for the courts to consider in deciding whether a limitation of a right is reasonable and justifiable.

[56] *Bernstein v Bester* NO 1996 (2) SA 751 (CC) [67].

[57] J De Waal, I Currie and G Erasmus, *The Bill of Rights Handbook*, 2nd edn (Kenwyn, Juta, 1999) 140.

[58] See Davis, *Democracy and Deliberation*, above n 21, 65.

[59] *S v Makwanyane* 1995 (3) SA 391 (CC) [144].

[60] *Dawood v Minister of Home Affairs* 2000 (3) SA 936 (CC) [35].

The foundational status of human dignity means that it serves also as a background principle in the interpretation and development of other rights. In this sense, there is a close link between the foundational aspects of human dignity and the specific right to dignity in the Court's jurisprudence. Arguing that the death penalty violates the right to dignity, Justice O'Regan of the Constitutional Court argued that 'the importance of dignity as a founding value of the new Constitution cannot be overemphasised ... [t]his right therefore is the foundation of many of the other rights that are specifically entrenched in [the bill of rights]'.[61] The link between the foundational place of the notion of dignity and the recognition of a specific constitutional right to dignity makes it difficult to disentangle a right to dignity from the protection of various associated rights. In order to explore the parameters of this interaction, it is helpful to divide the jurisprudence into three general categories: first, how the substantive right itself has shaped the outer limits of acceptable criminal sanctions; second, how the right is interconnected with the rights to freedom and equality; and third, how the right interacts with the control of information and speech rights.

First, in the area of criminal sanctions, the substantive right to dignity has had its most profound impact. The Constitutional Court has relied on the right to dignity to guide the court's imposition of limits on the state's ability to punish criminals. Because the death penalty was not explicitly precluded in the Constitution-making process, the Constitutional Court had to address the fate of the nearly 400 prisoners on death row at the time the Constitution was adopted. In *S v Makwanyane*, the new court's second decision, the Court struck down the death penalty on a number of grounds, including human dignity. The Court's decision addresses the relationship between dignity and capital punishment in a number of different ways. Justice Chaskalson, arguing for the majority of the Court, based his decision on the prohibition of cruel and unusual punishment. He cited both United States Supreme Court Justice Brennan's argument that 'the punishment of death ... treats members of the human race as nonhumans', and the Canadian Supreme Court's decision in *Kindler v Canada* in which a minority of judges described the death penalty as 'the supreme indignity to the individual, the ultimate corporal punishment, the final and complete lobotomy and the absolute and irrevocable castration ... the ultimate desecration of human dignity'.[62] In a subsequent case

[61] *Makwanyane* [328].
[62] See *Makwanyane* [57] and [60].

that challenged the sentence of juvenile whipping as cruel, inhuman and degrading, the Court argued, in part, that it is reasonable to expect the state to be:

> [f]oremost in upholding those values which are the guiding light of civilised societies. Respect for human dignity is one such value; acknowledging it includes an acceptance by society that . . . even the vilest criminal remains a human being possessed of common human dignity.[63]

Most recently, the Court struck down the common law criminalisation of sodomy as inconsistent with human dignity, arguing that:

> [As] a result of the criminal offence, gay men are at risk of arrest, prosecution and conviction of the offence of sodomy simply because they seek to engage in sexual conduct which is part of their experience of being human. Just as apartheid legislation rendered the lives of couples of different racial groups perpetually at risk, the sodomy offence builds insecurity and vulnerability into the daily lives of gay men. There can be no doubt that the existence of a law which punishes a form of sexual expression for gay men degrades and devalues gay men in our broader society. As such it is a palpable invasion of their dignity.[64]

Second, the right to dignity is closely associated with the rights to freedom and equality. In the first instance, Justice Ackermann drew on the link between dignity and personhood to emphasise the importance of freedom. In *Ferreira v Levin* he argued the following:

> [H]uman dignity cannot be fully valued or respected unless individuals are able to develop their humanity, their humanness to the full extent of its potential. Each human being is uniquely talented. Part of the dignity of every human being is the fact and awareness of this uniqueness. An individual's human dignity cannot be fully respected or valued unless the individual is permitted to develop his or her unique talents optimally.

He concluded that '[h]uman dignity has little value without freedom . . . to deny people freedom is to deny them their dignity'.[65] While the majority rejected Ackermann's atomistic conception of freedom and dignity, the Court did accept that the right to human dignity will flourish in the context of the 'multiplicity of rights with which it is associated' in the Bill of

---

[63] *S v Williams* 1995 (3) SA 632 (CC) [58].

[64] *National Coalition for Gay and Lesbian Equality v Minister of Justice* 1999 (1) SA 6 (CC) [28].

[65] *Ferreira v Levin* 1996 (1) SA 984 (CC) [49].

Rights. This strain of dignity jurisprudence (in which the right exists in a symbiotic relationship to other rights) has played an increasingly important role in the Court's equality jurisprudence.

Both in its definition of unfair discrimination and in its description of the purpose of the new constitutional order, the Constitutional Court has directly linked dignity and equality. The Court has adopted a specific three-stage enquiry, with a basic threshold test to decide whether there has been a differentiation between people or categories of people; followed by a two-step analysis of whether the differentiation amounts to discrimination and particularly unfair discrimination; and concluding with a determination of whether such unfair discrimination may be justified under the limitations clause.[66] Yet the very idea of unfair discrimination, and hence violation of the equality clause, remains linked to the concept of dignity. Addressing the question whether a differentiation made in the Forestry Act between owners of land within a fire-control area and those outside the area amounted to a violation of the equality clause, the Constitutional Court argued in *Prinsloo v Van der Linde* that unfair discrimination 'principally means treating persons differently in a way which impairs their fundamental dignity as human beings, who are inherently equal in dignity'.[67] Applying this rule, the Court held that the differentiation at issue in the case 'cannot by any stretch of the imagination, be seen as impairing the dignity of the owner or occupier of land outside the fire control area'.[68] The linkage between dignity and equality was also made in a case upholding President Mandela's decision to grant special remission of sentence to 'mothers in prison on 10 May 1994, with minor children under the age of twelve years',[69] while rejecting the claim that the decision discriminated against fathers in a similar position. In that case, the Court argued the following:

> [A]t the heart of the prohibition of unfair discrimination lies a recognition that the purpose of our new constitutional and democratic order is the establishment of a society in which all human beings will be accorded equal dignity and respect regardless of their membership in particular groups. The achievement of such a society in the context of our deeply inegalitarian past will not be easy, but that is the goal of the Constitution.[70]

---

[66] See *Harksen v Lane* NO 1998 (1) SA 300 (CC) [53].

[67] *Prinsloo v Van der Linde* 1997 (3) SA 1012 (CC) [31].

[68] *Prinsloo v Van der Linde* 1997 (3) SA 1012 (CC) [41].

[69] Presidential Act No 17, 27 June 1994.

[70] *President of the Republic of South Africa v Hugo* 1997 (4) SA 1 (CC) [41].

Third, the right to dignity has intersected quite dramatically with rights to information and freedom of expression. Here the right to dignity has been used by the Constitutional Court, in terms of its mandate in section 39(2) of the Constitution, to 'promote the spirit, purport and objects of the Bill of Rights' when developing the common law, to rewrite the long-established common law of defamation. The defendants to a defamation suit—a popular Sunday newspaper—argued for the adoption of the rule established in *New York Times v Sullivan*, which would limit the ability of public figures to claim defamation unless the publisher acted with 'actual malice'.[71] The Court acknowledged that '[f]reedom of expression is integral to a democratic society' as it is 'constitutive of the dignity and autonomy of human beings'. And it argued that the right to free speech must be 'construed in the context of the other values enshrined . . . [i]n particular, the values of human dignity, freedom and equality'.[72] Noting that the 'value of human dignity . . . values both the personal sense of self-worth as well as the public's estimation of the worth or value of an individual', the Court rejected the *Sullivan* approach and instead asked whether an appropriate balance had been struck 'between the protection of freedom of expression on the one hand, and the value of human dignity on the other'.[73] The Court found this balance in a rule adopted by the Supreme Court of Appeals that developed the common law to allow a public official to bring a defamation case in order to protect his or her dignity, but also allowed a defence of reasonable publication, in which the publisher only needs to demonstrate that either the statement was true and in the public interest (an existing common law defence) or that, if it was false, that publication was 'reasonable in all the circumstances'.[74]

V. SOCIO-ECONOMIC RIGHTS

The inclusion of justiciable socio-economic rights in the 1996 Constitution has been heralded internationally as a mark of this Constitution's extraordinary status. But this also raises questions about how these provisions are interpreted in a context of vast socio-economic inequalities and limited governmental capacity.

[71] *Fred Khumalo et al v Bantubonke Harrington Holomisa Case* CCT 53/01, decided by the Constitutional Court on 14 June 2002 [hereinafter *Khumalo*] [40].

[72] *Khumalo* [21]–[25].

[73] *Khumalo* [28].

[74] *Khumalo* [44].

A. Justiciability and the Implementation of Socio-economic Rights

Responding to concerns about the justiciability of these rights in the *First Certification* case,[75] the Constitutional Court rejected the rigid distinction between different types of rights. It argued instead that '[a]t the very minimum, socio-economic rights can be negatively protected from improper invasion'. In the defining case addressing the scope of socio-economic rights, the Court was called upon to define both the negative and positive obligations that the constitutional right to housing imposed on the government.[76]

In *Grootboom*, the first major socio-economic rights case decided positively by the Constitutional Court, the Court was required to review a local government's action in evicting squatters from private land that was to be used for low-income housing. In the process of eviction, the homes the squatters had erected were destroyed and much of their personal possessions and building material had also been deliberately destroyed. While the Constitutional Court upheld the claimant's argument that the municipality's action violated the negative obligation—the duty not to deprive them of shelter—owed to them under section 26(1), the Court proceeded to extrapolate on the positive duties placed on the state under section 26(2). Although the government was able to present a well-documented national housing policy that met the obligation to 'take reasonable legislative and other measures, within its available resources, to achieve the progressive realization of this right', the Court found that the failure to have a policy to address the needs for emergency shelter meant that the policy failed 'to respond to the needs of those most desperate' and thus was unreasonable.[77] At the same time, however, the Court emphasised that '[t]he precise contours and content of the measures to be adopted are primarily a matter for the legislature and executive' and stated that the Court 'will not enquire whether other more desirable or favourable measures could have been adopted, or whether public money could have been better spent'.[78]

---

[75] *Ex Parte Chairperson of the Constitutional Assembly: In re Certification of the Constitution for the Republic of South Africa, 1996*, 1996 (4) SA 744 (CC) [hereinafter *First Certification* case]

[76] *Government of the Republic of South Africa and others v Grootboom and others*, 2001 (1) SA 46 (CC) [hereinafter *Grootboom*].

[77] *Grootboom* [44].

[78] *Grootboom* [41].

B. Socio-economic Rights and the HIV/AIDS Pandemic

Faced with an HIV/AIDS pandemic—in which an estimated 19.6 per cent of the population or approximately 4.7 million people were thought to be HIV-positive as the country approached its first decade of freedom[79]—the debate about what to do covered a wide range of options: Some people remained in denial, while others dreamed of local vaccine breakthroughs. Still others, such as activists of the Treatment Action Campaign (TAC), engaged in public acts of lawbreaking, such as importing generic pharmaceuticals from Thailand in defiance of the patent rights guaranteed under South African law. At market prices of between R40,000 and R70,000 per year in 2001, it was estimated that providing antiretrovirals alone would cost between R168–294 billion per year—100 times the national public health budget.[80] Even with a 90 per cent discount (now offered by some of the pharmaceutical corporations), the cost of treating all 4.7 million patients would equal approximately 10 times the national public health drug budget. However, with Bangladeshi and Indian firms offering a 'generic' version of these drugs at 3 per cent the South African cost, it started to become more costly for the government not to provide treatment—given the expected costs of hospitalisation and the impact of work and skill losses on the economy. The consequence of this combined political and legal mobilisation was to dramatically alter the debate over access to antiretroviral treatment in South Africa. It set the stage, first, for a major reduction in the price of medicines and second, for the government's decision to provide antiretroviral treatment in the public sector.

i. Constitutional Rights and HIV/AIDS

On 21 March 2003, 600 volunteers under the banner of the TAC, a non-governmental organisation dedicated to ensuring access to treatment for the millions of South Africans infected with HIV/AIDS, commemorated Human Rights Day in South Africa by marching on the same police station in Sharpeville where police had gunned down anti-apartheid

---

[79] See T Barnett and A Whiteside, *AIDS in the Twenty-First Century: Disease and Globalization* (New York: Palgrave:MacMillan, 2002) 17.

[80] See N Nattrass, *The Moral Economy of AIDS in South Africa* (Cambridge, Cambridge University Press, 2004) 120.

protesters on 21 March 1960. Symbolising the number of South Africans dying each day from HIV/AIDS-related illnesses, the demonstrators demanded that the government immediately establish an antiretroviral treatment programme in the public health sector. At the same time, fellow TAC protesters in Durban and Cape Town highlighted the urgency of their demands by laying formal charges of culpable homicide against the Minister of Health and the Minister of Trade and Industry, whom they accused of negligently failing to act, thus causing the deaths of thousands of AIDS sufferers. This campaign reflected a context that contrasted to the day nearly a decade before in May 1994, when Nelson Mandela, in his first official exercise of power as President of South Africa, announced that the government would provide free health services to all children under the age of six and to pregnant women. Yet, unlike the struggle against apartheid, which lasted more than 40 years, within a year the government had conceded that the public sector must provide treatment and was embroiled in a debate over the pace of implementation. While it was indeed sad, as the Reverend Douglas Torr, the Anglican priest who led the TAC marchers in prayer at Sharpeville told the crowd, 'that those who fought to liberate South Africa from apartheid needed to fight again', the outcome—the largest government run HIV/AIDS treatment programme in the world today—is also a tribute to the way the people of South Africa have been able to mobilise and implement the promise of the Bill of Rights.

Given a history of racially structured deprivation, the ANC recognised during the democratic transition that a commitment to constitutionally enshrined civil rights would merely entrench the economic distributions of apartheid unless it was supplemented with a commitment to at least the basic guarantees of socio-economic rights. In an attempt to meet these constitutional commitments the newly elected government began in 1994 to implement its Reconstruction and Development Programme (RDP)—on which it had campaigned for election—as a way to address these inequalities. The mission of the RDP was to address the basic inequalities that had been legally enshrined by apartheid and to promote policies geared towards economic expansion, which would be key to absorbing the vast numbers of unemployed and underemployed people who had been marginalised during the apartheid era. In the health sector, the RDP immediately established a Presidential lead project to provide free health services to children under the age of six and pregnant women, while the ANC's National Health plan envisaged a broader goal of making 'basic health care available to all South Africans, giving priority to the most vulnerable groups'.[81] The plan emphasised '[m]aternal and child care, the protection of the environment, services in the rural areas, women's health and the care of the disabled' and it also promised that there would be 'a focus on the prevention and control of major risk factors and diseases, especially AIDS, tuberculosis, measles, gastrointestinal disease, trauma, heart disease and common cancers'.[82]

When Mandela's government took power in 1994, the South African health care system still reflected the impact of apartheid. Although 80 per cent of the population relied on the public health system for access to 'modern' medical treatment and the public sector consumed 60 to 70 per cent of pharmaceuticals (by volume), the private sector accounted for 80 per cent of the country's total expenditure on drugs.[83] In response to this situation, the government adopted a new National Drugs Policy that incorporated the World Health Organisation's (WHO) essential medicines programme. One year later, in 1997, the legislature amended the existing Medicines Act to allow for the parallel importation of medicines and compulsory licensing, among other measures, to implement this agenda. Although the new law passed the South African Parliament over the objections of the pharmaceutical industry and the United States government, and was signed into law by President Nelson Mandela in December 1997, implementation of the South African Medicines Amendment Act was soon put on hold and it was never implemented in its original form.[84]

The key features of the new law were 'measures to ensure [the] supply of more affordable medicines'.[85] One aspect of the law was designed to fundamentally change the distribution practices of the pharmaceutical manufacturers; for example, it prohibited industry employees from serving on the Medicines Control Board and blocked manufacturers and wholesalers from providing bonuses, rebates or other incentives to doctors. The Minister of Health was empowered 'to prescribe conditions for the supply of more affordable medicines . . . so as to protect the health of the public . . . notwithstanding anything to the contrary in the Patents

[81]   African National Congress, *A National Health Plan for South Africa*, prepared by the ANC with the technical support of WHO and UNICEF (May 1994).

[82]   Ibid.

[83]   Department of Health, *National Drug Policy for South Africa* (January 1996) 3.

[84]   See H Klug, 'Law, Politics and Access to Essential Medicines in Developing Countries' (2008) 36 (2) *Law & Politics* 207.

[85]   Medicines and Related Substances Control Amendment Act 90 of 1997 s 15C.

Act'. The Minister of Health was also granted the power to 'prescribe the conditions on which any medicine which is identical in composition, meets the same quality standard and is intended to have the same proprietary name as that of another medicine already registered in the Republic'[86] may be made available. The effect of these provisions would have been to allow the parallel importation of medicines and generic substitutions without the consent of the prescriber, and the issuing of compulsory licenses to allow for the importation or local manufacture of medicines without requiring the approval of the patent owner.

An opposition made up of 42 parties, including local companies, subsidiaries of transnational corporations and the multinational corporations themselves—and led by the Pharmaceutical Manufacturers' Association (PMA) of South Africa—challenged the constitutionality of the 1997 Act. They made a number of constitutional claims, but argued most specifically that the Act's provisions—empowering the government to determine the extent to which rights granted under a patent in South Africa shall apply, and allowing the government to prescribe conditions for the supply of more affordable generic medicines—together deprived owners of intellectual property in the affected pharmaceutical products of their constitutionally protected property rights. While the PMA case was initially stalled in the courts, the mobilisation of a global campaign against the drug companies and the intervention of the newly formed TAC in the case itself led to the dramatic collapse of the case in 2001 when the drug companies withdrew their suit.

Victory in this case did not end the domestic struggle over access to affordable medicines in South Africa. Despite their shared victory in the PMA case, the government and local social movements soon parted ways as the government balked at the demand to provide access to antiretroviral medicines in the public sector. Instead, the government poured resources into a controversial prevention campaign and newly elected President Mbeki began to question the scientific consensus on HIV/AIDS and to doubt the probity of providing access to the new treatment regime in the public sector. President Mbeki's infamous 'denialism' was focused on questioning the scientific basis of HIV/AIDS as well as raising questions about the toxicity of the new drugs.[87] A furious debate

[86] Medicines and Related Substances Control Amendment Act 90 of 1997 ss 15C(a) and (b).

[87] See, N Nattrass, *Mortal Combat: AIDS Denialism and the Struggle for Antiretorvirals in South Africa* (Durban, University of KwaZulu-Natal Press, 2007).

ensued over the government's stance, with some parties being highly critical and others defending President Mbeki and the Minister of Health Tshabalala-Msimang. Yet there can be no doubt that denialism seriously undermined efforts to effectively address the pandemic in South Africa. In response, civil society, led by the TAC, which had been launched in December 1998—and joined at key moments by the People Living with AIDS organisation, the trade union movement, churches and the Communist Party—began to directly challenge the government's mishandling of the HIV/AIDS pandemic.

ii. The Right to Health Before the Courts

The TAC brought its first legal challenge by demanding that the government provide mothers and their newborn babies access to Nevirapine, an antiretroviral that more than halved the rate of mother-to-child transmission of HIV when it was administered to both mother and child during birth and shortly thereafter. Second, the TAC brought a complaint before the Competition Board that alleged that a number of the major pharmaceutical corporations had colluded in maintaining the high price of particular medicines. Meanwhile, the HIV/AIDS crisis in South Africa continued to explode. Applying the legal arguments that were developed in the *Grootboom* case in the area of health and in the context of HIV/AIDS in particular, posed a major problem for the courts. In the *Treatment Action Campaign*[88] case, the Court was asked to require the government to provide Nevirapine to HIV-positive women in childbirth and their newborn babies—and not merely to have a reasonable policy to address the overwhelming HIV/AIDS pandemic within the confines of the state's resources. The Court decided to require the government to provide Nevirapine, marking an important extension of the principles laid out in *Grootboom* and an extraordinary reversal in the Court's approach to health rights, which only a short time earlier had seemed frozen by the combination of medical prerogatives and resource scarcity.

The 1996 Constitution's introduction of a constitutional right to health,[89] in a context of vast inequality and limited resources, soon produced a tragic confrontation between the health authorities and a patient

---

[88] *Minister of Health v Treatment Action Campaign* (2) 2002 (5) SA 721 (CC) [hereinafter *TAC*].

[89] 1996 Constitution s 27(1): 'Everyone has the right to have access to—(a) health care services, including reproductive health care.'

who required access to renal dialysis in order to prolong his life. When Thiagraj Soobramoney reached the Constitutional Court,[90] the Court denied his claim, drawing a distinction between the right not to be refused emergency medical treatment in terms of section 27(3)[91] of the Constitution and the progressive realisation of the right to health care guaranteed in section 27(2).[92] By rejecting Soobramoney's claim of a right to receive treatment, the Constitutional Court, in effect, recognised that certain medical decisions—in his case, the decision to limit access to a dialysis machine to those patients whose medical condition made them eligible to receive kidney transplants—are best made by medical personnel and should not be second-guessed by the courts.[93] Only a few years later, however, in the *TAC* case, the Constitutional Court essentially bypassed the *Soobramoney* decision by upholding a High Court decision, although not its reasoning, when it required the government to provide Nevirapine to mothers and newborns in public health facilities. Relying on the constitutional guarantee of a right to the progressive realisation of access to health care services, the Constitutional Court argued that, under the circumstances, the cost of Nevirapine and providing the appropriate testing and counselling to mothers was less burdensome to the state than the failure to provide the drug; therefore, the government had a constitutional duty to expand its programme beyond the 18 test sites the Department of Health had already planned.

The court's response effectively rejected the government's attempt to draw an analogy between the 'medical decision' in *Soobramoney* and the question of whether Nevirapine should be made available beyond the 18 test sites. In the High Court—the court of first instance in the *TAC* case—Judge Botha argued that while the medical status of individuals who needed kidney transplants was a medical question (involving the relationship between the availability of donated kidneys and the possibility of a successful transplant, as determined by the health condition of the donee), the issue of whether public sector doctors may prescribe a registered drug,

[90] *Soobramoney v Minister of Health (KwaZulu-Natal)* 1998 (1) SA 765 (CC) [hereinafter *Soobramoney*].
[91] 1996 Constitution s 27(3): 'No one may be refused emergency medical treatment.'
[92] 1996 Constitution s 27(2): 'The state must take reasonable legislative and other measures, within its available resources, to achieve the progressive realisation of each of these rights.'
[93] *Soobramoney*, above n 90, [3], [4] and [32]–[34].

where medically indicated, was not.[94] In its judgment, the Constitutional Court went even further, arguing that where the public sector fails to provide a particular treatment regime (medically indicated and available in the private sector), then the issue is clearly one of health policy and resources and thus implicates the progressive realisation of the right to health care services. Here, the Court built on its central decision in *Grootboom* by placing the review of the reasonableness of government policy and implementation at the centre of its socio-economic rights jurisprudence.

iii. The Role of Social Movement Activism

In April 2004, 10 years after South Africa's historic democratic election and shortly before the country's third national election, there was an extraordinary public meeting in Johannesburg City Hall. The TAC organised the meeting as part of a countrywide campaign calling on the government to implement the national executive's 2003 decision to provide antiretroviral treatment to HIV-positive patients in the public health service whose viral count had dropped below 200. TAC had earlier succeeded in its Constitutional Court challenge demanding that the government extend its programme to prevent mother-to-child-transmission to all public health institutions with the medical capacity to provide the treatment and beyond the eighteen established government test sites. The campaign to pressure the government to more effectively address the national HIV/AIDS pandemic had led to a Cabinet decision to roll out antiretroviral treatment in the public sector, yet in early 2004 there was little evidence that the government was moving to implement this policy. Now the TAC was mounting a national campaign, focused on the provincial governments and their departments of health, which are the front-line institutions in the health sector. I attended the meeting in the City Hall, and I was struck by both the tactics of the TAC and the response of the Gauteng provincial government, represented by its Premier, Sam Shilowa, former Secretary-General of the Congress of South African Trade Unions (COSATU) and the executive member responsible for health in the provincial government.

Johannesburg City Hall, in all its ornate colonial splendour, echoed with stomping feet and chants of hundreds of 'toyi-toying'[95] HIV-positive

---

[94]   TPD Case no 21182/2001, unreported, per Botha J.

[95]   This is an energetic high stepping dance that became a symbol of anti-apartheid resistance in the townships of South Africa in the 1980s.

activists of the TAC. For those old enough to have come of age in the anti-apartheid movement—including all the government officials and community leaders sitting on the stage—the meeting had all the resonances of the struggle against apartheid. Yet the demonstrators also reflected a fundamental change in the politics, strategies and tactics of TAC, the most effective of the new post-apartheid social movements. Instead of merely denouncing a bad government policy and demanding access to antiretroviral treatment in the public health services, the TAC leadership, its activists and supporters, continually reminded the government officials present—as well as the world—that they were loyal ANC members who would shortly be going to the polls to vote for the ANC, and that they were constituents whose needs the government had a duty to address. The meeting began with the showing of a short video documenting the TAC's protests against the government and pharmaceutical industry, and theTAC members who went to the stage to talk about living with HIV and AIDS constantly emphasised either their own histories as anti-apartheid activists or their continuing loyalty to the ANC, despite the government's failure to adequately address the HIV/AIDS pandemic.

Following the TAC speakers, a series of community, church and trade union representatives spoke of the urgency of the problem and expressed solidarity and support for TAC demands. The trade union speaker, in particular, said he had just rushed over from a meeting of the COSATU central committee, which had just decided to call upon the government to provide antiretrovirals to HIV-positive patients in the public health sector. At this point, the TAC invited the provincial government officials present to address the gathering. Although it had been previously announced that the provincial executive member in charge of the health portfolio would be speaking, the provincial Premier insisted on taking her place. Standing up before the chanting crowd, Premier Sam Shilowa announced that he was prepared to meet with representatives of the TAC that same afternoon and was committed to ensuring that the provincial government would begin to roll out antiretroviral treatment in the provincial hospitals, regardless of the status of the promised national plan. He added that he would use existing provincial funds, if necessary, until such time as the national government managed to secure the needed medicines as part of its own programme. This announcement and the subsequent implementation of the provincial roll out was a dramatic breakthrough for the TAC. Not only was it possible for Gauteng—the richest and most organised of the provincial governments—to actually follow through on its promise, but this would break the resistance of the national Department of Health, which had been tardy in its implementation of the national policy. The TAC demonstrated that it was possible to begin the roll out at the provincial level, and it was able to indicate its own willingness to assist with the rollout and to justify its continuing support of the ANC, despite rather sharp differences and ongoing conflict with the national Minister of Health.

The success of this campaign was premised on a holistic vision of the role constitutionally guaranteed rights might play in securing access to basic resources such as health care. First, the TAC had already mounted a successful constitutional challenge to the government's failure to provide broad access to antiretroviral treatment designed to prevent or limit mother-to-child transmission of HIV/AIDS. Second, instead of merely asserting a constitutional right to a broader treatment regime in the public health sector, the TAC recognised that there were limits to what could be achieved in asserting a right to health before the courts. Third, the TAC now employed a multifaceted strategy of political mobilisation and legal action, which focused on addressing the high price of medicines. In this regard, the Aids Law Project, which does most of the legal support work on behalf of the TAC, lodged a complaint before the country's newly energised Competition Commission, challenging the monopoly pricing practices of the major pharmaceutical companies active in the South African market. Finally, by switching from a legal strategy to a political strategy, timed to the approaching national elections, the TAC was able to take into account the relative capacities of the different regions of the country. The organisation was able to use its own strength and the capacity of the Gauteng provincial government and health services to initiate the implementation of the national rollout policy to which the national government was formally committed. This provided a demonstration effect for other provinces and isolated the resistance of the national Minister of Health, who had remained opposed to the extensive provision of antiretroviral treatment in the public sector.

In the first instance, activists and their lawyers asserted constitutional rights and relied upon the Constitutional Court to essentially impose an obligation on the state to provide mothers and newborns in public health facilities access to Nevirapine or other available medication to prevent mother-to-child-transmission of HIV/AIDS. And in the second instance, these same parties turned to a different process and legal resource—the Competition Commission—to bring down the prices of drugs for all those in need of antiretroviral and related treatments. In the *TAC* case, the social movement relied on the constitutional guarantee of a right to the progressive realisation of access to health care services and persuaded the Constitutional Court to hold that under the circumstances—in which the cost of the drug and providing appropriate testing and counselling to mothers was less burdensome then the failure to provide Nevirapine—the government had a constitutional duty to expand its programme beyond the 18 planned test sites. In the second case, the TAC pursued its aim to reduce drug prices and thus expand access to antiretroviral treatment by launching a complaint with the newly created Competition Commission against two of the major pharmaceutical corporations active in South Africa: GlaxoSmithKline (GSK) and Boehringer Ingelheim.The TAC accused them of engaging in excessive pricing of medicines. After the Commission found that the companies had colluded to fix prices, the companies reached an out-of-court settlement with the government that included granting at least three generic pharmaceutical companies voluntary licences on three major antiretrovirals, thus allowing more competition and lowering the price of the drugs in the South African market. Despite these dramatic political interventions and legal victories, the problem of access remains unsolved. For the majority of HIV-infected South Africans, the drugs are unaffordable, even at the reduced prices, and until they get access to the public sector programme being rolled out by the government, they will continue to be denied access.

C. Socio-economic Rights and Reasonableness Review

The Constitutional Court's socio-economic rights jurisprudence has coalesced around a standard of reasonableness. The standard of reasonableness is clearly drawn from the language of the socio-economic rights clauses of the Constitution, which explicitly frame the state's positive obligations in terms of a duty to 'take reasonable legislative and other measures, within its available resources, to achieve the progressive realization'[96] of the particular right; and the Court has held that both the legislative scheme and the implementation of any measures adopted by

[96] See 1996 Constitution ss 26(2) (housing) and 27(2) (health care, food, water and social security). Ss 24(b) (environment), 25(5) (land) and 29(b) (education) all use the language of reasonable measurers but in specifically modified forms.

the government must be reasonable.[97] Although the Court states clearly in its *Grootboom* decision that it will grant wide discretion to both the legislature and the executive when it comes to the means they adopt to achieve these goals,[98] the government still has a burden to justify its decisions and the Court has demonstrated its willingness to scrutinise and even reject the government's approach if the Court finds it to be unreasonable—as it did in the *TAC* case. The Court has also incorporated other approaches within its analysis of socio-economic rights—as in *Khosa* in which non-citizen permanent residents challenged the denial of social welfare benefits.[99] In that case, the Court adopted an analysis of intersecting rights that brought together the Court's concerns for equality and access to social resources. Yet the Court's ongoing reliance on a form of reasonableness review in this area has continued to draw critical concern.[100]

Some academic critics and activists and public interest lawyers have called upon the Court to adopt an approach to socio-economic rights similar to the United Nations Committee on Economic, Social and Cultural Rights, which monitors state compliance with the International Covenant on Economic, Social and Cultural Rights of 1966. In its General Comment 3, on the nature of the member state's obligations under the Covenant, the Committee has advocated for a 'minimum core' approach,[101] which would require states to achieve 'minimum essential levels' of these rights.[102] South Africa's Constitutional Court has made clear its resistance to these calls to define the 'minimum core' of these rights in the Constitution, although this rejection was initially framed in terms of the availability of contextual evidence and not as a matter of principle.[103] As a result, activists continued to assert that the inclusion of

[97] See *Grootboom* [41] and [42].

[98] *Grootboom* [41].

[99] *Khosa v Minister of Social development; Mahlaule v Minister of Social development* 2004 (6) SA 505 (CC).

[100] See D Davis, 'Adjudicating the Socio-Economic Rights in the South African Constitution: Towards "Deference Lite"?' (2006) 22 *South African Journal on Human Rights* 301.

[101] UN Committee on Economic, Social and Cultural Rights, General Comment 3 (1990), 'The Nature of State parties Obligations', UN Doc HRI/Gen 1/Rev1 at 45 (1994) [4].

[102] See D Bilchitz, *Poverty and Fundamental Rights: The Justification and Enforcement of Socio-Economic Rights* (Oxford, Oxford University Press, 2007) 183–87.

[103] See *Grootboom*, above n 76, [32] and [33].

these rights in the Constitution would be meaningless unless they supported some substantive content. When Judge Tsoka of the South Gauteng High Court struck down Johannesburg's policy of installing prepaid water meters in Phiri, Soweto, and issued an order in April 2008 that required the city to provide each resident with 50 litres of free water each day, it seemed as if the idea of a minimum core had finally been accepted.[104] And when the Supreme Court of Appeals essentially upheld Judge Tsoka's decision—while reducing the minimum supply of free water to 42 litres—and the City of Johannesburg appealed to the Constitutional Court, the question of whether the right to water required the supply of a specific minimum amount was placed squarely before the Court.

The Constitutional Court overturned the lower court decisions and found that the 'City's Free Basic Water policy falls within the bounds of reasonableness and therefore is not in conflict with either section 27 of the Constitution or with the national legislation regulating water services'.[105] This opinion, which greatly disappointed many activists, demonstrates the limits of a rights strategy that relies simply on constitutional litigation. [105] In response to the argument that the Court should quantify 'the amount of water sufficient for dignified life',[106] Justice Kate O'Regan pointed out that the Court had previously 'rejected the argument that the social and economic rights in our Constitution contain a minimum core'.[107] She reaffirmed this stance on the basis of two arguments. First, she argued that the 'text of the Constitution' requires that sections 27(1) and (2) be read together in order to 'delineate the scope of the [state's] positive obligation to provide access to sufficient water'—making the content of the right dependent upon the state's reasonable efforts to progressively realise the right. Second, she urged 'an understanding of the proper role of courts in our constitutional democracy'.[108] Justice O'Regan concluded by emphasising the centrality of context to the Court's approach, writing that

[104] See *Mazibuko and Others v City of Johannesburg and Others (Centre on Housing Rights and Evictions as amicus curiae)* (2008) 4 SA 471 (W).

[105] *Lindiwe Mazibuko and Others v City of Johannesburg et al* CCT 39/09, 2009 ZACC 28, decided on 8 October 2009 (CC) [hereinafter *Mazibuko*] [9].

[105] ibid.

[106] *Mazibuko*, above n 105, [51].

[107] *Mazibuko* [53].

[108] *Mazibuko* [57].

what the right requires will vary over time and context. Fixing a quantified content might, in a rigid and counter-productive manner, prevent an analysis of context. The concept of reasonableness places context at the centre of the enquiry and permits an assessment of context to determine whether a government programme is indeed reasonable'.[109]

VI. BILL OF RIGHTS, RULE OF LAW AND STATES OF EMERGENCY

While there is a great deal of continuity between the Bill of Rights in the interim and final Constitutions, the inclusion of a commitment to a 'rule of law' and constitutional supremacy in the founding provisions of the final Constitution highlight post-apartheid South Africa's formal commitment to a particular culture of rights and justification. In practice, the Constitutional Court has developed a two-fold analysis in applying both the rights guaranteed in the Bill of Rights and the more general requirement of 'legality' or the rule of law in reviewing the constitutionality of the exercise of governmental power. While the Court had argued in earlier cases that Parliament must abide by the rule of law[110]—that is, it must not act capriciously or arbitrarily—the Court took the opportunity, in a case addressing the power of the President to appoint commissions of inquiry, to clarify its approach.[111] The Court rejected the claim that the President's action was subject to the Administrative Justice clause of the Bill of Rights as it was not an administrative act: it did not involve the implementation of legislation. The Court nevertheless argued that the President was bound by the more general requirement of legality. In laying down its approach the Constitutional Court noted that first,

> the exercise of the powers [of the President] must not infringe any provision of the Bill of Rights; [and second] the exercise of the powers is also clearly constrained by the principle of legality and, as is implicit in the Constitution, the President must act in good faith and must not misconstrue the powers.[112]

---

[109]   *Mazibuko* [60].

[110]   See *Fedsure Life Assurance Ltd v Greater Johannesburg Transitional Metropolitan Council* 1999 (1) SA 374 (CC) and *New National Party v Government of the Republic of South Africa* 1999 (3) SA 191 (CC).

[111]   See *President of the Republic of South Africa v South African Rugby Football Union* 2000 (1) SA 1 (CC).

[112]   *South African Rugby Football Union*, above n 111, [148].

In a second case challenging the President's exercise of non-administrative power, the Constitutional Court described the general constraints the Constitution places on the exercise of public power. It argued that

> it is a requirement of the rule of law that the exercise of public power by the executive and other functionaries should not be arbitrary. Decisions must be rationally related to the purpose for which the power was given, otherwise they are in effect arbitrary and inconsistent with this requirement.[113]

In effect, then, the Court 'treats the provisions of the Bill of Rights as an elaboration of general principles implied by the rule of law' and requires that these 'specific provisions which concretise, elaborate on and implement the rule of law must be applied in legal disputes before the general norm is invoked'.[114] Nevertheless, it is clear that the Court is employing the founding principles' guarantee of the rule of law to require that—in addition to respect for the specific rights guaranteed in the Bill of Rights—when it comes to the exercise of governmental power (legislative or executive) there must be a rational relationship between the scheme adopted and the achievement of a legitimate purpose.[115]

A. States of Emergency and the Derogation of Rights

Given the apartheid regime's extensive use of emergency powers, it is not surprising that the Constitutional Assembly would seek to place limits on the ability of the government to violate rights under the guise of a State of Emergency. Not only does the Constitution limit the conditions under which a valid State of Emergency may be declared, but it also requires particular procedural steps and provides a list of non-derogable rights in its attempt to limit the effect of an emergency. While it may be argued that in a true emergency there is little likelihood that those in power will abide by constitutional niceties, these provisions do clarify the procedures and means the state may employ in addressing a national emergency. They also provide explicit ways in which individuals and groups may challenge the determination of a State of Emergency and the particular actions

---

[113] *Pharmaceutical Manufacturers Association of South Africa: Re ex p President of the Republic of South Africa* 2000 (2) SA 674 (CC) [85].

[114] De Waal, Currie and Erasmus, *The Bill of Rights Handbook*, 4th edn, above n 27, 14–15.

[115] See courts discussion in *New National Party* [19]–[24].

taken under it. Of course these constitutional measures assume that the courts and legislature will still be available as institutional resources for those challenging executive action. However, if they were to be bypassed or prevented from exercising their authority, these provisions would serve as an obvious means to deny the legitimacy of any alternative claims to authority.

Procedurally, a declaration of a State of Emergency must be made in accordance with existing legislation and is only valid if '[t]he life of the nation is threatened by war, invasion, general insurrection, disorder, natural disaster or other public emergency; and the declaration is necessary to restore peace and order'.[116] Furthermore, the declaration is only valid 'prospectively; and . . . for no more than 21 days . . . unless the National Assembly resolves to extend the declaration'.[117]

Importantly, while the National Assembly may extend the declaration for three months at a time, any extension beyond the first three-month extension must have the support of at least 60 per cent of the members of the National Assembly. Additional safeguards include provisions that limit the extent of the derogation of rights allowed under a State of Emergency,[118] prohibit the passage of legislation granting indemnification to 'the state or any person, in respect of any unlawful act'[119] and an explicit prohibition on any derogations from these limiting provisions.[120] Finally, in a clear response to the history of detention without trial under apartheid, the Constitution-makers accepted that there might be detentions without trial under a State of Emergency but they were careful to include a specific list of provisions designed to protect detainees from forms of abuse that characterised the apartheid era. As a result, detainees are guaranteed the right to see a doctor and lawyer of their choice 'at any reasonable time'[121] and the state has a duty to report detentions to an adult family member or friend within five days.[122] The only exceptions to these guarantees apply to non-citizens detained as prisoner of war, who must be held according to the standards of international humanitarian law.

---

[116] 1996 Constitution s 37(1)(a) and (b).
[117] 1996 Constitution s 37(2)(a) and (b).
[118] See 1996 Constitution, Table of Non-Derogable Rights, s 37(5).
[119] 1996 Constitution s 37(5)(a).
[120] 1996 Constitution s 37(5)(b) and (c).
[121] 1996 Constitution s 37(6)(c) and (d).
[122] 1996 Constitution s 37(6)(a).

VII. CONCLUSION: PURSUING RIGHTS IN A LAND OF VAST INEQUALITIES

Significantly, the struggle for rights in post-apartheid South Africa is not limited to litigation or political lobbying. The activists of the TAC, for example, have mobilised their members and communities through a variety of campaigns and actions, including the illegal importation of 'generic' medicines and the establishment of demonstration sites where they have proven to communities and the government, through experience, that another way is possible. In the latter case, the TAC collaborated with Médicins Sans Frontières (MSF) to establish an HIV/AIDS clinic in Khayelitsha, an impoverished community outside Cape Town, where free antiretroviral treatment for destitute individuals provided a model for the country. As Steven Friedman and Shauna Mottiar have argued, the TAC, with its 'politics of the moral high ground', has demonstrated that 'it remains possible to use the rights guaranteed and institutions created by liberal democracy to win advances for the poor and weak'.[123]

The failure of government to effectively protect the rights of welfare recipients,[124] property owners,[125] indigenous land-claiming communities,[126] women (in the context of intestate succession in indigenous law),[127] or to adequately protect newborns against the mother-to-child transmission of HIV,[128] or to recognise the marital rights of same-sex couples[129] have all led to extraordinary decisions by the courts and created intense debates about the types of remedies the courts should provide.[130] Although there has been a constant clamouring for bolder judicial action—demands that courts award mandatory relief and retain

[123] See S Friedman and S Mottiar, 'The Treatment Action Campaign and the Politics of Morality' in R Ballard, A Habib and I Valodia (eds), *Voices of Protest: Social Movements in Post-Apartheid South Africa* (Scottsville, South Africa: University of KwaZulu-Natal Press, 2006).

[124] *Khosa v Minister of Social Development* 2004 (6) SA 505 (CC).

[125] *President of the Republic of South Africa v Modderklip Boerdery (Pty) Ltd* 2005 (5) SA 3 (CC).

[126] *Alexkor Ltd v The Richtersveld Community* 2004 (5) SA 460 (CC).

[127] *Bhe et al v Magistrate, Khayelitsha et al* 2005 (1) SA 563 (CC).

[128] *TAC,* above n 88.

[129] *Minister of Home Affairs and Another v Fourie et. al* 2006 (1) SA 524 (CC).

[130] See K Roach and G Budlender, 'Mandatory Relief and Supervisory Jurisdiction: When is it Appropriate, Just and Equitable?' (2005) 122 (2) *South African Law Journal* 325.

supervisory jurisdiction—the Constitutional Court in particular has been careful to frame its orders in ways that encourage compliance but also attempt to bring the democratic organs of government into the decision-making process. The Court has asserted its right to provide appropriate relief, including mandatory orders and structural relief; yet it has also used its ability to suspend declarations of invalidity to give the legislature or executive the time and the flexibility to formulate constitutional alternatives.[131] In this way, the Court has effectively engaged in a dialogue with the other branches of the government in its attempt to assert its power while preserving and protecting its own institutional authority against potential popular and political backlashes.

The incorporation of justiciable socio-economic rights among other political and civil rights in a context of vast and continuing inequality has provided an extraordinary example of the multiple roles that the protection of constitutional rights in a Bill of Rights might play. On the one hand, rights advocacy has served as a key ingredient in the multilayered strategies of activists, politicians and government officials. However, the legal nature of these provisions has meant that even when political mobilisation has failed or simple enforcement by the courts has not been possible, the mere fact that the right is claimed, asserted and become part of political discourse has kept alive the claims of those seeking more equal access to social resources. Even when courts have offered little support for an initial claim—as in the sad case of Mr Soobramoney who desperately sought access to a dialysis machine in his attempt to survive renal failure—the very existence of the promise of a right to health meant that courts remained open to further attempts to define the right and to use the promise of a right to health to shift the debate over access to medicines to address the HIV/AIDS pandemic. The success of this particular campaign was the result of a multilayered strategy by the TAC, but it was the constitutional promise of a right to health in the Bill of Rights that formed a key element in that struggle.

---

[131] Roach and Budlender, 'Mandatory Relief', above n 130.

FURTHER READING

Currie, I and De Waal, J, *The Bill of Rights Handbook*, 5th edn (Lansdowne, Juta, 2005)

Ballard, R, Habib, A and Valodia I (eds), *Voices of Protest: Social Movements in Post-Apartheid South Africa* (Scottsville, University of KwaZulu–Natal Press, 2006)

Davis, D, 'Adjudicating the Socio-Economic Rights in the South African Constitution: Towards "Deference Lite"?' (2006) 22 *South African Journal on Human Rights* 301

Murienik, E, 'A Bridge to Where? Introducing the Interim Bill of Rights' (1994) 10 *South African Journal on Human Rights* 31

Sparks, A, *Beyond the Miracle: Inside the New South Africa* (Johannesburg, Johnathan Ball, 2003)

6

Parliamentary Democracy

———✦———

Introduction – Electoral System, Political Rights and the Formation of Government – Parliament as Law-Giver – Parliament as Watchdog – Conclusion: Democratic Participation and the Challenge of Post-apartheid Democracy

I. INTRODUCTION

DEMOCRACY IS ONE of the founding principles of post-apartheid South Africa. While the Constitution establishes a multi-party electoral democracy as a founding value of the Republic, South Africa has a long history of alternative notions and experiences of democracy. From the qualified franchise that existed in parts of South Africa prior to 1936 to today's universal franchise and electoral system based on proportional representation, the ideas and practices of democracy among South Africans have been quite diverse. These experiences include the racist, first-past-the-post constituency-based representative democracy of the apartheid era; the democratic centralism of the Communist Party and the underground structures of the liberation movement; the directly accountable shop-floor representatives of the trade union movement; and the community-based, participatory notions of democracy claimed by social movements, non-governmental organisations and even some traditional leaders. Given this diversity of experience and the demands for democratic accountability, the choice to adopt a purely representative form of democracy in post-apartheid South Africa must be understood as the consequence of the weight of cultural, legal and political continuity, inherent in the decision to retain a parliamentary system and the post-1989 context, in which the exercise of democratic choice through national elections had become the only basis for legitimate government in the eyes of the international community.

Historically, the notion of parliamentary sovereignty, which colonial South Africa inherited along with many other aspects of British public law, made the legislature a central organ of government. Unlike many other authoritarian societies, whose locus of power lies within the executive branch of the state, the legal and political authority of the colonial and apartheid regimes in South Africa was firmly located within the legislative branch and its exercise of parliamentary sovereignty. It was only after the 1976 uprisings and the attempt by the apartheid state to broaden its social base through the inclusion of the 'Coloured' and 'Indian' communities in the 1983 Constitution, that the locus of power shifted towards the executive branch though the creation of an executive President as head of government, rather than a Prime Minister serving under a symbolic head of state. The post-apartheid Constitutions would retain an executive President, indirectly elected by Parliament, but there was a general assumption that the legislature, as the representative branch of government, would be the dominant institution of South Africa's new popular democracy.

Although parliamentary sovereignty has been explicitly displaced by the embrace of constitutional supremacy, democracy is entrenched in the Founding Provisions of the Constitution, which define the country as a 'sovereign, democratic state founded on particular values', including 'universal adult suffrage, a national common voters role, regular elections and a multi-party system of democratic government'.[1] Although this provision does not entrench the system of proportional representation, which is incorporated in section 46(1)(d) of the Constitution, it does specify a number of criteria that establish a basic system of representative democracy—including a common voters' roll and a multi-party system of government. While this is not the only possible interpretation of these provisions, the three elections South Africa has held since it began its democratic transition have all been conducted in terms of these basic criteria to establish a formal system of representative democracy. Despite the abandonment of both the 'tricameral' legislative structure of the 1983 Constitution and the constituency-based structure of representative democracy that had shaped the legislative branch of government since

---

[1]   Constitution of the Republic of South Africa Act 108 of 1996 [hereinafter 1996 Constitution] s 1(d).

the introduction of representative government at the Cape in 1854, both the 1993 interim and 1996 final Constitutions retained South Africa's long-standing parliamentary system. This embrace of an existing institution with long-standing traditions has fundamentally shaped the procedural practices and format of the legislative function under the Constitution.

Parliament is a bicameral institution with the National Assembly and the National Council of Provinces (NCOP) playing distinct roles in the legislative and oversight functions that are at the core of this branch of government. The National Assembly is composed of between 350 and 400 women and men elected as members, according to the terms of an electoral law that is framed by three constitutional requirements: a national common voters' role; minimum voting age of 18 years; and which 'results, in general, in proportional representation'.[2] The Constitution states that the National Assembly is elected for a term of five years[3] and that it should represent the people and ensure government

> by the people under the Constitution . . . by choosing the President, by providing a national forum for public consideration of issues, by passing legislation and by scrutinizing and overseeing executive action.[4]

The NCOP, in contrast to other parliamentary systems, is not a Senate or upper House but rather the institutional embodiment of the principles of co-operative government and intergovernmental relations that attempt to mediate among different levels of government without explicitly embracing a federal system of government. The purpose of the NCOP is to integrate the provinces into the national legislative process, thus achieving a level of integrated law-making that is central to the constitutional principle of co-operative government that envisions three 'spheres of government which are distinctive, interdependent and interrelated'.[5]

In this scheme, the NCOP represents the provinces and is composed of provincial delegations appointed by the provinces. While this body has different roles depending on the type of legislation it is considering, its essential function is to represent the interests of the provinces at the national level. Each province is represented by a 10-person delegation made up of 4 special delegates and 6 permanent delegates. The permanent

---

[2] 1996 Constitution s 46(1)(a)–(d).
[3] 1996 Constitution s 49(1).
[4] 1996 Constitution s 42(3).
[5] 1996 Constitution s 40(1).

delegates come from the different political parties represented in the provincial legislature in proportion to their representation in that legislature and serve until the first meeting of the next elected provincial legislature. The special delegates include the Provincial Premier, or his or her designated representative as well as three additional members of the provincial legislature who may be designated from time to time, allowing the legislature to send different delegates depending on the issues to be addressed in the NCOP. In addition to provincial representation, the Constitution also provides for a tenth non-voting delegation to represent organised local government in the NCOP.

II. ELECTORAL SYSTEM, POLITICAL RIGHTS AND THE FORMATION OF GOVERNMENT

Regular democratic elections were not the generally expected outcome of the conflict over apartheid in South Africa. While the apartheid regime had long claimed to be a bastion of Western democratic principles at the tip of Africa, it had simultaneously and steadfastly rejected the liberation movement's demand for majoritarian democracy. Under these circumstances, many considered a violent conflagration and an ethnically divided polity to be the most predictable outcomes of the conflict.[6] The essence of this problem was that any political structure that was genuinely democratic would obviously transfer power away from the white minority once and for all time. But even when it was finally accepted that only a democratically elected government in South Africa would be acceptable to the international community and the majority of South Africa's inhabitants, the problem of how to produce an electoral system that would determine the will of the people without reproducing patterns of racial representation remained, at first, unsolved.

A. Origin and Nature of the Electoral System

The demand for full citizenship, including the right to participate in the government of the country, was first formally articulated in December 1943 when the ANC adopted a document entitled 'Africans Claims in

---

[6] See RW Johnson, *How Long Will South Africa Survive?* (New York, Oxford University Press, 1977).

South Africa', the findings of its Atlantic Charter Committee. Established to provide a response to the Atlantic Charter, the committee produced both a point-by-point interpretation of the Charter, from the perspective of the majority of South Africans, as well as a Bill of Rights claiming 'full citizenship rights such as are enjoyed by all Europeans in South Africa'. The Atlantic Charter was issued in August 1941 after a shipboard meeting between US President Franklin D Roosevelt and British Prime Minister Winston Churchill and became the reference point for African leaders in South Africa in the lead-up to the Allied Peace Conference, which was to be attended by the government of South Africa. While the Atlantic Charter was described as a statement of Allied war aims, ANC leaders were aware that there was no agreement among the Allied powers about whether the Charter's promise to 'respect the right of all people's to choose the form of government under which they will live'[7] applied equally to either domestic minorities within their own nations or to the inhabitants of their overseas colonies. Nevertheless, subjugated peoples around the world—including African patriots in South Africa—enthusiastically embraced this promise.

Perfectly aware of the different interpretations given by Roosevelt and Churchill to the promise of self-determination,[8] the African Claims document directly addressed the question of settler colonies in Africa, arguing that the 'demands of the Africans for full citizenship rights and direct participation in all councils of the state should be recognized'.[9] Despite the failure of the allies to fully embrace these demands—and the victory of the National Party in the 1948 elections that heralded the coming of apartheid—the demand of full citizenship and democratic rights would remain central in the struggle against apartheid over the next 40 years. Over this period, during the Cold War and the era of military coups and one-party states that swept post-independence Africa, different views of democracy were debated and practised within the liberation movement. But by the time the Berlin Wall fell and South Africa's transition away from apartheid began in 1990, a new, invigorated notion of democracy

[7]   E Borgwardt, 'Atlantic Charter' in her *A New Deal for the World: America's Vision for Human Rights* (Cambridge, MA, Belknap Press of Harvard University Press, 2005) 303–04.

[8]   See AB Xuma, 'We Fight for World Democracy: Introduction to African Claims in South Africa', reprinted in K Asmal, with D Chidester and C Lubisi (eds), *Legacy of Freedom: The ANC's Human Rights Tradition* (Johannesburg, Jonathan Ball, 2005) 7–21.

[9]   Xuma, 'We Fight for World Democracy', above n 8, 14.

had already begun to take hold among activists fighting apartheid. The experience among trade unionists of shop-floor organising as well as the organisation of the United Democratic Front emphasised demands for democratic accountability. At the same time, the ANC in exile and among underground cells in South Africa had begun to formulate its own vision of a post-apartheid polity. In 1987, the ANC adopted a set of Constitutional Guidelines that were taken up and embraced by the international community in the Harare Declaration and subsequent United Nations Convention on Apartheid.

The international community's embrace of electoral democracy as a precondition to South Africa's re-admission to the international community helped to preclude demands for group-based options, such as consociational democracy. However, it did not provide guidance for an acceptable institutional structure of representative democracy. For those who assumed there would be a simple first-past-the-post, geographically based electoral system—as had been the tradition among those who could vote before and during the apartheid era—the question of constituency boundaries soon became overwhelming. Apart from the problem of agreeing upon a process of demarcation that would be acceptable to the different parties in the negotiations, the fact that apartheid had divided the country into racially designated residential areas meant that any demarcation would have to balance the ideal of a non-racial election with the realities of a racially defined geography. While some people suggested that the cities could be demarcated to create constituencies that would be integrated—which would mean that they would have a clear black majority—this action would have effectively precluded the established white parties, which would not be expected to gain even a plurality in most parts of the country where the ANC was expected to receive a significant majority of the votes. In Zimbabwe, this dilemma had been resolved by guaranteeing the white minority 20 seats in Parliament for the first decade of independence. In South Africa, however, this option was unacceptable both for its explicit reliance on racial representation and for its potentially relatively short-term guarantee of ethnic minority representation. In this context, the option of proportional representation became a means to avoid the contentious task of immediate demarcation and a way to guarantee the effective participation of small parties, including those with minority ethnic or racially based constituencies.

B. Proportional Representation and Political Parties

Despite the fear among its detractors that proportional representation would result in a splintered electorate, in which no party would have sufficient support to govern alone, in the first three post-apartheid elections—in 1994, 1999 and 2004—the African National Congress, led first by Nelson Mandela and then by Thabo Mbeki, captured the vast majority of votes. In fact, the ruling party's percentage of votes and hence seats in the national legislature increased from 62.56 per cent in 1994 to 69.69 per cent in 2004. In contrast, the opposition remained highly fractured. The old ruling National Party, which withdrew from the Government of National Unity in 1996 and renamed itself the New National Party in 1997, disbanded on 9 April 2005 after making the decision to merge with the ANC. The Democratic Party thus assumed the mantle of the formal parliamentary-style opposition in 1997, despite having placed fifth and having received a mere 1.73 per cent of the vote in 1994. However, after transforming itself into the Democratic Alliance (DA) and embracing many of the disgruntled former National Party's supporters, the DA received 12.73 per cent of the vote in the 2004 election. The 19 other opposition parties standing for election received a further 17.94 per cent of the vote and were allotted 71 seats in the 400 seat National Assembly, the lower house of Parliament. Despite a period of heightened political tensions and the split in the ANC which led to the emergence of the Congress of the People (COPE) as a new political contestant, the basic pattern remained unchanged in the 2009 national election. ANC support fell a mere 3 percentage points to 65.9 per cent, while the official opposition increased its support to 16.66 per cent of the vote.[10] The failure of COPE to obtain more than 7.42 per cent of the vote came as a surprise to many who had assumed that the split in the ANC might produce an opposition party within the fold of the liberation movement tradition. While the official opposition now holds 67 seats, the functional committees, debates and votes in Parliament are overwhelming dominated by the 264 members of the ruling ANC.

The practical effect of these lopsided numbers is that the effective locus of power in Parliament is located in the ANC Caucus and among the party officials who serve as both parliamentary and party officials,

---

[10] See, R Southall and J Daniel (eds), *Zunami!: The 2009 South African Elections* (Johannesburg, Jacana Media and Konrad Adenauer Stiftung, 2009).

such as the Speaker of Parliament and the ANC Chief Whip. The Speaker of Parliament is a constitutional position,[11] voted into office by the members of the National Assembly. In contrast, the party caucuses elect the political party Whips, who play a significant role in the political life of the institution. While the German Basic Law envisions a particular integrative role for political parties in the system of government, South Africa's 1996 Constitution does not explicitly regulate the role of political parties. Instead, the Constitution, in both its founding provisions and in the Bill of Rights, makes multi-party democracy a basic value of the Constitution and guarantees the rights of individuals to make free political choices, including the right to form political parties, to participate and recruit members and to stand for elected office and vote in elections. The only provision of the Constitution that explicitly addresses political parties per se is the requirement that the national legislature must provide funding for political parties to enhance multi-party democracy. This funding, which is to be available for parties participating in both provincial and national legislatures, must be provided on an 'equitable and proportional basis'.[12] At least for the present, this too, overwhelmingly benefits the ANC, which has until now dominated the electoral results.

C. Floor-crossing, Founding Principles and Democracy

The political dominance of the ANC was further strengthened in the period before the 2004 election by the adoption of floor-crossing in the legislatures in both the national and provincial spheres of government as well as at the municipal level. While the parties had debated the question of changing party affiliations among Members of Parliament in the five years between national elections during the Constitution-making process, the outcome was the inclusion of a specific anti-defection clause in the 1996 Constitution.[13] Critics of proportional representation argued that the effect of the closed-list system was to empower political parties so that party priorities would effectively dominate the behaviour of elected representatives. As a result, elected representatives were not free to represent the potentially changing desires of the electorate but were instead beholden to the hierarchy of the political party. The opposition

[11] 1996 Constitution s 52(1).
[12] 1996 Constitution s 236.
[13] 1996 Constitution s 23A(1), as included in s 13 of Sch 6A.

Democratic Party argued that one way to lessen this problem would be to allow elected representatives to switch political parties if they felt that the party they represented in the legislature no longer served the interests of those they represented. As a result, the Constitution included a specific provision empowering Parliament to amend the anti-defection clause, if it wished, so as to enable Members of Parliament to change parties without losing their membership in the legislature. While at first the ANC was opposed to this idea, it eventually embraced the notion of floor-crossing as it sought to strengthen its majority in Parliament to achieve the two-thirds majority required to amend the Constitution.

The impetus for change came initially from the opposition parties—the New National Party (NNP) and the Democratic Party (DP)—which formed an alliance after the 1999 elections. The parties wanted to preclude the ANC, which had for the first time won a plurality of the votes in the Western Cape provincial election, from taking power in that province. The two parties also formed an alliance to contest the local government elections in 2000. The new Democratic Alliance (DA) made surprising gains in the local government elections and as a result DA officials were elected at the local level. But at the national and provincial levels the two parties continued to remain legally separate while operating as one entity. Despite arguments that the DP and NNP be allowed to formally merge, the ANC remained opposed to changing the anti-defection clause, feeling that the DA represented the 'congealing of a race and class-based, right-wing opposition'.[14] One year later, however, when the alliance between the DP and the NNP soured, the ANC saw the opportunity to capture the Western Cape provincial government and build a super-majority in the National Assembly and threw its support behind the idea of floor-crossing. According to the then ANC National Chairperson, Mosiuoa Lekota, the ANC's change of heart reflected discussions indicating that the adoption of floor-crossing would lead to a political realignment that would break up existing 'racial power blocs'.[15]

As a result, in June 2002 four pieces of legislation were introduced to facilitate the adoption of floor-crossing in all spheres of government. These included two constitutional amendments and two pieces of implementing legislation, which together allowed elected representatives

[14] J Faull, 'Floor-crossing', presentation to Democracy Development Programme Workshop, Royal Hotel Durban, 13 October 2004 (IDASA, 2004) available at www.idasa.org.za.
[15] Ibid.

to cross the floor to another party within the legislature without losing their seats during a particular15-day period in the second year following any election. New parties could be formed and existing parties could merge or subdivide during this period. In addition, the seats of those who switched to new, other or merged parties would be regarded as belonging to those parties, even if it meant that the proportional representation defined in the pervious election would, to a certain degree, be distorted.

The amendments allowing floor-crossing contained two significant limitations that had the effect of favouring the ANC. First, any particular member could only cross the floor once without losing his or her seat. This also applied to parties, which were only allowed to subdivide, merge or both subdivide and merge with other parties once while retaining their status in the legislature. A second, more significant limitation required at least 10 per cent of the membership of a party to cross the floor before a legitimate floor-crossing would be recognised. This meant that before any individual member of the ANC could cross the floor she would have to mobilise at least 29 others to join her; while 10 per cent of any of the other parties was a much smaller number and therefore much easier to achieve. As a result, the ANC was able to poach large numbers from other parties, assisted by its position as the governing party that could offer Cabinet posts and other advantages to a prospective defector from another party. It also ensured that it was very difficult for individual ANC members to cross the floor to the opposition.

Since 2002 there have been four floor-crossing window periods, two at the national and provincial levels and two at the municipal level, resulting in approximately 1,100 public representatives crossing to other parties. Predictably, the ANC lost no national or provincial members and gained the vast majority of cross-overs at the municipal level. In most cases, this has had little effect on governance, since most were at the municipal level. However, in a number of cases, the floor-crossings led to changes in the control of some local municipalities—such as the Cape Town City Council in 2002 and the provincial governments in the Western Cape and KwaZulu-Natal. At the national level, the 2003 floor-crossing window led to an increase in ANC membership and gave the governing party a two-thirds majority in Parliament for the first time. The net effect thus far has been to increase the dominance of the ANC at all levels of government.

Floor-crossing was controversial from the beginning. While the ANC initially opposed the idea, once the required legislation was adopted in June 2002 the United Democratic Movement (UDM), a small regionally based party, challenged the validity of the new legislation before the courts. When the Constitutional Court issued its unanimous, unattributed opinion in October 2002, it provided no opinion on the validity of floor-crossing. Instead, the Court focused on whether the constitutional amendments were adopted by the correct amending procedures and majorities, for if they were, they 'become part of the Constitution ... [and] cannot be challenged on the grounds of inconsistency with other provisions of the Constitution'.[16] The amended Constitution, the Court argued, 'must be read as a whole and its provisions must be interpreted in harmony with one another'.[17]

The Court rejected any suggestion that it would consider the appropriateness of floor-crossing as a policy matter, stating that this is a 'political question of no concern to the Court'. It did agree, however, to address three issues appropriate to the constitutionality of the legislation under attack.[18] First, it examined the claim that the amendments undermined the basic structure of the Constitution. Second, it addressed the notion that they were inconsistent with the Founding Principles of section 1 of the Constitution and therefore could only be amended by a supermajority of 75 per cent of the National Assembly and six of the nine provinces in the NCOP, as required under section 74(1). Third, it considered whether the amendments violated the political rights of citizens protected in the Bill of Rights, amendment of which requires a two-thirds majority and the vote of six provinces. The floor-crossing amendments had been passed by a simple two-thirds of the National Assembly as required for all matters not within the founding provisions, Bill of Rights or that pertaining specifically to the provinces.

In an earlier decision Justice Mahomed, then Deputy President of the Constitutional Court, had suggested that even duly passed constitutional amendments might not qualify as amendments at all if they were to have the effect of 'radically and fundamentally restructuring and reorganizing the fundamental premises of the Constitution'.[19] As in the earlier case, the Constitutional Court refused to address the basic structure question. Instead, it argued that 'proportional representation, and the anti-defection

[16] *United Democratic Front v President of the Republic of South Africa* et. al, CCT 23/02, decided 4 October 2002, [hereinafter *UDM* case] [12].

[17] Ibid.

[18] *UDM* case, above n 16, [11].

[19] *Premier of KwaZulu-Natal and Others v President of the Republic of South Africa and Others* 1996 (1) SA 769 (CC) [47].

provisions that support it' are not so fundamental to the South African constitutional order such that amending these provisions would 'undermine democracy itself, and in effect abrogate or destroy the Constitution'. As the Court noted, the electoral system adopted in South Africa is 'one of many that are consistent with democracy', whether they contain anti-defection clauses and are organised on the basis of proportional representation or not.[20]

The second challenge, which argued that the floor-crossing amendments and statutes violated the Founding Principles of the Constitution, had two separate prongs. It argued that these laws were at odds with the guarantee that South Africa would be a multi-party democracy and that they violated the guarantee of the rule of law.[21] The Constitutional Court addressed these arguments by noting that while there is no single meaning to the idea of a multi-party democracy—beyond the prohibition of the legal imposition of a one-party state—the claim that proportional representation and adherence to an anti-defection rule are essential components of the guarantee of a multi-party system in the Founding Provisions of the Constitution is unsustainable. Specifically, the Court pointed out that the guarantee of proportional representation, which was included in the Constitutional Principle VIII, was not incorporated into the founding values of the 1996 Constitution. Furthermore, while an anti-deflection provision is not a prerequisite for either a multi-party system or even proportional representation, the explicit inclusion of an anti-defection clause in the transitional provisions of the Constitution, with the explicit provision that it might be amended within a reasonable time by a simple act of Parliament to allow for floor-crossing, negates any implication that an anti-defection provision is implicit in the founding values. Finally, the Court repeated its holding from prior cases that the 'Constitution requires legislation to be rationally related to a legitimate government purpose' or else it will be 'inconsistent with the rule of law and invalid'. And the Court rejected the claim that the political motives of the ANC and NNP legislators, who may have voted for these laws in order to gain political advantage, made them illegitimate. The Court explicitly noted that it is the purpose of the legislation—what it seeks to achieve—that must be rational and that the motives of the individual legislators are irrelevant.

---

[20]   *UDM* case, above n 16, [17].
[21]   *UDM* case, above n 16, [20].

The Court did, however, strike down the Loss or Retention of Membership of National and Provincial Legislatures Act, which enabled floor-crossing in the national and provincial legislatures. It did so because the transitional provisions under which the Act was passed as ordinary legislation required that changes to the anti-defection clause be made within a reasonable time. The legislature waited five years after the report of the parliamentary committee that had originally investigated the question to act. The Court ruled that this time period was not reasonable, believing it reflected more a change in political climate than the passage of a reasonable period of time as required by the transitional provisions of the Constitution. In response to the Court's decision, Parliament adopted the Constitution Amendment Act 2 of 2003, which introduced a new schedule 6A to the 1996 Constitution, thus enabling the floor-crossing to proceed. The result, as Glenda Fick has argued, is that the 'will of the electorate expressed at the time of an election—for parties and their policies—morphs into the will of the individual representatives and the parties and policies for whom they express a preference'.[22]

Despite the regular flow of elected officials across the floor at each window of opportunity, and the fact that this flow has clearly benefited the ruling ANC, the practice of floor-crossing has remained controversial. Opposition to floor-crossing was raised once again during the tenth anniversary celebration of the Constitution in 2006. Responding to calls for Parliament to introduce legislation to abolish floor-crossing, President Thabo Mbeki insisted that there was nothing inherently undemocratic about floor-crossing, as the Constitutional Court had found. However, he indicated that the government was open to revisiting the issue. He argued that the political parties in Parliament (rather than the government) should take up the issue. As a result of this initiative, new constitutional amendments were introduced to abolish floor-crossing in 2008 and signed into law by President Kgalema Motlanthe on 9 January 2009, thus ending the era of floor-crossing.[23] These amendments abolishing floor-crossing demonstrate that South Africa's democracy remains a work-in-progress but also show that it has not stagnated, despite the overwhelming dominance of a single party.

[22] G Fick, 'Elections' in Stuart Wooman et al, *Constitutional Law of South Africa*, 2nd edn (Kenwyn, Juta, 2004) 21.

[23] See Constitution Fourteenth Amendment Act of 2008 and Constitution Fifteenth Amendment Act of 2008, signed into law on 9 January 2009, Government Gazette nos. 31791 and 31792.

D. Dissolving Parliament and Calling New Elections

The National Assembly is elected for a set term of five years and the President must set the date for an election within 90 days of the expiry of the legislature's mandate.[24] To ensure political and legal continuity, the National Assembly remains competent to exercise its powers 'until the day before the first day of polling for the next Assembly'.[25] In the event that the Electoral Commission fails to deliver the results of an election within the required period or if a court sets aside an election, the President must once again call a new election within 90 days of these events.[26] Significantly, Parliament may be dissolved before the end of its term under very specific conditions. In the first instance, the President must dissolve the National Assembly if a simple majority of the members of that body adopt a resolution to dissolve.[27] However, this cannot be done within the first three years of its term.[28] This provision provides an element of stability in the event that the legislature becomes closely divided and the governing coalition is unable to maintain a simple majority within the legislature. This is a fairly unique and innovative response to the concern that proportional representation may create political instability through the promotion of political factions. It also opens the possibility of a situation in which the National Assembly is composed of so many factions that no political party or coalition is able to muster a numerical majority. Yet it must be understood that this possibility is confined to the legislative branch. If the legislature fails to elect a President or if there is a vacancy in the presidency and the National Assembly fails to elect a new President within 30 days of the vacancy, the three-year limitation on dissolution does not apply. In order to ensure effective governance, failure to reach agreement on the election of a President requires the Acting President to dissolve the National Assembly and call a national election so the people may decide the fate of the country.[29]

---

[24] 1996 Constitution s 49(1) and (2).
[25] 1996 Constitution s 49(4).
[26] 1996 Constitution s 49(3).
[27] 1996 Constitution s 50(1)(a).
[28] 1996 Constitution s 50(1)(b).
[29] 1996 Constitution s 50(2)(a) and (b).

III. PARLIAMENT AS LAW-GIVER

Parliament has historically been the main location of inter-election political contestation between the governing and opposition parties in the Westminster model. However, the increasing complexity of public policy issues and the decline of parliamentary debate on the one hand, and the rising importance of the media and civil society as checks on government conduct, on the other hand, means that Parliament is becoming increasingly focused on the production of law. The speed of technological change and global interdependence means that legislatures around the globe are called upon to constantly update the statutory framework as well as enter into whole new realms of political, legal and ethical questions that seem to arise and transform the social and political landscape at an increasing pace. In its first two electoral terms, from 1994–99 and 1999–2004, Parliament passed just over 800 Bills, the vast majority of which were promulgated into law. While many of these were aimed at removing the legacy of discriminatory laws that dominated South Africa's pre-democratic statute book, others began to build a 'framework for democratic rights and improved delivery of services'.[30]

Although national legislatures in many countries have been swept up in processes of legal change driven by global imperatives, there is also a growing devolution of authority within nation states as it becomes increasingly clear that national institutions are often too distant, geographically and politically, from the regional and local government spheres to adequately comprehend and address local problems. Within this context, the debate over legislative authority in South Africa has moved towards the notion of subsidiarity, which allows the ANC to avoid demands from other parties for the creation of a federal system, in which sovereign authority would be formally divided between national and regional governments. It has simultaneously recognised that issues are often best dealt with at the level of government that, in the particular context, is the most appropriate location for a decision to be made.

---

[30] G Fick, 'Is There Free and Fair Selection of Decision-makers?' in R Calland and P Graham (eds), *Democracy in the Time of Mbeki* (Cape Town, IDASA, 2005) 170.

A. Legislative Authority and Process

The Constitution explicitly distributes legislative authority to all three spheres of government: the national, regional and local. At the same time it ensures that the ultimate law-giving authority is vested in Parliament, which is empowered to override even the exclusive legislative competence of a province if it is necessary to maintain national security, economic unity, essential national standards, minimum standards of service delivery or 'to prevent unreasonable action taken by a province which is prejudicial to the interests of another province or to the country as a whole'.[31] It is important to understand, however, that the NCOP, which directly represents provincial governments in the national legislature, is a full participant in the legislative process and therefore plays a central role in the exercise of this override function. Ultimately however, the NCOP cannot prevent the National Assembly from passing legislation affecting the provinces if the legislation is supported by a two-thirds vote in the Assembly. However, such a vote may only take place after a complex procedure in which the legislation is voted on by both houses,[32] submitted to a mediation committee[33] and then if no agreement is reached, either lapses, or is passed by a two-thirds majority in the National Assembly.[34] All other legislation, not directly affecting the provinces as defined in the Constitution, is the preserve of the National Assembly, although the NCOP does have a deliberative role and formally votes on these issues. Voting procedures in the NCOP depend on the subject matter before the Council. In the case of matters affecting the provinces and in the case of constitutional amendments, each provincial delegation has a single vote. In matters of general interest, in which the NCOP has a primarily deliberative role, the members of the Council cast individual votes.

National legislative action is divided into three categories with related procedural rules: amendments to the Constitution; ordinary bills, including those addressing areas of concurrent provincial and national jurisdiction; and finally, money bills and legislation providing for the 'equitable division of revenue ... among the national, provincial and local spheres of government'[35] which may only be introduced by the Finance

[31] 1996 Constitution s 44(2)(a)–(e).
[32] 1996 Constitution s 76(1).
[33] 1996 Constitution s 76(1)(d)–(h).
[34] 1996 Constitution s 76(1)(e), (i) and (j).
[35] 1996 Constitution ss 73(2) and 214(1)(a).

Minister. All members and committees of Parliament may introduce legislation, yet in practice, new legislation tends to be introduced by the specific departments of government responsible for the particular subject matter or for implementing the policies or programmes the legislation is designed to address. This practice tends, as in many other countries, to shape the law-making agenda of the legislature. While this is not unusual in parliamentary systems the explicit ring-fencing of money bills, which makes them the sole prerogative of the Ministry of Finance, means that the legislature has limited power over the national purse. In effect, Parliament is simply called upon to vote on the budget as a single package and is unable to exercise its authority over particular spending decisions, unless it is prepared to vote down the budget in toto. Although it was justified as necessary to maintain financial discipline and also on the grounds that the budget process is just too complicated for most parliamentarians to fully grasp, this provision came to symbolise the weakness of Parliament in the constitutional scheme.

Frustration among parliamentarians, who have increasingly felt that their inability to seriously challenge the distribution of resources effectively limits their capacity to shape government action, gave impetus to demands that Parliament be given a larger role in defining government expenditures. Moreover, the Constitution, as amended in 2001, provides that procedures for Parliament to amend money Bills must be provided for by legislation. This legislation was finally put forward as a bill in July 2008 as part of a wholesale revival of Parliament's authority and autonomy from the executive branch. This political shift was one of the products of the division within the ANC between the Mbeki and Zuma camps. After the December 2007 party conference at Polokwane, in which Jacob Zuma defeated President Mbeki in the election for ANC President, power seemed to split between the executive branch, which remained in Mbeki's hands, and Luthuli House (the ANC headquarters in Johannesburg) and Parliament, where the majority of MPs seemed to support Zuma and the ANC policy shifts that were adopted in Polokwane. One of the most significant legislative consequences of this split was the Money Bills Amendment Procedure and Related Matters Act of 2008, which was finally signed into law by Mbeki's successor, President Kgalema Motlanthe, on 16 April 2009.

The new law requires Parliament to establish separate committees on finance and appropriations in both the National Assembly and in the NCOP, and sets out an elaborate process for the passage of the national budget and related laws.[36] To support this process the law also creates a Parliamentary Budget Office to provide research assistance to the committees as well as 'advice and analysis on proposed amendments to the fiscal framework, the Division of Revenues Bill and money Bills and policy proposals with budgetary implications'.[37] While this is an important step forward in the empowerment of the legislature, the statute is designed to ensure that the appropriations process remains constrained within a clear budgetary framework. To this end, Parliament is required to first approve a general fiscal framework, which ensures that all subsequent spending proposals remain within the broader economic strategy of the government. Only once there is agreement on the fiscal framework may Parliament tackle both the Division of Revenue Bill, which provides for the distribution of finances between the different spheres of government—national, provincial and local governments—and the Appropriations Bill. Amendments to the Appropriations Bill may only be made after the Division of Revenue Bill has been agreed upon. Finally, the Revenue Bills must be considered and must be consistent with the approved fiscal framework and Division of Revenue bills. While the strict procedural process and the complexity of government finances will constrain Members of Parliament, the availability of procedures to approve the overall fiscal framework and to amend and adopt the different aspects of the government's budget holds the promise of fundamentally altering the relationship between the legislature and the executive. At the same time, however, the ANC's continuing domination of Parliament by the ANC, through its overwhelming electoral support, means that the real power in Parliament continues to reside in the ruling party's parliamentary caucus.

B. Constitutional Amendments

Apart from some specific procedural guarantees—such as notice periods and the requirement that an amending Bill may not contain other subject matter—most provisions of the Constitution may be simply amended by a Bill passed by a two-thirds vote in the National Assembly. In fact the Constitution was amended more than 11 times in its first decade of existence. This general amending procedure does not, however, cover amendments to a number of specific clauses guaranteeing the nature and

[36] Money Bills Amendment Procedure and Related Matters Act 9 of 2009.
[37] Ibid s 15(2)(b).

structure of the state, including the founding provisions in section 1, the Bill of Rights in Chapter 2 or any provisions affecting the provinces either singularly or generally, all of which require higher majorities in the National Assembly and the NCOP. Even if these majorities are achieved, the President may—as with all other legislation—refuse to give his or her assent to the Amendment Bill. In such a case, the President may either send the bill back to Parliament for reconsideration or refer it to the 'Constitutional Court for a decision on its constitutionality'.[38] Furthermore, a third of the members of the National Assembly may, within 30 days of the President's assent, ask the Constitutional Court to review the constitutionality of an Act of Parliament. These latter provisions, which allow for abstract review, raise the possibility that the Constitutional Court's role in deciding on the appropriateness of a proposed constitutional text may not have been exhausted by the Court's extraordinary role in certifying that the final constitution met the requirements of the Constitutional Principles contained in Schedule 4 of the 1993 interim Constitution.

The founding provisions of the Constitution receive the highest degree of protection. Any bill to amend either the subsection of the amending provisions guaranteeing the founding provisions of Section 1 or Section 1 itself requires a 75 per cent vote in the National Assembly and the support of at least six of the nine provinces. Section 1 of the Constitution defines the Republic of South Africa as 'one, sovereign, democratic state' founded on certain basic values:

> (a) human dignity, the achievement of equality and the advancement of human rights and freedoms; (b) Non-racialism and non-sexism; (c) Supremacy of the Constitution and the rule of law; [and] (d) Universal adult suffrage, a national common voters roll, regular elections and a multi-party system of democratic government, to ensure accountability, responsiveness and openness.

The Bill of Rights is also entrenched, with any amendment requiring at least a two-thirds vote in the National Assembly as well as the support of six of the nine provinces in the NCOP. South Africa's 'federal' structure is also given greater constitutional protection. Any amendments affecting the NCOP, altering 'provincial boundaries, powers, functions or institutions' or that deal 'specifically with a provincial matter' require the support of six of the nine provinces. In the event that the amendment Bill 'concerns only a specific province or provinces', the NCOP may not pass

[38]   1996 Constitution s 74(4)(b).

the amendment unless it has been approved by the relevant provincial
legislature or legislatures.[39]

C. Parliamentary Practice

As in legislatures elsewhere, the essential work of Parliament is conducted
in the approximately 65 parliamentary committees that exist in both
the National Assembly and the NCOP. In the National Assembly there
are approximately 30 portfolio committees that track the functional
departments of the national government in addition to the specific coordination, oversight and joint committees required by the Constitution.[40]
The NCOP is a break from the Westminster tradition because it is not a
second, higher, house but rather a version of the German *Bundesrat* that
represents the provinces in the national legislative process. However, the
fact that six of the nine provinces had ANC governments from 1994
and all the provinces were governed by the ANC between 1999 and
2009 means that the NCOP has never served as a counterbalance to the
dominant National Assembly.

When South Africa's Parliament first convened on 24 May 1994, its
Members inherited a tradition that was lacking in democratic pedigree
and steeped in particular institutional habits that many of the old guard,
representing the old regime and the former white opposition, assumed
would continue. The first change came with the reinvigoration of the
committee system.[41] Creating new committees and opening them up for
the first time to the public and press was relatively simple; the lack of
resources for research and other staff assistance would take longer to
overcome. A single clerk served the 13 parliamentary committees inherited from the old Parliament. As the parliamentary rules were rewritten to
simultaneously expand the number of committees and to empower them,
the lack of parliamentary experience among the newly elected MPs—as
well as the lack of researchers and other staff—meant that the effectiveness of any committee often depended on the personal experience,
energy and ambition of the committee chairpersons. Some committees,
such as the Justice Committee, which counted a number of lawyers

[39]   1996 Constitution s 74(8).

[40]   See 1996 Constitution ss 45(1), 55(2), 92(2) and 199(8).

[41]   See R Calland (ed), *The First Five Years: A Review of South Africa's Democratic Parliament*
(Cape Town, IDASA, 1999) 29–42.

among its members and had a close relationship with the new Minister of Justice, became deeply involved in the redrafting of legislation, such as the law establishing the Truth and Reconciliation Commission in 1995 and the Human Rights Commission. Others had far less capacity and would either just adopt what the executive presented or rely on bureaucrats testifying before the committee for guidance on what could or could not be amended.

In the 15 years since its inauguration, the National Assembly has continued a high rate of statutory production but at the same time has faced increased criticism for its seeming failure to effectively exercise oversight of the executive. Critics argue that Parliament became increasingly ineffective and deferential as many of the senior ANC leaders who had participated in the Constitution-making process until 1996 were redeployed by the ANC into the executive or the government bureaucracy or they simply left to join the private sector.[42] Others argue that in comparative perspective, Parliament has functioned relatively well. The National Assembly, they argue, reflects the demographics of the country, for the first time; it has amended between 75 and 80 per cent of the legislation presented to it by the executive since 1994; and it has established a system of committees, a third to a half of which are functioning well. And while it remains a work-in-progress and has not fully established its status as an independent branch of government with the capacity to check the executive, it is nevertheless not a rubber stamp and compares favourably with its sister institutions across Africa and around the globe.[43]

IV. PARLIAMENT AS WATCHDOG

The greatest source of controversy over Parliament's role is its weak performance in serving as watchdog over the policies and practices of the executive. While Parliament has always been the primary source of formal law-making in South Africa, it has historically never managed to serve very effectively as a watchdog. This may, of course, be attributed in part to the parliamentary tradition in which government-appointed Commissions of Enquiry have always served to investigate and address questions of

---

[42] See R Calland, *Anatomy of South Africa: Who Holds the Power?* (Cape Town, Zebra Press, 2006) 94–102.

[43] JD Barkan, 'The South African National Assembly in Comparative Perspective' (2007) 47 *Focus* 8–11

government failure and malfeasance. At Westminster, the parliamentary custom of ministerial responsibility—and quick, quiet resignation at the slightest hint of impropriety—has historically narrowed the institutional space for robust investigation or confrontation of a ruling party and its conduct in government. Instead, a government may fall or call an early election, but even in London there is an increasing tendency for the executive to brave its way through by actively attempting to 'spin' public opinion while abandoning the custom of taking formal responsibility and accepting the resignation of those identified as culprits.[44] Instead, governments are increasingly leaving the process of managing political and public service malfeasance to the courts through various processes of judicial review—either administrative law or, where appropriate, constitutional review.

Even if parliamentary systems have never served as effective watchdogs, given the dominance of the ruling party and members of government within the institution, this does not mean that parliamentarians do not at times take up this role with some forcefulness. South Africa's pre-1994 apartheid Parliament did not, however, have such a tradition. Instead, the colonial and apartheid regimes that governed until 1994 maintained an 'entire social edifice . . . structured to enrich a powerful few at the expense of the majority'.[45] In the period between 1948 and 1994 Parliament served as a rubber stamp for the decisions of the National Party and executive. There were many pressure groups,

> such as the wine farmers . . . who used their close proximity to Parliament to 'take people to parties' and provide them with a quota of wine annually—this continued in the immediate post-1994 period, when MPs had access to cost-price wines . . . These were all subtle forms of influence-buying that could be compared with contemporary private sector-subsidized golf days for politicians and public sector officials.[46]

Furthermore, the increasing secrecy of the apartheid regime and the expansion of covert operations after 1976—as well as the 'history of

[44] See P Leyland, *The Constitution of the United Kingdom: A Contentual Analysis* (Oxford, Hart Publishing, 2007) 128–32.

[45] D O'Meara, *Forty Lost Years: The Apartheid State and the Politics of the National Party, 1948–1994* (Randburg, South Africa, Ravan Press; Athens, Ohio University Press, 1996) 231.

[46] HV Vuuren, *Apartheid Grand Corruption: Assessing the Scale of Crime of Profit in South Africa from 1976–1994*, A Report prepared by Civil Society at the Request of the Second Annual Anti-Corruption Summit, May 2006' (Cape Town, Institute for Security Studies, 2006).

routinised corruption'[47] in central government departments and the 'homeland' administrations—provide ample evidence for the following claim by Speaker of Parliament Frene Ginwala:

> [I]n South Africa we inherited an intrinsically corrupt system of governance . . . To survive, it created a legal framework that was based on and facilitated corruption. It has taken years in Parliament to repeal old laws and introduce even the basic legal framework that would enable us to deal with corrupt bureaucrats, politicians and police. The private sector also operated in a closed society and profited by it. There were partnerships with international criminals and the corruption that was built into the system is very difficult to overcome.[48]

In contrast to this history, South Africa's first truly democratic legislature seemed in its early years to be committed to diligently exercising its duty to act as a public watchdog. The relative strength of the legislature during these early years may be attributed to two factors. First, the initial post-apartheid Parliament, established under the interim Constitution, served simultaneously as the national legislature and as the Constitutional Assembly responsible for writing South Africa's final Constitution. Given this historic Constitution-making responsibility, it is no surprise that many of the most prominent politicians and anti-apartheid activists, from across three generations, were nominated and elected to serve in this first Parliament. Second, these individuals were held in high esteem and wielded enormous political authority within the ANC, which meant that there was a de facto as well as formal distribution of power between the legislature and the executive. This balance was also enabled by Nelson Mandela's explicit plea that even he, as President, be held accountable by the collective leadership of the ANC.

The confidence of these parliamentarians was evident in the early practice of the parliamentary committees, which would ask probing questions of high-ranking civil servants and Ministers and, at times, take them to task. At the same time, however, the committees lacked the resources to adequately research and investigate issues. This problem was exacerbated by the historic physical separation of government: the executive and administrative departments were located in Pretoria, while the legislature

---

[47] T Lodge, *South African Politics Sine 1994* (Cape Town, David Philip, 1999) 60.

[48] F Ginwala, 'Speaker of Parliament, Remarks to the Opening Session, Global Forum II, The Hague' (28 May 2001), cited in HV Vuuren, *Apartheid Grand Corruption*, above n 46, 5–6 and fn 13.

was situated more than one thousand miles away in Cape Town. In a short time, however, the tendency of the executive to recruit many of the most effective politicians into the Cabinet and the tendency of Committee Chairs to use their positions to promote their political careers meant that those members who were within the government increasingly dominated Parliament. The ruling party became correspondingly more centralised and concerned with protecting the image of the government rather than raising questions about the implementation of policy or the integrity of government programmes and officials.

A. *Sarafina* II

Parliament's first major oversight challenge arose when it was revealed in the press that the Department of Health was spending R14.2 million on a musical that was to tour the country providing education on the growing HIV/AIDS pandemic. Commissioned from world-class South African playwright Mbongeni Ngema in 1995, the budget for the show represented a significant portion of the health department's HIV/AIDS prevention efforts. The musical itself, *Sarafina II*, was criticised for failing to impart a clear public health message. But the scandal focused on the high costs of production—including the salaries, luxurious facilities and what was seen as the inappropriate grandeur of the production itself. When the Portfolio Committee first asked the Minister of Health, Dr Nkosazama Zuma, to justify this expenditure, she purportedly refused to attend the hearing. Zuma's appearance before the committee, after government realised that her refusal to attend would be politically embarrassing, merely demonstrated how new the concept of oversight was for the legislature. First, the MPs relied mainly on press reports to challenge the Minister, instead of demanding access to the official documentation, which was their right. Second, the ANC members remained extraordinarily passive, caught between the exercise of their parliamentary duty and loyalty to the government. As one ANC member later admitted,

> It was still early days. We did not know how to deal with something like this. Perhaps we should be condemned for it, perhaps we should be forgiven, but we were more concerned with damage control than we were with parliamentary accountability.[49]

[49]   Calland, *The First Five Years*, above n 41, 36.

The Committee's failure was further highlighted when the Public Protector issued a report in June 1996 that documented the mismanagement of tender procedures and the 'unauthorized expenditure of foreign aid' in this project.[50]

In contrast to the *Sarafina II* affair, there were numerous cases in which parliamentary committees began to show their potential, in both their legislative and oversight functions. A dramatic example of legislative intervention was the fight over the introduction of a State Maintenance Grant for children between the ages of 0–6 years. Minister of Welfare Geraldine Fraser-Moleketi had gone directly to Cabinet with a proposal to adopt a flat-rate per-child grant of R75 per month. This proposal was the culmination of a process initiated by an intergovernmental coordinating group or MINMEC, ad-hoc bodies established in 1995 to bring together the provincial and national officials who shared responsibility for particular areas of governance. In this case, the Minister of Health initiated a MINMEC that brought together the health and social welfare departments at national and provincial levels. This body then appointed a Committee (later named for its chairperson, Francie Lund, as the Lund Committee) to produce a critical appraisal of the existing system of state support and to report on possible policy options aimed at providing effective support to families and children. Reacting to the Minister's announcement and the outrage of civil society groups who felt that 'an important and far-reaching policy [was] being implemented without consultation', the Portfolio Committee called public hearings in April 1997. The Minister attended the hearings, but publicly insisted that '[t]here is no turning back', noting that the 'department had already printed leaflets setting out details of the new benefit before the hearings took place'.[51] These actions demonstrated a form of executive decision-making that stood at odds with the new Constitution. Persuaded by civil society submissions, which pointed out that the Lund Committee itself had suggested R125 per child, per month, the ANC-chaired Portfolio Committee opposed the government's announced policy and unanimously proposed that the benefit be set at R135 per month. This was the first time a parliamentary committee, with support from civil society and the ANC caucus 'took on an ANC Minister and successfully challenged and changed government policy'.[52]

[50] Calland, *The First Five Years*, above n 41, 35.
[51] Calland, *The First Five Years*, above n 41, 38.
[52] Calland, *The First Five Years*, above n 41, 39.

B. Travelgate and the Arms Deal

Parliament's ability to act as an effective watchdog was further undermined by its own dalliance in addressing a pattern of systematic abuse by Members of Parliament (MPs) from across the political spectrum. The first inklings of what would come to be known as 'Travelgate' surfaced in the year 2000 when Speaker of the House Frene Ginwala publicly rebuked two Members of Parliament for abusing travel vouchers, granted annually in a checkbook type format, so that MPs could travel between Parliament in Cape Town and their constituencies or homes around the country. When the issue was later raised in the ANC caucus, Essop Pahad, a close associate of President Mbeki, attacked the Speaker, objecting to the public reprimand on the grounds that the ANC MP involved had used the travel vouchers for ANC Party business that the ANC leadership considered legitimate.[53] But this was only the tip of the iceberg, and by the time the scandal unravelled in 2007, it embroiled more than 100 MPs who were forced to resign, plead guilty and enter into plea-bargains to repay millions of Rands to Parliament for fraudulent claims; or were brought to trial and convicted as a result of their misuse or even the sale of their parliamentary travel allocations for private benefit. Even more damaging has been the fact that 'senior ANC leaders and Cabinet members involved have, in most instances, quietly paid back the money that was defrauded from Parliament'.[54] As a result the integrity of the institution was severely compromised.

However, the most egregious and consequential failure of oversight occurred at the dawn of the new century when Parliament's attempt to assert its oversight of a major arms-procurement process led to repeated interventions by the executive, and the ANC's highest officials in the legislature, which effectively undermined the ability of the legislature to perform its constitutional role. The 'arms deal', as it has been christened, involved a simple—if extremely expensive—government procurement process. But it was also a complex policy of military modernisation and hoped-for economic investment for the country, coupled with possible kickback funding for the ruling party and a plethora of secondary contracts providing multiple opportunities for simple old fashioned graft.

---

[53] See A Feinstein, *After the Party: A Personal and Political Journey inside the ANC*, (Cape Town, Jonathan Ball, 2007) 241–42.

[54] Feinstein, *After the Party* 242.

Deputy President Thabo Mbeki chaired the Cabinet sub-committee from 1996 to 1999, and headed the official procurement process that oversaw and 'commissioned the purchase of R30 billion worth of armaments—specifically, submarines and frigates—from a French-German consortium and fighter-jets from a British-Swedish one'.[55] The government justified such vast expenditures on armaments by arguing that they provided an opportunity for industrial investment and job creation, since the bidders promised that the deal would lead to investments in the South African economy worth approximately R104 billion and would create around 65,000 jobs. In the end, the arms deal cost twice the amount originally agreed upon, produced only 13,000 jobs by 1996, and became what Mark Gevisser has described as the 'poisoned well of post-apartheid South African politics'.[56] It led to the demise of some institutions, massive legal battles and the eventual ousting of Thabo Mbeki from the presidency.

The controversy that would become the arms-deal scandal had its roots in the early years of the democratic transition. Gevisser even suggests that the decision to modernise the military might have been based as much on concerns over a 'disaffected military' and the threat of internal destabilisation it posed, as it was based on concern about external threats to national security. The scandal first hit the headlines when Member of Parliament Patricia de Lille (then of the opposition Pan Africanist Congress) stood up in the National Assembly and announced that she had in her possession a 10-page briefing authored by 'concerned' ANC MPs accusing senior ANC politicians of corruption and questioning whether the promised 'off-sets' would ever become a reality.[57] In fact, the Auditor General had already raised questions about the arms deal in November 1998. And while Defence Minister Mosiuoa Lekota derided Lille's claims in public, privately he gave approval for the Auditor General to have access to all relevant documentation for audit purposes. However, within days, the Cabinet sub-committee countermanded the defence Minister's decision, claiming that the Auditor General first had to clear his terms of reference with the Committee. When the Auditor General released the first official report on the arms deal on 15 August 2000, questioning the 'off-sets' and arguing that the 'practice of choosing

---

[55] M Gevisser, *A Legacy of Liberation* (New York, Palgrave MacMillan, 2009) 256.
[56] Ibid.
[57] See P Holden, *The Arms Deal In Your Pocket* (Jeppestown, South Africa, Jonathan Ball, 2008) 38.

the Hawk [aircraft] did not meet standard regulations on acquisitions',[58] the issue was formally placed in the hands of the National Assembly's Standing Committee on Public Accounts (SCOPA).

While there is no constitutional duty to do so, the ANC's initial commitment to open government and accountability led to the practice of giving the chair of SCOPA to an opposition member of the National Assembly. When the Auditor General's report came before SCOPA in late 2000, the chair, Gavin Woods of the Inkatha Freedom Party— together with the leading ANC member of the Committee, Andrew Feinstein and the remaining members—agreed that further investigation was necessary. When Feinstein reported this decision to senior ANC leaders in the legislature he met with a mixed reaction. Jacob Zuma, then Deputy President and the leader of Government's Business in Parliament was at first supportive and insisted to Feinstein that the Committee continue with its constitutional role, while the ANC's Chief Whip in Parliament Tony Yengeni argued that a public hearing was not a good idea and that the matter be considered an internal matter.[59] The government turned defensive when SCOPA insisted on continuing its investigation and recommended that Judge William Heath, who then headed the Special Investigating Unit (an independent statutory body reporting directly to Parliament and empowered to investigate maladministration and corruption in government at the President's request)[60] be brought in to investigate the arms deal. In a series of moves, the ruling party and government attacked the recommendation, contained in SCOPA's Fourteenth Report to Parliament, and once President Mbeki rejected Judge Heath's application to investigate the arms deal, the ANC leadership in Parliament moved against SCOPA. First, Feinstein was removed from his role as head of the ANC Study Group in SCOPA; then the Committee was stacked with loyalists who would be sure to follow instructions. As ANC Chief Whip Tony Yengeni told a press conference, 'there was no committee in respect of the ANC which is above party political discipline'.[61]

Despite this initial victory, it was only a matter of months before the revelations of corruption related to the arms deal would bring down

[58] Holden, *The Arms Deal In Your Pocket*, above n 57, 40.

[59] Feinstein, *After the* Party, above n 53, 160–61.

[60] See, Special Investigating Units and Special Tribunals Act 74 of 1996.

[61] See Feinstein, *After the Party*, above n 53, 195, quoting *Business Day* (7 February 2001).

some of the very leaders who had acted against SCOPA. The first casualty was Tony Yengeni, who would after long denials eventually plead guilty to fraud and was sentenced to four years in prison for defrauding Parliament by failing to disclose a 47 per cent discount he received from Daimler Benz on a luxury 4×4 Mercedes Benz.[62] President Thabo Mbeki dismissed Jacob Zuma from his position as Deputy President following the conviction of his financial advisor Shabir Shaik for corruption arising out of one of the arms deal's secondary contracts. However, Zuma refused to serve as the fall guy. In his legal and political fight to avoid accusations of corruption, he was eventually elected President of the ANC and had a judge state that the executive had illegally interfered in his prosecution. As a result, President Thabo Mbeki was forced to resign from office[63] and the National Prosecuting Authority dropped all charges against Jacob Zuma[64] before he was elected President of South Africa in April 2009. While the arms-deal scandal would prove much more resilient than the Standing Committee on Public Accounts and its oversight function, the removal of Thabo Mbeki as President of the ANC at Polokwane in December 2007 represented a brief revival of legislative authority and a renewed willingness to challenge the executive. Whether the oversight function of the National Assembly will be fully restored any time soon remains a matter of continuing political contestation. However, the entrance into the National Assembly of the Congress of the People (COPE)—a new opposition party that broke away from the ANC and received eight per cent of the votes in its first electoral contest in 2009— has raised some hopes that this function will be revived.

V. CONCLUSION: DEMOCRATIC PARTICIPATION AND THE CHALLENGE OF POST-APARTHEID DEMOCRACY

While the legislature clearly serves as the embodiment of South Africa's representative democracy, the single-party dominance of the ANC within the legislature and the Constitution's guarantee of a 'multi-party system of democratic government, to ensure accountability, responsiveness and

[62] See Holden, *The Arms Deal In Your Pocket*, above n 57, 68–86.

[63] While the Judge's decision and statements, which led to Mbeki's resignation, would be later reversed and severely criticised by the Supreme Court of Appeals, the political momentum had clearly shifted against Thabo Mbeki and his allies in the ANC.

[64] See Gevisser, *A Legacy of Liberation*, above n 55, 320–39.

openness' have stimulated debate over the exact nature and depth of the country's hard-fought constitutional democracy. Concerns over ANC party dominance of Parliament and executive or party authority over public affairs reached a fever pitch in 2007, when the ANC divided into competing factions. On one side was President Mbeki, and on the other a range of opponents, including Jacob Zuma and others who may not have agreed with Zuma but felt excluded by Mbeki and his supporters. Despite the highly charged politics that led up to Mbeki's defeat at Polokwane—and his subsequent resignation on 24 September 2008—the ousting of President Mbeki and the election of his replacement by Parliament remained within the parameters of the constitutional order. This situation presents a distinct contrast to the many extra-legal outcomes of political conflict that have bedevilled many newly independent and developing countries in the post-colonial era. In this context of formal adherence to representative democracy, questions over the role of proportional representation, floor-crossing and democratic participation are being raised.

Although the recent Constitutional Amendments have returned the system of representative democracy in Parliament to the era before floor-crossing—ensuring a truer reflection of the system of proportional representation inherent to the electoral system—the question of participatory democracy has played out in some unexpected ways. On the one hand, there has been an attempt to institutionalise participatory democracy at the local level through the statutory requirement that local governments establish ward committees through which local residents should participate in the formulation of local development plans. On the other hand, different social movements and political groups have challenged the government for failing to ensure public participation in the legislative process. The most dramatic of these challenges came when an anti-abortion group went to court to oppose a number of health laws that they claimed had gone through Parliament without opportunity for public engagement.[65] Less dramatic but more consequential was the Constitutional Court's decision to raise questions about the validity of a Constitutional Amendment that effectively redrew the boundaries of a province against the wishes of the residents of the Matatiele Municipality, who found themselves removed from one province and placed in another against their wishes.[66] While the

---

[65] See, *Doctors for Life International v Speaker of the National Assembly and Others* 2006 (12) BCLR 1399 (CC) [hereinafter *Doctors for Life*].

[66] See, *Matatiele Municipality and Others v President of the Republic of South Africa and Others* 2006 (5) SA 47 (CC) [hereinafter *Matatiele Municipality*].

Court agreed that Parliament had the authority to redraw provincial boundaries and thus relocate municipalities, it refused to accept that mere formal adherence to the process of Constitutional Amendment—even if accepted by the parties to the litigation—would dispose of the question of whether the Amendment was in fact constitutional.

The Constitutional Court issued two important decisions one day apart in mid-August 2006, both of which addressed questions of public participation and participatory democracy. First, the Court declared both the Choice on Termination of Pregnancy Amendment and the Traditional Health Practitioners Acts of 2004 invalid on the grounds that the manner in which they were adopted was inconsistent with the Constitution. Second, the Court invalidated the Twelfth Amendment to the Constitution to the extent that it changed the borders of the province of KwaZulu-Natal on the grounds that the provincial legislature had failed to hold public hearings as required by its role in the National Council of Provinces and the national legislative process through which the Constitutional Amendment had been adopted. In both cases, the Constitutional Court emphasised that the history of South Africa and the struggle against apartheid in particular, as well as the founding principles of the Constitution, require a generous reading of the requirements that the National Assembly and the NCOP 'facilitate public involvement in the legislature'.[67] While the Court emphasised in the *Matatiele* case that 'the democratic government that is contemplated' in the Constitution is 'partly representative and partly participatory, accountable, transparent and makes provision for public participation in the making of laws by legislative bodies',[68] it acknowledged that legislative bodies have wide discretion in choosing particular means of participation. Even as the Court held that in these two cases the legislature had failed to provide reasonable means for participation—having in both cases failed to hold public hearings—the Court nevertheless suspended its orders of invalidity for 18 months to allow the legislature to provide the requisite democratic participation that would validate the legislation.[69]

The significance of these judgements for the future of South Africa's fledgling democracy cannot be overstated. While the electoral dominance of the ANC has meant that there has been little concern that electoral fraud or extra-constitutional action is likely to threaten the formal

---

[67] See 1996 Constitution ss 59(1)(a) and 72(1)(a) and *Doctors for Life* [207].

[68] *Matatiele Municipality*, above n 56, [65].

[69] *Doctors for Life*, above n 55, [225(c)] and *Matatiele Municipality*, above n 56, [99].

process of representative democracy any time soon, there have been serious concerns that this same dominance at the polls has led to a practical exclusion of minority and opposition voices. This became evident in the long failure of ANC public representatives to challenge the government's bizarre stance on HIV/AIDS as well as the government's increasingly dismissive attitude to public criticism. Although Doctors for Life might have been a classic minority group (anti-abortion activists), the Matatiele Municipality represented a clear case of democratic malfunction. In that case, the government ignored the wishes of a local community, manifested in demonstrations and other public expressions of discontent, while distant politicians cut deals and made decisions that were detrimental to their constituents' interests. Justice Sandile Ngcobo's insistence for the Court that the people must have a voice in the democratic process and be allowed to be heard, as well as his deference to the legislature in allowing them time to reconsider and rectify the infirmities of these laws, is a clear manifestation of the form of constitutional democracy Justice Ngcobo intends to continue to fight for as the newly appointed Chief Justice of South Africa.

The split in the ANC that saw the emergence of COPE as a political party in the 2009 election led many commentators to hope that a more serious political opposition would emerge to challenge the ANC's dominance. Unlike the many existing opposition parties, whose former roles during the years of apartheid hang like albatrosses around their political necks, COPE is predominantly made up of former ANC members who either supported Thabo Mbeki against Jacob Zuma and left the ANC when Zuma won, or who had become disaffected with the ANC more generally. Despite initial excitement that the ANC might face a serious political challenge, COPE's 8 per cent showing and its own continuing leadership conflicts have raised questions about its future prospects. Nevertheless, there is a chance that the threat of COPE, as well as the presence of legitimate opposition figures with significant black support, might reinvigorate the legislature more generally. Even as President Zuma asserts control over the ANC, the Parliamentary Caucus has continued to display a greater degree of engagement and oversight, indicating that there is potentially increasing political space for Parliament.

FURTHER READING

Calland, R, *Anatomy of South Africa: Who Holds the Power?* (Cape Town, Zebra Press, 2006)

Fick, G, 'Elections' in S Woolman et al, *Constitutional Law of South Africa*, 2nd edn (Kenwyn, Juta, 2004)

Gevisser, M, *A Legacy of Liberation: Thabo Mbeki and the Future of the South African Dream* (Basingstoke, Palgrave Macmillan, 2009)

Holden, P, *The Arms Deal in Your Pocket* (Jeppestown, Jonathan Ball, 2008)

Lodge, T, *South African Politics Since 1994* (Cape Town, David Philip, 1999)

Southall, R and Daniel, J (eds), *Zunami!: The South African Elections of 2009* (Auckland Park, South Africa, Jacana Media, 2009)

7

Executive Government

<hr>

**Introduction – The President – Cabinet Government – Governing
Principles, Independent Institutions and Executive Governance –
Conclusion**

I. INTRODUCTION

IN ORDER TO achieve the goals of the Constitution, executive
power is centralised in the President and Cabinet and dispersed
among a number of constitutionally defined institutions. While the
Constitution clearly states that the executive authority of the Republic is
vested in the President,[1] power is in fact formally distributed more
broadly between the traditional executive branch of government and a
number of independent or relatively autonomous institutions. These
include the state institutions that support constitutional democracy, commonly referred to as the Chapter 9 institutions, as well as the Public
Service Commission, Central Bank and the Financial and Fiscal
Commission. This attempt to disperse executive power marks South
Africa's post-apartheid Constitutions as part of the post-Cold War wave
of constitutional changes that sought to protect democratic governance
by breaking up executive power within a state rather than simply relying
on the traditional separation of powers among the three branches of
government. Understanding executive governance under the final
Constitution thus requires an exploration of the interactions of these
different institutions and their overall relationship to political parties and
other sources of political power in the society.

[1] Constitution of the Republic of South Africa Act 108 of 1996 [hereinafter 1996
Constitution] s 85(1).

As in all modern Constitutions, the 1996 Constitution provides specifically for executive government in a chapter entitled 'The President and National Executive'. These sections of the Constitution define how power is to be exercised in the governance of the country. However, unlike traditional parliamentary systems and some presidential-type Constitutions—which rely on the legislative branch and judiciary to check and balance executive power—South Africa's post-apartheid Constitutions have included a set of constitutionally independent institutions to protect and advance good governance and human rights. Some of these institutions have historically existed under executive control, but the establishment of a range of independent institutions is an innovative attempt to constitutionalise a higher level of accountability and to insulate some decisions from the vagaries of everyday politics. The exercise of power to govern the country will be the central focus of this chapter's discussion of executive government; however, we will also consider some of the constitutionally defined institutions that are either empowered to govern in specific areas—such as finance and elections—or are supposed to serve as checks on the decisions of the executive. It is also important to consider the Constitution's creation of principles and institutions to guide specific areas of governance—such as public administration and security—areas that have traditionally been within the sole purview of the executive. And it will also be necessary to consider the relationship between the formal constitutional provisions and political parties that serve to organise and legitimate the exercise of political power.

In South Africa, public law—which includes both constitutional law and administrative law—is a legacy of British colonialism. Although a number of the historic entities that were eventually subsumed into the Union of South Africa may have offered alternative models or adopted aspects of different traditions of governance—such as in the Zulu Kingdom or the Boer and Griqua Republics—the historically dominant form of executive government was modelled on Westminster. From the earliest period of representative government in the Cape Colony until the waning days of apartheid, a ceremonial head of state, with limited authority, stood symbolically over a Cabinet government led by a Prime Minister. From 1910 until the declaration of a Republic in 1961, the Governor-General, as representative of the King or Queen of England, served as South Africa's ceremonial head of state. After 1961, a State President served as head of state but had extremely limited executive powers. It was only in 1983 that the apartheid regime adopted a quasi-presidential form of government, combining the Prime Minister's role with the head of state and empowering the new President with extraordinary authority as a means of overcoming the potential limits of the 1983 Constitution's 'tricameral' Parliament. Despite the illegitimacy of this first presidential experience, the dynamics of the democratic transition seemed to preclude any return to the parliamentary form of executive rule.

Negotiations over the nature of the executive were, in fact, a key ingredient in the agreement establishing the 1993 interim Constitution. Debate over the structure of the executive was initially stalled by the National Party's insistence that the presidency be 'shared by the three largest parties'[2] in a form of triumvirate, in which FW de Klerk imagined 'an executive committee of party leaders, with a rotating chair, to deal with fundamental principles'.[3] The ANC accepted that participation in government remained one of the National Party's non-negotiable demands, yet it sought to meet this demand with its 'sunset proposal', a key element of which was the guarantee that each party receiving 5 per cent of the vote in the election would have a right to nominate Ministers to the Cabinet. This proposal was subsequently incorporated into the Constitutional Principles, together with the provision that there would not be another national election before 30 April 1999—unless Parliament passed a vote of no confidence in the executive—providing the framework for a five-year government of national unity. Section 84 of the interim Constitution guaranteed '[e]very party holding at least 80 seats in the National Assembly' the right to designate an Executive Deputy President. And if no parties or only one party were to hold 80 seats, 'the party holding the largest number of seats and the party holding the second largest number of seats shall each' have the right to designate one Executive Deputy President. This guaranteed the deal struck between the ANC and the National Party, which ensured that FW de Klerk had a right to be an Executive Deputy President and part of the executive branch of government while precluding the formal power-sharing arrangements that the National Party had long sought in the negotiations.

Despite agreement on the structure of the executive, the problem of executive decision-making remained unresolved. When de Klerk argued

---

[2] D Atkinson, 'Principle Born of Pragmatism?' in S Friedman and D Atkinson (eds), *The Small Miracle: South Africa's Negotiated Settlement*, South African Review 7 (Johannesburg, Ravan Press, 1994) 103.

[3] Atkinson, 'Principle Born of Pragmatism?', 104.

that decision-making in the new Cabinet would have to be by con-sensus—resurrecting the demand for a minority veto over government decisions—Mandela put his foot down. He assured de Klerk that he was committed to seeking consensus, but he was adamant that if there were disagreement, 'the majority (50 per cent) would decide'.[4] Formal agree-ment on executive decision-making came in a final bilateral meeting between de Klerk and Mandela only hours before the Multi-Party Negotiating Forum adopted the interim Constitution. Making this pos-sible was the 'six-pack' agreement, a last-minute deal reached between negotiators that resolved a number of key issues that had remained outstanding. While the National Party agreed to majority decision-making in the Cabinet, the ANC also made a number of concessions. These included the need for a 60 per cent majority to adopt a final Constitution in a referendum if the Constitutional Assembly were to deadlock; a two-thirds majority in the Senate before any changes could be made to the boundaries, powers and functions of the provinces; an agree-ment that the provinces would be permitted to adopt their own Constitutions so long as they did not conflict with the Constitutional Principles in the interim Constitution or the provisions of a future national Constitution; a guarantee that whites would have 30 per cent of seats in local Councils in the first phase of democratically elected local governments, combined with a requirement that there be a two-thirds majority for budget decisions, which gave whites an effective veto over spending at the local level; and finally, an agreement that the wording of the amnesty clause in the postamble to the Constitution would read 'shall' rather than 'there may be amnesty'.[5]

According to Mac Maharaj, who participated in these last-minute negotiations, 'the trade-off . . . was: How does cabinet function versus this last item they are concerned with—amnesty?'[6] The Cabinet decision-making agreement was captured in Section 89(2) of the interim Constitution, which stated that the

> Cabinet shall function in a manner which gives consideration to the consen-sus-seeking spirit underlying the concept of a government of national unity as well as the need for effective government.

[4] P Waldmeir, *Anatomy of a Miracle: The End of Apartheid and the Birth of a New South Africa* (London, Penguin Books, 1997) 231.
[5] P O'Malley, *Shades of Difference: Mac Maharaj and the Struggle for South Africa* (London, Penguin Books, 2007) 401.
[6] O'Malley, *Shades of Difference* 401.

This wording left enough ambiguity that some elements of the old regime could later claim that this formulation, taken together with the requirements that the President 'shall consult the Executive Deputy Presidents' and 'exercise and perform all functions . . . in consultation with cabinet'[7] meant that President Mandela was bound to govern by consensus. Yet, despite these efforts to pursue the National Party's original demands, even beyond last minute negotiations, a key element of the deal remained Mandela's insistence that he would attempt to govern inclusively, but if consensus could not be reached, Cabinet decisions would be made by majority vote. This outcome, reached in a final face-to-face negotiation between de Klerk and Mandela on the night of 17 November 1993, according to Patti Waldmeir, was 'the moment when de Klerk accepted majority rule, finally and forever'.[8]

Other elements of the deal, however, recognised the existence of other sources of power beyond the politicians and had consequences that long outlasted the general guarantee of a Government of National Unity (GNU). These additional 'sunset clauses' gave particular guarantees of job tenure, pensions and remuneration to incumbent members of the public service, police and defence forces.[9] Although the National Party withdrew from the GNU in June 1996, the ability of the ANC to transform the public service—as the operational arm of the executive—was still constrained by the sunset clauses, which 'forc[ed] the state to carry many senior civil servants who were anxious, de-motivated and, in some instances, hostile'[10] until at least 1999. However, beyond the sunset clauses and the guarantee in the Constitutional Principles that the GNU would frame the structure of the executive for a full five years (until April 1999), no limitations were placed on the future structure or composition of the executive. The Constitutional Principles adopted in Schedule 4 of the interim Constitution thus placed no limitations on the choices open to the Constitutional Assembly in framing the structure of executive government in the final Constitution. It was, however, the interim Constitution's continuation of a quasi-presidential form of government—in which

---

[7] Constitution of the Republic of South Africa Act 200 of 1993 [hereinafter 1993 interim Constitution] s 82(2) and (3).

[8] Waldmeir, *Anatomy of a Miracle*, above n 4, 231.

[9] 1993 interim Constitution ss 236, 237 and 238.

[10] Developing a Culture of Good Governance: Report of the Presidential Review Commission on the Reform and Transformation of the Public Service in South Africa, February 1998, ch 2, para 2.1.3.

Nelson Mandela became the first democratically elected President of South Africa—that left little incentive for the Constitutional Assembly to reopen the debates over executive governance.

II. THE PRESIDENT

Nelson Mandela set an extraordinary example as South Africa's first democratically elected President, both in his role as head of state for all South Africans and by his decision to step aside after serving only one term in office. While many Constitution-makers in the post-Cold War era placed limits on the terms of office for Presidents, there have been repeated attempts by popular incumbents—in Africa, Latin America and Russia—to obtain constitutional changes that would enable them to extend their time in power. Mandela, like George Washington before him, was in a unique position to claim political authority. Yet, time and again, he declared his commitment to abide by the Constitution as he sought to provide an example for the country and the world. Not only did Mandela welcome the determinations of the Constitutional Court that struck down his own decisions, but he also voluntarily subjected himself to the jurisdiction of the courts as an individual—at one time placing himself under the authority of a court as a witness.

Despite extraordinary political strains in the years that have followed, South Africa has continued to offer an example of constitutional constraint. For example, when Thabo Mbeki, a second-term President, lost an internal party election, his own party pressured him to resign from office. President Mbeki could have stood his ground, rejecting the party's decision to 'redeploy' him and forcing the National Assembly to pass a vote of no confidence in him if they wished. However, he chose to resign and allow the National Assembly to simply replace him by voting in Kgalema Motlanthe to serve as President for the remaining months of the legislature's term. Even President Jacob Zuma, who was engaged in intense conflict with Mbeki within the ANC and faced great legal controversy around his own fitness to serve—but led the ANC to another landslide election victory in 2009—promised to serve only one term in office. While it is far too soon to know whether this pattern will be maintained, it is extraordinary, particularly in the post-colonial context, for a newly emergent democracy to witness a political struggle so intense as to effectively remove a President from office and for that struggle to remain within the broad confines of the law and Constitution. Executive power has so often been taken and so rarely relinquished voluntarily that the formal commitment to the rules of the game provides a hopeful talisman for South Africa's young Constitution.

A. Election, Appointment and Term of Office

The National Assembly elects the President. While COPE, the newly formed political party, campaigned in the 2009 elections for a constitutional change that would allow for a directly elected President, the Constitution provides for the indirect election of the President. After each national election, and 'whenever necessary', the National Assembly is required to 'elect a woman or a man' from among its members to serve as President.[11] The Chief Justice or another judge appointed by the Chief Justice (in the event of a vacancy) presides over the election of the President at the first sitting of a newly elected National Assembly, according to a procedure laid out in Schedule 3 of the Constitution. Once elected, the President ceases to be a member of the National Assembly and takes on the dual role of head of state and head of government.

In theory, the legislature may elect any one of its members to the post of President; but in practice, the leader of the political party that wins the most seats in Parliament is elected. Although Nelson Mandela was elected unopposed under the interim Constitution and Thabo Mbeki was twice elected unanimously in 1999 and 2004, the election of Jacob Zuma following the 2009 election was, with the nomination of the leader of the COPE, contested. The elections of constitutional office bearers—the President, Speaker of Parliament and a number of other constitutional office bearers in the National Council of Provinces (NCOP) and provincial legislatures—are conducted according to a set procedure.[12] This process requires a formal nomination as well as a method of electoral elimination if no candidate receives a simple majority of all votes cast in the first round of voting. The repeated elimination of the lowest vote-getter in the unlikely case of multiple nominations will, in most cases, produce a President elected by the majority of members. A tied vote at the end of the process requires a new round of nominations and voting at a follow-up meeting within seven days, while the nomination of

[11] 1996 Constitution s 86.
[12] 1996 Constitution, Sch 3, Part A.

a single candidate requires the presiding officer to declare that candidate elected.

The President must assume office within five days of being elected to the post, by taking the oath of office specified in Schedule 2 of the Constitution. The President's term of office is defined by the life of the legislature that elects the President, unless there is a vacancy due to the resignation, death or removal of the President. While 'no person may hold office as President for more than two terms',[13] the period a person serves as President as a result of a vacancy within the term of the legislature is not counted and he or she may go on to serve two full terms thereafter. President Thabo Mbeki's resignation within months of the end of his second term created the first vacancy in the office of President, which was quickly filled when Parliament elected Kgalema Motlanthe. Although President Motlanthe was understood to be serving in a transitional role pending the 2009 national elections and the expected election of Jacob Zuma (who was heading the ANC's candidate list), in constitutional terms Motlanthe served as South Africa's third democratic President. Motlanthe's appointment as Deputy President by President Zuma raises the possibility that Motlanthe may serve two further full terms as President in the future.

Despite Thabo Mbeki's effective political removal by the ANC, in fact, the constitutional mechanisms for removal were not readily available to his political enemies. The only way they could have legally removed him would have been for a majority of the members of the National Assembly to pass a vote of no confidence in the President or to pass a resolution dissolving Parliament. This action would have required the President to dissolve the National Assembly and call an election within 90 days of the dissolution. Since President Mbeki retained some support among ANC parliamentarians and opposition members of Parliament, it is unclear whether his detractors could have obtained the necessary majority to dissolve the National Assembly or pass a vote of no confidence. Furthermore, it seems even less likely, on the existing evidence, that the National Assembly could have removed him from office by a two-thirds vote of the National Assembly on any of the three grounds specified in the Constitution: 'a serious violation of the Constitution or the law; serious misconduct; or, inability to perform the functions of office'.[14]

[13] 1996 Constitution s 88(2).
[14] 1996 Constitution s 89(1)(a)–(c).

Even with the required two-thirds support from members of the National Assembly, the effective removal of the President would require the Constitutional Court to agree that the basis for the vote met the requirements of at least one of the three grounds for removal. The likelihood of a constitutional challenge to a vote for removal is especially high, given the fact that removal from the office of President on either of the first two grounds has severe consequences for the individual. Removal for misconduct or violation of the Constitution or law results in both the denial of any benefits of having served—including pension etc—and perhaps most significantly, preclusion from serving in any public office.[15]

If, on the one hand, President Mbeki's decision to resign in September 2008 cut short any process of constitutional removal, it provided, on the other hand, a clear example of how political developments within a ruling political party may have an impact on the constitutional system without Parliament resorting to the existing constitutional mechanisms for removal. Judicial criticism by Judge Nicholson in the Zuma corruption case, which implied that Mbeki had interfered in the decisions of the National Prosecuting Authority, might have provided evidence of Mbeki's failure to abide by the Constitution and law. The political impact of that decision within the ANC—on top of Mbeki's electoral loss to Jacob Zuma in the ANC election for party President at the organisation's national conference the previous December—led to Mbeki's resignation. While Mbeki and his supporters may have chosen to fight, the proximity to the upcoming 2009 election, in which he would not be a candidate for President, made this an unlikely scenario. The dramatic impact of these internal party politics on the presidency is, however, less a reflection on the constitutional arrangements than a consequence of the single-party political dominance of the ANC within the system.

In a purely parliamentary system, the ruling party may appoint any of its Members of Parliament to the position of Prime Minister at any time during its electoral term. However, in a presidential system, the individual holding that office is usually protected from shifting political winds until the next election. This is usually achieved by setting a fixed term in office and making the President subject to direct election by the voting public— even if it is mediated through a formally indirect electoral process, like the electoral college in the United States. In South Africa, the tying of normal presidential terms to the temporal life of the National Assembly means

---

[15] 1996 Constitution s 89(2).

that to force the President out of office on purely political grounds, a majority of the members of the national legislature must agree to once again subject themselves to the electorate or a majority of members must support a no-confidence vote in the President. A decision to dissolve the National Assembly is, however, restricted by the requirement that the President must only dissolve Parliament if the National Assembly's resolution to dissolve is adopted at least three years after the election of that Assembly.[16] One exception to this requirement arises when there is a vacancy in the office of President—due to the President's removal or resignation—and the National Assembly fails to elect a new President within 30 days. In this case, the Deputy President, who serves as Acting President in the event of a vacancy, is required to dissolve the National Assembly and call a new election.

The political dominance of a single party—the ANC—means that for the moment these restraints are less effective at protecting a President who loses political support within the party, especially after the first three years of his term. This dominance might also limit the ability of the President to pursue policies that do not have the full support of the ruling party, despite the relative autonomy that the Constitutional scheme provides for the executive. It was precisely Thabo Mbeki's pursuit of more neoliberal economic policies—as well as his centralisation of power within the executive and the office of the presidency in particular—that led to his increasing alienation from Shell House (the party headquarters of the ANC) and significant factions within the broader ANC political alliance. These developments produced increasing unhappiness and finally open conflict within the ANC. Yet the ANC's sheer numerical dominance of the National Assembly meant that there was little hope that a small faction of the ANC could align in Parliament with the opposition to pass a vote of no confidence in the President. Instead, opponents of Mbeki ignored the formal constitutional mechanisms and worked inside the party to challenge the power of the President, thus effectively forcing his resignation. A less-dominant ruling party might thus have the paradoxical effect of strengthening the presidency under the 1996 Constitution.

The possibility of obtaining the support of the majority of Members of Parliament to either dissolve the National Assembly—after three years of their five year term—or to pass a no-confidence vote in the President seems unlikely in a context where the ruling party holds most of the seats

---

[16]   1996 Constitution s 50(1)(b).

in the Assembly. This is likely to be the case even if the party is split, unless the opposition party members of the Assembly were to share the same political goals as a very large group within the ruling party that comes to oppose the President. The relative autonomy of the President, in respect to his or her own party, is enhanced in theory by the fact that, once elected, the President gives up his or her seat in the National Assembly. Additionally, through the power of appointment, he or she is able, if he or she wishes, to forge a government that is relatively independent of the ruling party in Parliament. Furthermore, the provision that allows the National Assembly to pass a vote of no confidence in the Cabinet alone—which forces the President to reconstitute the Cabinet—allows for a majority of the members of the National Assembly to send a clear message of displeasure at the policies or actions of the executive branch without having to obtain the level of political agreement necessary to replace the President. Yet, despite rank-and-file unhappiness among ANC Members of Parliament with the neoliberal policies Mbeki's government enacted with the Growth, Employment and Redistribution (GEAR) strategy, there was no attempt to follow this path.

B. Duties, Powers and Functions

As head of state and head of the national executive, the President is burdened with duties and endowed with powers and functions that frame the scope of legitimate constitutional action. Unlike South Africa's predemocratic republican Constitutions, the role of the President as head of state does not entail the exercise of prerogative powers, which AC Dicey described as 'the residue of discretionary or arbitrary authority, which is at any given time legally left in the hands of the crown'.[17] Instead, the President is encumbered with the duty to 'uphold, defend and respect the Constitution as the supreme law of the Republic' and is bound to exercise only such powers as have been 'entrusted by the Constitution and legislation, including those necessary to perform the functions of head of State and head of the national executive'.[18] This might seem a broad grant of executive power, but the founding provisions declare the supremacy of the Constitution, stating that 'law or conduct inconsistent with it is

[17] AC Dicey, *Introduction to the Study of the Law of the Constitution*, 10th edn (London, Macmillan Education, 1959; reprinted 1987).
[18] 1996 Constitution ss 83(b) and 84(1).

invalid', making it clear that these powers are circumscribed by the boundaries of the constitutional order. Even the notion of legal exception, asserted by some to justify the extra-constitutional deployment of power in cases of National Emergency or martial law, is limited by the constitutional provisions that provide a map for exceptional circumstances; all else is extra-constitutional and thus outside the law.

Presidential powers may be divided between acts that are undertaken in the President's capacity as head of state and those assumed as head of the national executive. The significance of this distinction lies in the requirements of collective action and responsibility when acting as a member of the national executive on the one hand, and the relatively autonomous actions the President is empowered and required to take as head of state. Listed in Section 84(2) these head-of-state functions include agreeing to and signing legislation into law; calling the legislature into session; making appointments required by legislation or the Constitution; appointing commissions of inquiry and calling national referenda; appointing diplomatic representatives; receiving and recognising foreign representatives; pardoning criminals and conferring honours. These presidential functions involve limited, if any, political discretion by the President.[19] The presidency has itself adopted this view of these functions in *The Manual of Executive Acts of the President,* which states that the

> [o]ffice of the President interprets . . . Head of State appointments to be those appointments that the President makes for ceremonial or similar reasons such as when he is required to merely confirm candidates selected by another body or when he appoints persons under his powers listed under section 84(2) of the Constitution.[20]

This view of the President's head-of-state powers does not, however, fully take into account two significant areas of discretionary authority granted to the President. First, a truly important exercise of political discretion lies in the President's duty to appoint the Deputy President and members of the Cabinet. While formally outside of the section 84(2) framework, it is clear from the Constitution that this power is not formally exercised in collaboration with any other constitutional authority

---

[19] See, C Murray and R Stacey, 'The President and the National Executive' in S Woolman et al (eds), *Constitutional Law of South Africa,* 2nd edn (Cape Town, Juta, 2007) ch 18.2.

[20] Executive and Legal Services: Office of the President, *The Manual of Executive Acts of the President* (March 1999) para 3.10, cited in Murray and Stacey, 'The President and the National Executive' in Woolman et al, above n 19, ch 18.2(a) fn 27.

but is, rather, a central aspect of political power to be exercised at the President's discretion. Under section 91(2), the President has the duty to appoint these members of his government as well as determine their powers and functions. Although there are some specific requirements—such as the limit on the number of Ministers that may be appointed from outside of Parliament and the duty to 'appoint a Member of the Cabinet to be the leader of government business in the National Assembly'—the President's explicit authority to dismiss them at his discretion ensures that the President is empowered to retain control over the composition of the government. This authority—and the fact that the Ministers are beholden to the President for their appointments—has, at times, exacerbated the inherent tensions between Presidents and their own political party.

Second, another constitutionally significant element of these powers and functions is the authority to either refer a Bill passed by Parliament 'back to the Assembly for reconsideration of the Bill's constitutionality', or to refer a 'Bill to the Constitutional Court for a decision on the Bill's constitutionality'.[21] These powers are not comparable to the veto power exercised by the President of the United States, but the effect is similar. On the one hand, the return of a Bill for reconsideration by the National Assembly is a clear political statement by the President that there is a problem with the legislation. Even if it is simply a technical issue, it clearly gives the President a significant role in the legislative process. On the other hand, a referral of a Bill to the Constitutional Court clearly indicates the President is questioning the decision of the legislature. Even if the exercise of this power is restricted to constitutional questions, and cannot be based on a mere political objection to the legislation, the President may use this authority to achieve important political results.

Presidents have referred legislation back to the National Assembly at least four times since the adoption of the Constitution. The first case was when President Mandela raised questions about the constitutionality of a Bill passed by the national Parliament in 1998 to regulate the production, distribution and consumption of liquor.[22] When the legislature returned the bill unchanged to the President, Mandela referred it to the Constitutional Court. Responding to the President's concerns, the Constitutional Court found that aspects of the Bill that sought to regulate

[21] 1996 Constitution ss 79(1) and 79(4)(b).
[22] Liquor Bill B131-98.

the purely intra-provincial distribution of liquor violated the scheme of co-operative governance in which the provinces are afforded some degree of autonomy.[23] While the Court produced a nuanced conception of the distribution of authority between the national and regional legislatures, the decision by the President to send the Bill for 'abstract' review was an important political indicator that the President and his government remained committed to the system of co-operative government established in the Constitution, despite the determination of an ANC-dominated Parliament to unilaterally impose its own scheme of liquor regulation. More recently, President Mbeki referred the Independent Communications Authority of South Africa Amendment Bill of 2005 back to the National Assembly; however, once the legislature made changes that were acceptable to him, he signed the Bill into law.[24]

The President's broadest powers are, however, reserved for his role as head of the national executive. While the exercise of executive authority in this context must be undertaken in conjunction with members of the Cabinet, the extent of this authority is fairly all-encompassing. It includes developing and implementing national policy; preparing and initiating legislation; implementing legislation, except where the Constitution or national legislation 'provides otherwise'; coordinating the functions of state departments and administrations; and finally, 'performing any other executive function provided for in the Constitution or in national legislation'.[25] The exercise of joint authority between the President and members of Cabinet is formalised by the requirement that all legally consequential decisions by the President, including decisions taken in terms of statutory authority, must be in writing and 'be countersigned by another Cabinet member if that decision concerns a function assigned to that other Cabinet member'.[26] The requirement that the President act in his role as head of the national executive together with the Cabinet is emphasised in those provisions of the Constitution that define the President's role in appointing the judiciary. These provisions require consultation with specific individuals and institutions, and the overall requirement that these appointments are made on the basis of the

---

[23] *Ex parte President of the Republic of South Africa: Re Constitutionality of the Liquor Bill* 2000 (1) SA 732 (CC).

[24] Independent Communications Authority of South African Amendment Bill B32-2005.

[25] 1996 Constitution s 85(2).

[26] 1996 Constitution ss 101(1) and (2).

President's role as head of the national executive makes it clear that these are Cabinet decisions, not made purely at the discretion of the President. Despite this, it is clear that the power to appoint and dismiss Cabinet members ensures that the President has an authoritative role within the Cabinet structure. This was particularly evident in the practice of President Mbeki, who followed both his inaugurations with late-night processes of Cabinet appointments in which serving Cabinet members were called into meetings right through the night to hear their fates—either being dismissed, retained or appointed to new ministries.

C. The Presidency

When Nelson Mandela arrived in the Union Buildings—the executive building in Pretoria (now Tshwane) designed by Sir Herbert Baker—he found that he had far fewer administrative resources than his predecessor FW de Klerk, who was his second of two Deputy Executive Presidents under the interim Constitution, the first being Thabo Mbeki. Not only did Mandela have to share his office with the two Deputy Presidents and consult with them on all issues, but he also faced a far greater task of restructuring the inherited system of governance, including the public service. To address this issue, Mandela appointed a Commission of Inquiry Regarding the Transformation and Reform of the Public Service in 1996. According to its 1998 report, the role of the Presidential Review Commission

> was to assist in the processes of transforming the state and its principal executive arm, the public service, from an instrument of discrimination, control and domination to an enabling agency that would consolidate democracy and empower communities in ways that were demonstrably accountable and transparent.[27]

The report's recommendations focused in part on what it termed the 'apex and core of government'. It argued that

> the transformation and development of the governance of South Africa requires a radical re-appraisal of the functions, structures, personnel and management of the Office of President, taken together with the Office of the

[27] Report of the Presidential Review Commission on the Reform and Transformation of the Public Service in South Africa, Pretoria, 1998, para 1.3, available at www.info.gov.za/otherdocs/1998/prc98/index.html.

Deputy President, to ensure greater direction and co-ordination in government policy at all levels'.[28]

The government did not embrace all of the Commission's recommendations, but the transformation of the office of the President saw the emergence of the presidency as a key locus of policy-making and co-ordination. During Mandela's term there was an unofficial division of tasks in which President Mandela focused on nation-building while Deputy President Mbeki served as 'Nelson Mandela's de facto Prime Minister',[29] taking most of the responsibility for the day-to-day running of the country. Although Mandela and Mbeki worked within the strictures of the Government of National Unity, in practice, as the National Party's power and influence declined, de Klerk was privately sidelined and the office of First Executive Deputy President Mbeki was transformed, going from a base of zero to a staff of 96 by April 1997. That staff included Chief Director Dr Frank Chikane, parliamentary councillor Essop Pahad as well as a number of legal, economic and political advisors.[30] The policy-making role of Mbeki's office was further enhanced after the Cabinet reshuffle in April 1996, which led to the scrapping of the office of the Reconstruction and Development Programme (RDP) in the President's office and the redeployment of Minister without Portfolio Jay Naidoo, who was in charge of the RDP. Instead, a new unit—the Co-ordination and Implementation Unit (CIU)—was established in Mbeki's office with the goal of co-ordinating government policy. The merger of the offices of the President and Deputy President, which took place after the May 1999 elections and the end of a constitutionally guaranteed Government of National Unity, saw the creation of the presidency through the formal integration of the offices.

Some of President Mbeki's critics saw the creation of the presidency as a product of Mbeki's desire to centralise authority and questioned its 'excessive concentration of power'.[31] But others believed it represented the

---

[28] Report of the Presidential Review Commission on the Reform and Transformation of the Public Service in South Africa, above n 27,Conclusions and Recommendations, para 7.2.1.4.

[29] M Gevisser, *A Legacy of Liberation: Thabo Mbeki and the Future of the South African Dream* (New York, Palgrave Macmillan, 2009) 1.

[30] See, F Chothia and S Jacobs, 'Remaking the Presidency: The Tension between Co-ordination and Centralization' in S Jacobs and R Calland (eds), *Thabo Mbeki's World: The Politics and Ideology of the South African President* (Pietermaritzburg: University of Natal Press; London, Zed Books, 2002) 147–49.

[31] Chothia and Jacobs, 'Remaking the Presidency', above n 30, 150.

structural embodiment of the final Constitution's vision of executive government. From this perspective, the emergence of the presidency was a
response to the demise of the Government of National Unity—both politically and as a constitutional guarantee—and a means to implement the
recommendations of the Presidential Review Commission. This structural
analysis placed less emphasis on Mbeki's motives and focused instead on
how executive governance has been transformed by the particular ways in
which the government has chosen to implement the 1996 Constitution's
provisions regarding the President and the national executive. The three
most consequential features of this transformation were the creation of the
Cabinet Office to co-ordinate the functioning of Cabinet from within the
Presidency; the upgrading of the CIU into the Policy Co-ordination and
Advisory Services (PCAS), an agency tasked with vetting all new policies
and draft legislation before tabling at Cabinet meetings;[32] and the decision
to have the Directors-General—the most senior civil service post in each
government department—enter into their five-year contracts of appointment directly with the President and not with the Cabinet Minister
responsible for their department, as was previously the case.

President Mandela's 1994 appointment of Jay Naidoo to head the RDP
as Minister without Portfolio in the President's Office was understood at
the time to provide a central co-ordinating function for the implementation of the ANC's electoral programme. Government departments under
the control of individual Cabinet members, however, proved relatively
unresponsive to this centralised effort. Instead, Naidoo faced the problem of trying to implement the RDP without a public service bureaucracy
under his control. The government first responded to this situation by
attempting to prompt government departments into action by creating
presidential lead projects as a means to kick-start the RDP. The inherent
limitations of this project-centred approach to implementation—as well
as changing economic and political conditions—led first to the demise of
the RDP office, to a shift in government economic policy and then to a
reformulation of the government's approach to co-ordination.

When Thabo Mbeki became President he elevated Essop Pahad,
his close friend and ally, to the position of Minister without Portfolio
and placed him in control of the Government Communications and
Information Service, which had originally been established in Mbeki's
Deputy President's office to co-ordinate government communications.

---

[32] Chothia and Jacobs, 'Remaking the Presidency', above n 30, 151.

Policy co-ordination in the presidency was left to the PCAS, which is divided into five units shadowing each of the Cabinet committee clusters established in October 1998 and reorganised in September 1999 to implement government polices in specific sectors.[33] These ministerial clusters or sectoral committees—social; economics; investment and employment; international relations, peace and security; justice, crime prevention and security; and governance and administration—are, in turn, shadowed by five Directors-General clusters 'to ensure that the deliberations of Ministers translate into the design, approval and implementation of practical policy and legislative measures'.[34] These processes of centralised co-ordination were further enhanced after the election of President Jacob Zuma in 2009, as a response to the global economic crisis and local concerns about the need 'to achieve visible and tangible socio-economic development within the next five years'.[35]

President Zuma introduced changes to both the presidency and the Cabinet. The presidency has been enhanced by the addition of a second Minister in the Presidency. The first Minister in the Presidency will head the newly created National Planning Commission (NPC), which, according to President Zuma, 'will be responsible for strategic planning for the country to ensure one National Plan to which all spheres of government would adhere', enabling the government 'to take a more comprehensive view of socio-economic development in the country'.[36] The importance of this new Commission was made evident by the appointment of the powerful former Minister of Finance, Trevor Manuel, to serve as the Minister in the Presidency in charge of the NPC. The second Minister in the Presidency is responsible for monitoring and evaluating government performance in all spheres of government as well as being in charge of administration in the presidency. The net effect of these changes is that the presidency—with four principle political players: the President, Deputy President and two Ministers serving as the central planning and co-ordinating structure of government—has become the most powerful

[33] While there are six cabinet committees, there are only five units within the PCAS and only five Directors-general clusters, since economics and investment and employment clusters are served by a single PCAS unit and DG cluster.

[34] The Presidency, *Democratic Governance: A Restructured Presidency At Work* 2000/2001 (Pretoria, GCIS, 1 March 2001) 15, available at www.info.gov.za.

[35] Statement by President Jacob Zuma on the appointment of the new Cabinet, May 10, 2009. Issued by Government Communications (GCIS) and available at www.info.gov.za.

[36] Ibid.

political institution in the country. Despite the Constitution's formal statement that 'the President exercises the executive authority together with other members of the Cabinet'[37]—and the requirement that executive decisions by the President must be 'countersigned by another Cabinet member if that decision concerns a function assigned to that other cabinet member'[38]—in reality, the presidency will increasingly serve as the central location of government decision-making.

III. CABINET GOVERNMENT

The Cabinet is the formal decision-making centre of the executive—playing the role of 'political decision-maker'.[39] At its fortnightly meetings, Cabinet members review and discuss draft laws and policies that are presented to the Cabinet in the form of cabinet memoranda, which are produced by the relevant Ministers with the assistance of the Cabinet secretariat. In response to concerns over the lack of co-ordination in the 1998 Report of the Presidential Review Commission, President Mbeki introduced the system of Cabinet clusters to address each of the major areas of governance.[40] In addition to these Cabinet committees, which were initially chaired by designated Ministers but more recently by either the President or Deputy President, the presidency has organised bi-annual Makgotla, 'extended strategy planning or review meetings', at which the Cabinet, Directors General and special advisors to the President review and discuss government policy and programmes across all sectors. These forms of co-ordinated policy-making and review of government action were supplemented by President Mbeki's introduction, in his 2004 State of the Nation address, of 'several dozen long-term objectives to guide his administration'. These included 'clear targets, promises of open government, and a concern for efficient administration'.[41] At the same time, a new Cabinet Office was established within the presidency in order to

[37] 1996 Constitution s 85(2).
[38] 1996 Constitution s 101(2).
[39] See, R Calland, *Anatomy of South Africa: Who Holds the Power?* (Cape Town, Zebra Press, 2006).
[40] See, The Presidency, *Annual Report 2002–2003*, ch 5.1, available at www.thepresidency.gov.za/docs/reports/annual/2003/chapt5.pdf.
[41] D Hemson and M O'Donovan, 'Putting Numbers to the Scorecard: Presidential Targets and the State of Delivery, in S Buhlungu et al (eds)*State of the Nation: South Africa 2005–2006* (Cape Town, HSRC Press, 2006) 11.

ensure the co-ordination of the Cabinet and—as some have argued—the President's control over Cabinet in the name of efficiency and public service delivery.

It is generally argued that the 1996 Constitution 'establishes a system of cabinet government',[42] and that South Africa has a parliamentary rather than presidential system of government, even if it constitutes a somewhat hybrid form.[43] The emergence and strengthening of the presidency highlights the power of the President within this constitutional system. The President's relative power is evident in the very design of the executive branch, in which the President is given the sole power to appoint and dismiss the Deputy President and members of Cabinet.[44] Furthermore, the President assigns powers and functions to each member of Cabinet and has the authority by proclamation to transfer functions between Ministers.[45] The President can also temporarily assign 'any power or function of another member who is absent from office or is unable to exercise that power or perform that function'.[46] Even as the President serves as a member of Cabinet and as such is accountable to Parliament for the exercise of executive powers and functions, the power of the President in relation to other members of Cabinet is indisputable. This is amplified by the fact that it has been only in fairly extreme circumstances—such as when President Mbeki 'withdrew from the AIDS debate'[47] in 2002 and allowed the Cabinet to go ahead and adopt a national HIV/AIDS treatment programme that he did not support—has there been any real evidence of Cabinet influence over the President.

Even within the Cabinet, as is the case in other parliamentary systems, there is a distinction between more senior members of Cabinet, who often hold the most important posts, and those who are not part of the inner circle. However, Minister of Finance Trevor Manuel has, until recently, been first among Ministers. The unique power of the Department of Finance or Treasury—as it is termed in the Constitution—was built not only on the astute political acumen of Manuel, but also on the technical capacity of the department and the ministerial budget committee that

[42] GE Devenish, *A Commentary on the South African Constitution* (Durban: Butterworths, 1998) 158.

[43] Murray and Stacey, 'The President and the National Executive', above n 19, ch 18.1.

[44] 1996 Constitution s 91(2)

[45] See 1996 Constitution ss 91(2) and 97.

[46] 1996 Constitution s 98.

[47] Gevisser, *A Legacy of Liberation*, above n 29, 291.

recognises Treasury's engagement with the whole spectrum of government decisions that have budgetary impacts.[48] This 'government within a government' quality of the Treasury was further enhanced by the constitutional provision that precluded all but the Minister of Finance from introducing a Money Bill in the National Assembly[49] and the adoption of the Public Finance Management Act in 1999.[50] The authority of the executive was enhanced by the legislature's mistaken assumption that it could not amend a Money Bill until Parliament passed a specific procedure for doing so, as provided for in section 77(3) of the Constitution. Meanwhile, the Finance Management Act imposed a system of 'financial probity and sound procedure' throughout government that gave a central role to the Treasury in Mbeki's administration.[51]

President Zuma's restructuring of Cabinet—which is reflected in a steady increase in the size of Cabinet from 40 Ministers and Deputy Ministers in Nelson Mandela's 1994 government to 62, as well as the addition of six new government departments—has further increased the authority of the presidency. While the Department of Finance may have been a 'government within a government' during the Mbeki presidency, the creation of a National Planning Commission headed by Trevor Manuel as one of the two Ministers within the Presidency, suggests that there will be a greater emphasis on economic ordering and less of a focus on formal financial control, which marked the era of Finance's ascendancy. The appointment of Pravin Gordhan, the extremely competent former head of the South African Revenue Services—the semi-privatised tax agency—as the new Minister of Finance indicates, however, that there might be a greater balance of power within the central core of government than the simple shifting of Manuel to the National Planning Commission suggests.

Along with the restructuring of various government departments to reflect the new priorities of the ruling ANC, a further shift in the location of policy-making power within the system of governance has occurred. Unlike many parliamentary systems—in which the ruling party's representatives constitute the leading decision-making body of the party—decision-making within the ANC has remained within the party's National Executive Committee. As a result, there has been a constant fluctuation of decision-making power between the executive branch

[48] See, Chothia and Jacobs, 'Remaking the Presidency', above n 30, 159.
[49] 1996 Constitution s 73(2)(a).
[50] Public Finance Management Act 1 of 1999.
[51] See, Calland, *Anatomy of South Africa*, above n 39, 58.

of government and the party. Enormous power gravitated to Mandela during the democratic transition, but Thabo Mbeki effectively separated policy-making from the internal decisions of the party through a combined strategy of political centralisation, bureaucratisation and an emphasis on the technical complexity of policy-making and implementation. The political revolt at the ANC's National Conference at Polokwane in December 2007 was a consequence of a grassroots rejection of the government's policies, and it had the effect of reasserting the authority of the political party over government. This led, until Mbeki's resignation in September 2008, to what was described as the 'two centres of power' problem—one being the President of the country, the other being the President of the ANC (or more generally, the National Executive Committee and Shell House, the ANC's leading political organ and party headquarters in downtown Johannesburg).

IV. GOVERNING PRINCIPLES, INDEPENDENT INSTITUTIONS AND EXECUTIVE GOVERNANCE

In addition to the regular constitutional structures and provisions for executive governance, the Constitution employs a series of principles, mechanisms and institutions to enhance the practice of government by promoting the values of participation, openness, transparency and accountability. Among these are a series of independent institutions that include the Chapter 9 'State Institutions Supporting Democracy'; the Public Service Commission; civilian secretariats for defence and police; an independent commission to make recommendations concerning remuneration for persons holding public office; a Central Bank; and a Fiscal and Financial Commission to make recommendations on the equitable division of revenue among the local, regional and national spheres of government. These different institutions are granted varying degrees of constitutional independence and authority, and they represent an attempt to insulate particular governmental decisions from the realm of competitive party politics. They are also designed to avoid obvious conflicts of interest or concerns of political influence. A parallel mechanism used in the Constitution is the articulation of basic values, governing principles, primary objectives and duties as a means of framing the role of particular mechanisms and institutions. The Chapter 9 institutions for 'strengthening constitutional democracy in the Republic' have a common set of governing principles aimed at securing their independence and impartiality, while the chapters on public administration and the security services are each headed by sets of principles that frame the scope of constitutionally legitimate goals and means of operation for these vital operational branches of the state.

A. Assignment, Delegation and Intervention

The most direct means of addressing failures in executive governance are the powers given to the President, Provincial Premiers, Cabinet members and the national executive to reassign or delegate executive power to a different Minister, executive body or sphere of government. Even more dramatic is the power given to the national and regional governments to intervene—under particular circumstances—in provincial and municipal administrations, respectively. The President always has the power to allocate duties and areas of responsibility among Cabinet members. And the provisions that allow the transfer or temporary assignment of functions by the President (or the permanent assignment by a member of Cabinet of authority over particular functions or legislation) provide a significant degree of flexibility in governance. Compared to the delegation of authority—when the delegated authority is exercised in the place of the original authority—the assignment of administrative authority over particular laws to the provincial or municipal governments fully transfers the responsibility of governance over the specified functions or laws. This constitutional scheme provides a flexible approach to the implementation of government programmes and legislation, so that these laws and programmes may, in accordance with the constitutional imperative of co-operative government, be implemented at the most appropriate level of governance. At the same time, the power given to the national and provincial governments to intervene in provincial or municipal administrations—when these spheres of government either 'cannot or do[es] not fulfill an executive obligation in terms of the Constitution or legislation'[52]—ensures a formal means for tackling failures in governance at all subordinate levels of the public administration.[53]

[52] 1996 Constitution ss 100 and 139.
[53] See, Department of Provincial and Local Government, Intervening in Provinces and Municipalities: Guidelines for the Application of Sections 100 and 139 of the Constitution, 26 April 2007, available at www.dplg.gov.za.

The March 1998 provincial intervention and takeover of Butterworth, a small industrial city in the Eastern Cape Province, and the more recent threat by Sicelo Shiceka, the National Minister of Cooperative Governance and Traditional Affairs, to intervene in the failing municipalities of the Northwest Province provide an important view of the ways these mechanisms have been employed. In the case of Butterworth, there had been an ongoing conflict among political factions in the town that included ANC councillors in the Butterworth Transitional Local Council that led to a complete breakdown in local service delivery in February 1998. The last straw came when, on the verge of complete financial collapse, the Council failed to pay municipal workers their wages. The workers went on strike, refuse went uncollected and for three days there was no water in the taps. In response to continuous public protests as well as allegations of mismanagement, fraud and corruption, the Provincial Member of the Executive Council (MEC) for Local Government and Housing stepped in. When initial negotiations failed to produce a solution, the MEC issued a directive on behalf of the provincial executive that detailed the inability of the Council to fulfil its executive obligations and replaced the councillors and town clerk (manager) with administrators appointed by the MEC.

The provincial executive followed the substantive and procedural requirements detailed in the Constitution, obtaining the unconditional approval of the National Minister and seeking the approval of the NCOP. But it soon became clear that the MEC had overstepped his authority by claiming both the executive and legislative powers of the Council. The NCOP approved the intervention, but limited the power of the intervening administrators to the maintenance of 'essential national standards' and the establishment of 'minimum standards for the rendering of services'. The Council thus retained its legislative powers and ability to use municipal resources to carry out its legislative duties while the town clerk was reinstated and the outside administrators had to report to the Council on their activities. Finally, the NCOP's Select Committee on Constitutional Affairs and Public Administration took up the task of monitoring events in Butterworth and conducted a two-day study tour in May 1998 to ensure that the intervention was continuing within the guidelines issued by the NCOP.

Despite the restraints placed upon the intervention by both the NCOP and the courts, the effect was to return Butterworth to 'relative normality'.[54]

---

[54] See, J de Visser, *A Legal Analysis of Provincial Intervention in a Municipality*, LLM thesis University of Cape Town, 1999.

In response to this experience, the government introduced a Constitutional Amendment in 2003[55] that clarified the power of intervention and limited the roles of the National Minister and NCOP.[56] First, the Amendment provided for a limited administrative intervention; it also allowed the intervening provincial authority to completely dissolve the municipal council until the election of a new Council. Second, it limited the oversight role of the National Minister and the NCOP, to a form of veto that would bring the intervention to an end, rather than the approval process originally required by the Constitution. Finally, the amendment established a mandatory form of intervention in cases of financial crisis. These latter provisions dispensed with the discretionary powers of the provincial executive and instead required the province to intervene if a municipality failed to produce a budget or adopt necessary revenue-raising measures or could not provide essential services due to a financial crisis. If the provincial executive 'cannot or does not adequately exercise' these powers, the Constitution now requires the national government to intervene.

It was under these circumstances that the National Minister of Cooperative Governance and Traditional Affairs threatened to intervene to prevent the collapse of municipal governments in the Northwest Province in the second half of 2009. This threat was, however, challenged by provincial government officials, who claimed that the intervention of the ANC leadership through the redeployment or suspension of party members was in violation of the constitutional provisions that structure the nature of national intervention in provincial or municipal affairs.[57] This conflict highlights the interplay between the structures of the ANC, as a political party, and the role of the national government. On more than one occasion, the national leadership of the ANC has found itself in conflict with a provincial section of the party and has sought to intervene politically by exerting internal party discipline, redeploying officials and elected representatives or taking disciplinary action, including suspension or expulsion, against those who do not follow the decisions of the party's National Executive Committee. These intra-regional and regional–national conflicts have only intensified with the

[55] Constitutional Amendment Act 3 of 2003.

[56] See, N Steytler and J de Visser, 'Local Government' in S Woolman et al (eds), *Constitutional Law of South Africa*, 2nd edn (Cape Town, Juta, 2007) ch 22.1(e).

[57] M Mataboge, 'ANC North West Leaders Face Chop', *Mail and Guardian Online* (12 July 2009), available at www.mg.co.za/article/2009–07–12-anc-north-west-leaders- face-chop.

split in the ANC that led to the formation of the Congress of the People (COPE). This confusion, between the role of national government officials, who must act within the strictures of the Constitution, and the principles of co-operative government and the actions of the ANC as a political party in which the same individuals assert political authority, is especially fraught given the political dominance of the ANC in eight of the nine provinces.

B. Independent Institutions

As South Africa prepared for its first democratic elections after the political opening, announced by FW de Klerk in February 1990, questions arose about the management of the forthcoming elections. Up until 1990, the government had organised and managed all elections. But many people raised serious concerns about the legitimacy of the first democratic election if the apartheid regime was to conduct it, especially if conflict were to arise over the results. The liberation movement sought to resolve this problem by calling for the installation of an interim government, as called for in the internationally sanctioned Harare Declaration. However, the incumbent regime argued that there could be no handover of power until a negotiated solution, insisting on legal continuity between the existing state and any future legal order. Faced with an irresolvable tension, the ANC explored the option of creating a number of independent bodies to oversee the transition to democracy, including an independent electoral commission to manage the election. The democratic transition was thus facilitated in the period leading up to the first democratic election by establishing three independent institutions:[58] the Independent Electoral Commission,[59] the Independent Media Commission[60] and the Independent Broadcasting Authority.[61]

The embrace of this idea and the legal institutions it spawned fit well in this period with the global emphasis on expanding democratic constitutionalism. And it set the stage for a significant embrace of the idea of 'state institutions supporting constitutional democracy' that became an

[58] See, H Klug, 'Constitution-making, Democracy and the "Civilizing" of Unreconcilable Conflict: What Might we Learn from the South African Miracle?' (2007) 25 (2) *Wisconsin International Law Journal* 269.

[59] Independent Electoral Commission Act 150 of 1993.

[60] Independent Media Commission Act 148 of 1993.

[61] Independent Broadcasting Authority Act 153 of 1993.

important innovation in the final Constitution. Chapter 9 of the Constitution establishes six separate institutions: the Public Protector; South African Human Rights Commission; the Commission for the Promotion and Protection of the Rights of Cultural, Religious and Linguistic Communities; the Commission for Gender Equality; the Auditor General; and the Electoral Commission. The Constitution establishes these institutions as 'independent, and subject only to the Constitution and the law', and requires them to be 'impartial' and to 'exercise their powers and perform their functions without fear, favour or prejudice'.[62] However, the translation of this promise into the reality of functioning institutions has been more difficult. From internal personnel conflicts to external challenges to their functioning, legitimacy and financial independence, these institutions have remained embroiled in controversy. Apart from the Electoral Commission—which has now successfully managed four electoral cycles in addition to local government elections—and the Auditor General, which, as a pre-existing institution, had an institutional culture and staff in place, the remaining Chapter 9 institutions have struggled to define their constitutional roles. Issues of adequate financing and accountability—as well as the political careerism and resulting caution of some of the office-holders in these institutions—have led to questions about the degree of independence these institutions really enjoy or exercise.

When the government decided to initiate a review of these institutions after 10 years, it realised that it would not be appropriate for the executive to conduct such a review. Instead, the executive called upon the National Assembly, to which the Constitution makes these institutions accountable, to conduct a review. Thus, in September 2006 the National Assembly adopted a resolution appointing an ad hoc multi-party committee to review the Chapter 9 institutions and the Public Service Commission. In its mandate, the committee was asked 'to assess in broad terms whether the current and intended legal mandates of the institutions are suitable for the South African environment, whether their consumption of resources is justified in relation to their outputs and contribution to democracy' and most significantly, 'whether a rationalization of function, role or organization is desirable or will diminish the focus on important areas'.[63] The report of this committee, which was chaired by

---

[62] 1996 Constitution s 181(2).

[63] Republic of South Africa, Minutes of Proceedings of National Assembly, No 46–2006 Third Session, Third Parliament, Thursday, 21 September 2006, 4(2)(a).

ANC stalwart and Member of Parliament Kadar Asmal, was issued in mid-2007 and called for significant reform of these institutions.[64] The committee identified an apparent 'lack of consistency and coherence in approach' that it argued 'is ultimately undermining of . . . [these institutions'] individual, and even common, efforts'. And the report calls on Parliament to conduct an urgent review 'for the purposes of identifying a more systematic approach, particularly those regarding funding and budgets, the appointment of commissioners, collaboration between the institutions, internal governance arrangements and the relationship of the institutions with Parliament'.[65]

One of the report's key recommendations was that a number of the Chapter 9 and related institutions—such as the Pan-South African Languages Board and the National Youth Commission—be consolidated into the Human Rights Commission (HRC). Recognising that the existing plethora of human rights institutions were products of the particular circumstances of South Africa's democratic transition, the report argues that 'the present institutional framework has created fragmentation, confounding the intention that these institutions would support the seamless application of the Bill of Rights'.[66] Furthermore, the report notes that despite internal staff conflicts and a failure to amend the Human Rights Commission Act of 1994 to make it consistent with the requirements of the 1996 Constitution, the HRC has continued to expand and develop its activities. For example, the number of complaints the HRC has received from the public has increased from 5,762 in 1999–2000 to 11,710 in 2005–06.[67] The Committee also noted the progressive improvement in the six Socio-Economic Rights reports issued by the HRC, culminating in the 2006 report that showed a 'vast improvement in the manner in which information is solicited from government departments and the accuracy with which that information is reported'.[68] Despite the report and concerns that the Chapter 9 institutions continue to suffer internal tensions and overlapping mandates, there has been no attempt to make needed reforms. Two years after the release of the

[64] Parliament of the Republic of South Africa. Report of the ad hoc Committee on the Review of Chapter 9 and Associated Institutions. A Report to the National Assembly of the Parliament of South Africa, Cape Town, South Africa (2007), available at www.parliament.gov.za. [Hereinafter Report on the Review of Chapter 9].

[65] Report on the Review of Chapter 9, p 19.

[66] Report on the Review of Chapter 9, p 37.

[67] Report on the Review of Chapter 9, p 179.

[68] Report on the Review of Chapter 9, pp 179–80.

report, Kader Asmal, deeply distressed by the failure of the government and the National Assembly, in particular, to take up the report in a timely fashion, publicly accused Parliament of having no interest in his review of Chapter 9 institutions charged by the Constitution with protecting democracy, saying that the failure to debate the review was 'an appalling scandal'.[69]

In contrast to the Human Rights institutions, which have had internal problems but have largely remained outside of intense public controversy—except maybe the Human Rights Commission's investigation into racism in the media—the Auditor General and the Public Protector have both been directly involved in the intense conflicts over allegations of corruption in the 'arms deal' and 'oilgate', questions that implicate both the ANC as a party and senior members of government. While it was the Auditor General who first raised concerns about the 'arms deal' by declaring it a 'high risk' and requesting permission to investigate it, the Auditor General's office has also avoided direct confrontation with government agencies and institutions it is required to monitor by developing the practice of providing 'qualified audits', which are neither followed up upon or seen to be as serious as those cases in which the Auditor General declares an adverse audit indicating that severe problems have been detected.[70] The Public Protector has, however, remained a lightning rod of criticism for the institution's unwillingness to confront government—and most specifically for the 2005 report that the Public Protector issued in response to complaints about the misappropriation of public funds by the Petroleum Gas and Oil Company of South Africa (PetroSA), a state oil company accused of advancing R15 million in public funds to a private company, Invume Investments, which, in turn, donated R11 million to the ANC.[71] Concerns about the unwillingness of the Public Protector to investigate some of these allegations and the report's whitewash of other allegations were only heightened when the North Gauteng High Court set

[69] M Mateboge, 'Asmal Takes On Parliament', *Mail and Guardian Online* (20 July 2009), available at www.mg.co.za/article/20090720asmaltakesonparliament.

[70] See, Auditor General, National General report of the Auditor General: on the audit outcomes of Departments, Constitutional Institutions, Public Entities and other entities for the financial year 2007–08, RP 06/2009, available at www.agsa.co.za/audit-reports/National.aspx.

[71] The Report of the Public Protector on an Investigation into an Allegation of Misappropriation of Public Funds by the Petroleum, Oil and Gas Corporation of South Africa, trading as PetroSA, (the PetroSA Report) was submitted to Parliament as Report No 30 on 29 July 2005.

aside the report in a ruling on 30 July 2009. Concerns about the Public Protector were further exacerbated following strong public reaction to the news in early October 2009 that the outgoing Public Protector, Lawrence Mushwana, had received a golden handshake of R6.8 million in addition to the luxury car he was entitled to purchase from the government at the end of his seven-year non-renewable term. On 19 October 2009, President Zuma's appointment of Thulisile Madonsela—a well-respected human rights advocate and constitutional lawyer—as the new Public Protector provided some hope that this institution might yet fulfil the constitutional role it was envisioned to play.

C. The Fiscal Constitution

Much like other new post-Cold War Constitutions, the 1996 Constitution includes a range of provisions that together constitute a fiscal Constitution.[72] It created a number of specific institutions, including a Central Bank,[73] national treasury[74] and a constitutionally independent Financial and Fiscal Commission,[75] and it also mandated Parliament to create legislation providing for a range of fiscal functions.[76] While the independence and impartiality of the Financial and Fiscal Commission is constitutionally required, the South African Reserve Bank, as the central bank, is guaranteed a relative independence through the constitutional requirement that the Bank pursue its primary objective—protecting the value of the national currency—'independently and without fear, favour or prejudice'.[77] The Bank is required to consult regularly with the Minister of Finance, who is in charge of the national treasury, an institution that Parliament is constitutionally required to legislate into existence.

Significantly, the impetus for constitutionalising the financial structure of the post-apartheid state came from both without and within the borders of South Africa. Globally, the late 1980s and early 1990s saw an

[72] See, 1996 Constitution, c 13: Finance.
[73] 1996 Constitution ss 223–35.
[74] 1996 Constitution s 216.
[75] 1996 Constitution ss 220–22.
[76] 1996 Constitution ss 213 (National Revenue Fund), 214 (Equitable shares and allocations of revenue, 215 (National, provincial and municipal budgets), 217 (procurement), 218 (Government Guarantees) and 219 (Remuneration of persons holding public office).
[77] 1996 Constitution s 224(2).

emphasis on deregulation and the idea of market independence, requiring a loosening of currency controls and the segregation of the state's fiscal structures from the pressures of governmental and electoral politics. Domestically, the debate over regionalism and the demands for provincial autonomy in the democratic transition required the establishment of commitments and the creation of institutions that would guarantee the equitable distribution of resources to the different regions, even if they were politically hostile to the government. The result is a fiscal Constitution that guarantees a market-based valuation of the currency—which is so important to foreign investors and the domestic elite—as well as a national treasury that ensures that the bulk of income in the form of indirect taxes, such as the national value added-tax (VAT), is collected and gathered at the national level before it is distributed to the regions. The regions are guaranteed a fair share of national revenue through a national legislative process that has to consult with the Fiscal and Financial Commission and take a range of constitutionally determined factors into consideration, and the Constitution also provides for distinct aspects of provincial and local government finances.

D. Public Administration and Governing Principles

The distinct fragmentation of executive power that the Constitution seeks to achieve is further augmented by an attempt to frame the form of governance practised in these different institutional locations. The technique the Constitution adopts for achieving this common standard of governance is reflected in a series of provisions that prefigure the specific institutional and functional sections of the Constitution with a set of principles meant to guide those engaged in the different realms of executive authority. The Constitution contains a number of sets of principles, including those guiding intergovernmental relations and establishing the role of the independent institutions supporting constitutional democracy. However, the principles most pertinent to the exercise of executive authority are the 'basic values and principles governing public administration' as well as those governing national security. The principles of public administration include transparency, responsiveness, representivity, efficiency, participation and the admonishment that '[p]ublic administration must be develop-oriented'.[78] In order to institutionalise

---

[78] 1996 Constitution s 195(1)(c).

these principles, the 1996 Constitution consolidated the provincial and national public service commissions created under the interim Constitution into a single national Public Service Commission. More recently, efforts to improve the public service have led to calls for the consolidation of all civil servants into a single national civil service.

Concerns over capacity, especially at the local government level, have driven this process of consolidation. Yet the net effect has been to reduce local autonomy, as increasingly decisions about civil service appointments have been centralised. Antagonism to this consolidation of power is reflected in complaints and concerns over the ANC's policy of cadre deployment and the feeling by opposition parties and others that the outcome is an increasing conflation of state and party. In this regard, the ANC has also faced internal tensions when local and regional branches have refused to accept the designation of local candidates for election by the ANC head office or have resisted attempts by the party to intervene in intra-party conflicts at the local and regional levels. Although there is little evidence that the principles of public administration have been used to challenge any aspect of this process, it is clear that the consolidation of the public service into a single national public service will require a constitutional amendment. Section 197(4) specifically provides that the '[p]rovincial governments are responsible for the recruitment, appointment, promotion, transfer and dismissal of members of the public service in their administrations'. This provision also makes it clear that this local or regional authority is constrained by the general 'framework of uniform norms and standards applying to the public service'.[79]

In addition to the general principles of public administration, the governing principles that preface sections establishing various institutions—including the state institutions supporting constitutional democracy and the security services—include specific requirements that define the legitimate policy goals of these institutions. The principles governing national security specifically state that 'national security must reflect the resolve of South Africans ... to live as equals, to live in peace and harmony, to be free from fear and want and to seek a better life'.[80] Significantly, the security provisions of the Constitution also provide for different forms of civilian oversight of the defence, police and intelligence services. These include civilian secretariats for the defence force and police as well as a civilian

---

[79]   1996 Constitution s 197 (4).
[80]   1996 Constitution s 198 (a).

inspector—who is nominated by the President but must receive a two-thirds vote of approval in the National Assembly—to oversee the intelligence services. Finally, the idea of institutional and practical independence for different governmental institutions is highlighted by the recurring admonishment that particular institutions and government functionaries are 'subject only to the Constitution and the law' and must exercise their authority 'impartially and without fear, favour or prejudice'. This mantra is repeated in reference to the judiciary, the national prosecuting authority, the state institutions protecting constitutional democracy and the central bank.

E. Executive Governance and the Politics of Accusation

This repeated framing of the law as a neutral arbiter of power came under increasing stress during the latter years of the Mbeki presidency. The Constitution attempts to distribute executive authority among a variety of institutions to mediate the effects of concentrated power—particularly within a polity in which the dominance of a single political party seems relatively secure for the foreseeable future. However, the emergence of a unipolar democracy effectively limits the relative independence of these institutions. These effects were most evident in the political struggles among different factions of the ANC at every level of government. Most dramatic were the accusations of corruption that led to the dismissal of Jacob Zuma from the post of Deputy President and the counter-accusation that President Mbeki improperly influenced the National Prosecuting Authority in that case, an accusation that ultimately led to Mbeki's resignation as President. The fact that a High Court judge endorsed these claims of political interference hastened Mbeki's departure and thus had powerful political consequences, despite the fact that the High Court's decision was subsequently overruled and severely criticised by the Supreme Court of Appeals.

Aside from this dramatic example of the way in which law and legal process are being used to wage and resolve political struggles for power within the ruling party, there are also myriad examples where government officials, high and low, have been accused of corruption or other wrongdoing while the legal and administrative process has allowed different factions to gain access to positions of power and authority as those accused are suspended with full pay from their government positions.

The most notorious cases during this period included the suspension and later trial of Deputy President Jacob Zuma (for rape); the Commissioner of Police Jackie Selebi (for corruption); the Director-General of the National Intelligence Agency Billy Masetlha (accused of withholding information from the Inspector-General of intelligence and fraud). There were also official Commissions of Enquiry into accusations against the former head of the National Prosecuting Authority (NPA) Bulelani Ngcuka (accused of being an apartheid spy) and into whether Vusumzi 'Vusi' Pikoli (Ngcuka's successor as head of the NPA) was fit to hold office despite his firing by President Mbeki. The net effect is that while some officials are excluded from processes of procurement and authority that have become the lifeblood of patronage and power, they continue to receive their government salaries and benefits, thus allowing them to continue to engage in the political struggles that led to their unmasking or possibly malicious denouement. Add to this the fact that the government has, in many cases, covered the legal costs of those accused of wrongdoing in their official capacities, and the result is a new process of political struggle through law within the executive branches of the post-apartheid South African state.

The President is duty-bound to 'uphold, defend and respect' the Constitution,[81] and members of Cabinet are also formally responsible 'collectively and individually to Parliament'.[82] However, the task of achieving executive accountability remains a constant source of tension within the political and legal spheres in South Africa. In addition to these general constitutional forms of accountability, Cabinet members are required to abide by a code of ethics that the President published on 28 July 2000 as required by section 2 of the Executive Members Ethics Act adopted by Parliament in 1998. The Constitution specifies—and the Executive Ethics Code re-emphasises—that members of Cabinet must individually refrain from undertaking other paid work; they cannot use their positions to enrich themselves or others; or act in ways that are inconsistent with their offices or involve themselves in situations that might give rise to conflicts of interest between their 'official responsibilities and private interests'.[83] The Ethics Code furthermore requires Cabinet members to declare any 'personal or private financial interest' they might have in matters that are before the executive body, and in the

---

[81]   1996 Constitution s 83(b).

[82]   1996 Constitution s 92(2).

[83]   See 1996 Constitution s 96(2) and Executive Ethics Code para 2.3.

case of a conflict of interests either withdraw from the decision-making process or ask the relevant Premier or President for permission to participate. In addition, Cabinet members have a duty to report these interests to the Secretary of Cabinet. Nevertheless, accusations over violations of the Code of Ethics have led to a series of investigations by the Public Protector, including a general investigation into reporting failures where the Public Protector concluded that there had been no violation of the Code because the databases the Auditor General relied upon were not always up-to-date and there was a 'misunderstanding in regard to the interests that Ministers and Deputy-Ministers are obliged to disclose'.[84] Thus, despite an elaborate constitutional and legislative framework for ensuring executive accountability, the implementation of these processes is a continuing source of controversy. This situation led President Zuma to create a new anti-corruption Cabinet team in late November 2009.

V. CONCLUSION

Executive authority lies at the heart of effective government. The control of executive power remains one of the most difficult problems in any constitutional framework. The 1996 Constitution takes up this challenge by empowering the President and seeking to fragment executive authority by creating a range of independent institutions to exercise particular aspects of executive power and to serve as checks on the abuse of executive authority. While the more traditional checks on the executive have proven rather anaemic in the context of South Africa's unipolar democracy, the specialised institutions designed to protect constitutional democracy and disperse authority among relatively independent institutions have proven no less vulnerable. In the case of Parliament, major oversight committees were effectively neutered by party bosses while 'question time'—that mainstay of the Westminster system—was undermined by changing the rules to shorten the time devoted to questions and answers and by the tendency of Cabinet Ministers to avoid attending the relevant sessions of the National Assembly or to simply refuse to provide adequate responses. Again, the dominance of a single party makes it difficult to establish accountability in the face of party solidarity or outside

---

[84] See, Report on an Investigation in Connection with Compliance by Ministers and Deputy Ministers with the Provisions of the Executive Ethics Code relating to the Disclosure of Financial Interests, Report of the Public Protector, No 2/2006, p 4.

the party caucus. Despite these limitations, the executive structure provided by the Constitution has survived intense political conflict and managed to sustain stable governance over the first 15 years of democracy.

FURTHER READING

Calland, R, *Anatomy of South Africa: Who Holds the Power?* (Cape Town, Zebra Press, 2006).

Chothia, F and Jacobs, S, 'Remaking the Presidency: The Tension between Co-Ordination and Centralization' in S Jacobs and R Calland (eds), *Thabo Mbeki's World: The Politics and Ideology of the South African President* (Pietermaritzburg, University of Natal; London, Zed Books, 2002)

Gevisser, M, *A Legacy of Liberation: Thabo Mbeki and the Future of the South African Dream* (Basingstoke, Palgrave Mascmillan, 2009)

Murray, C and Stacey, R, 'The President and the National Executive' in S Woolman et al (eds), *Constitutional Law of South Africa*, 2nd edn (Kenwyn, Juta, 2007)

Parliament of the Republic of South Africa (2007). Report of the ad hoc committee on the Review of Chapter 9 and Associated Institutions. A Report to the National Assembly of the Parliament of South Africa, Cape Town, South Africa, available at www.parliament.gov.za.

8

Constitutional Role of the Courts

————————

Introduction – Historical Context – Creation of the Constitutional Court – Strategic Engagement and Judicial Pragmatism – Conclusion: Rights, Politics and the Margins of Judicial Power

I. INTRODUCTION

SOUTH AFRICA'S DEMOCRATIC transition fundamentally changed the role of courts in the constitutional system. The courts have been empowered by the introduction of constitutional review, and they have also been fundamentally reshaped as their demographics have slowly shifted to reflect the composition of the country. At the same time, there has been an increasing turn to the law and courts as a means and venue to resolve both political and social conflicts. While all levels of the courts—except the Magistrates' courts—are active in the project of constitutional review, it is only the Constitutional Court that has the ultimate power to overturn a legislative Act of the national Parliament or an action by the President. As the Constitutional Court has gained global recognition and respect, increasing concern over the criminal justice system and involvement of the judicial system in highly charged legal conflicts involving various constitutionally created institutions—and some of the country's senior politicians—has brought political tension to the new status and role of the courts.

A. Product of the Democratic Transition

The Constitutional Court is a product of the country's democratic transition away from apartheid in the early 1990s. The creation of a

Constitutional Court was an essential element in facilitating the democratic transition through a two-stage process of constitutional change. In the first stage, the country adopted an interim Constitution and held a democratic election to elect a new government and a legislative body whose two houses met jointly to form a Constitutional Assembly. The second stage saw the Constitutional Assembly produce a final Constitution for post-apartheid South Africa. This two-stage process was facilitated by an agreement to adopt a set of Constitutional Principles that would be attached as a schedule to the negotiated interim Constitution and which would provide the framework for the democratically elected Constitutional Assembly to formulate a final Constitution. The Constitutional Court was then required to certify that the Constitutional Assembly had remained loyal to the Constitutional Principles, thus completing the Constitution-making process established in the interim Constitution.

While both of the new Constitutions introduced extensive Bills of Rights as a response to the country's history of colonialism and apartheid, the Constitutional Principles promised those who would lose power in a democratic election that their fundamental concerns would still be addressed in the final constitutional dispensation, despite their loss of representative power. In order to guarantee this outcome, the negotiating parties agreed that a Constitutional Court would serve the unique function of certifying whether the final Constitution produced by the Constitutional Assembly conformed to the parameters of the Constitutional Principles. Furthermore, many participants in the struggle for democracy had experienced the failures of new post-independence governments in Africa and other post-revolutionary governments, which came to power with promises of freedom and liberation but became increasingly repressive. As a result, many in the liberation movement believed that institutional restraints on power, including constitutional review, were not merely a sop to those who were losing power, but an essential part of guaranteeing the promise of liberation itself. The Constitution thus formally proclaims that it is the supreme law of the land and explicitly grants the Constitutional Court the authority to act as the final arbiter of the meaning of the Constitution.

B. Paradox of Democracy and Constitutional Review

The rejection of tyranny and the embrace of rights seem to be logical reactions to a period in which rights were systematically violated. However, these aims do not explain why South African society would turn to the judiciary to protect such rights. This was particularly striking because the judiciary (and the law in general) was intimately associated with the construction and maintenance of the prior oppressive regime. In South Africa, judicial review of legislative authority had historically been explicitly rejected. And in the period just prior to the democratic transition all the major parties remained committed to notions of democracy that assumed a democratic South Africa would continue to embrace parliamentary sovereignty. In fact, the struggle against apartheid was always understood as a struggle against racial oppression and minority rule, and conversely, as a struggle for majoritarian democracy. This history makes the empowerment of judges in a democratic South Africa not just unnecessary to the goals of democratisation, but a rather unexpected outcome of the democratic transition.[1]

II. HISTORICAL CONTEXT

A. The Courts, Judiciary and the Rule of Law under Apartheid

Despite attempts by participants in the anti-apartheid struggle to defend themselves in the courts against the abuses of the state,[2] it was only in the last decade of the apartheid era that they began to actively engage the judiciary in an attempt to challenge apartheid laws and to create legal spaces for contesting the policies and actions of the apartheid state.[3] Even then, although there were significant victories in the Appellate Division of the Supreme Court against the State of Emergency—such as requiring the

---

[1] See, H Klug, *Constituting Democracy: Law, Globalism and South Africa's Political Reconstruction* (Cambridge, Cambridge University Press, 2000).

[2] See generally, M Benson, *Nelson Mandela: The Man and the Movement* (London and New York, WW Norton, 1986); L Foreman and ES Sachs, *The South African Treason Trial* (New York, Monthly Review Press, 1958); N Mandela, *No Easy Walk to Freedom: Speeches and Documents*, ed by R First (London, Heinemann, 1965).

[3] See, RL Abel, *Politics by Other Means: Law in the Struggle Against Apartheid, 1980–1994* (New York, Routledge, 1995).

police to account for their actions[4]—it is important to distinguish the Supreme Courts from the lower courts. In highly publicised inquest hearings and in what came to be described in the lower courts as a system of 'punishment by process'[5], the majority of participants in the legal system have experienced a different reality. For example, more than 70 political detainees are known to have died in security police detention between 1963 and 1990, and the courts repeatedly exonerated their torturers

> either because the conspiracy of silence and outright lying by police officers made it impossible to reach the truth or because the courts too readily believed the fairytales proffered as fact . . . [and] in the face of glaring evidence to the contrary, they resolutely declared that no one was to blame.[6]

Furthermore, critics charge that the Magistrates' Courts acted 'as part of the state's disciplinary machinery'.[7] This was most evident in the stream of 'public violence' (punishment by process) cases that passed through the Magistrates' Courts after 1985. Mass arrests, including 'substitute arrests—brother for brother, father for son, neighbour for neighbour'; assaults and torture, followed by detention while awaiting trial; and protracted court proceedings often ended in dismissals for lack of evidence.[8] Nine months of monitoring by the Black Sash (a human rights organisation made up predominantly of white women) revealed 'that 42% of those accused were juveniles, and that only 13% of adults and 17% of juveniles were found guilty'.[9] The Black Sash concluded that

> very large numbers of innocent people are arrested in random fashion and charged on flimsy evidence that cannot stand up to examination in court. They are thus made to endure a protracted period of punishment by process with little hope of redress . . . When the accused are acquitted or discharged, the family is too weary and disturbed to want to face any suit for wrongful arrest or further court proceedings: it is sufficient to be free.

Even the superior courts came under direct criticism in the mid-1980s, after anti-apartheid lawyers, who had gained early court victories against

[4] N Haysom and S Kahanovitz, 'Courts and the State of Emergency', in G Moss and I Obery (eds), *South African Review* 4 (Braamfontein, Ravan Press,. 1987) 192.

[5] M Crewe, *Punishment by Process*, SASH (May 1987), 19–20.

[6] G Bizos, *No One to Blame?: In Pursuit of Justice in South Africa* (Cape Town, David Philip, 1998) 6–7.

[7] Haysom and Kahanovitz, 'Courts and the State of Emergency', above n 4, 191.

[8] Ibid.

[9] Haysom and Kahanovitz, 'Courts and the State of Emergency', above n 4, 20.

the worst restrictions of the State of Emergency, began to lose their cases in the Appellate Division. A wave of successive judgments by the Appellate Division demonstrated that the state had virtually unlimited power under Emergency provisions.[10] Criticism came particularly from external bodies such as the International Commission of Jurists, whose observer at the treason trial of Helene Passtoors in 1986 concluded that there is 'justification to the viewpoint of black people and concerned whites that most South African courts in their uncritical and "positivist" approach to apartheid legislation merely serve as instruments of repression'.[11] Thus, while it may be reasonable to believe that the victims of apartheid would support the introduction of a Bill of Rights in response to the massive denial of rights under apartheid, there is less reason to believe that there should be an equivalent faith in the judiciary as the upholder of such rights.

Despite this legacy, it has been argued that black South Africans retained a significant degree of confidence in the legal system and the courts in particular.[12] This confidence, Stephen Ellmann argues, lent a 'measure of legitimacy to the legal system', which—coupled with the history of anti-apartheid lawyering—'might have encouraged South Africans to see virtue in the ideals of fearless advocacy, independent judging, and the rule of law' offering the 'promise that these same ideals would be honoured in a post-apartheid South Africa'.[13] These conclusions may seem strained, given the contrary evidence and nature of the opinion polls that Ellmann himself notes. But they do suggest that the turn to the judiciary may indeed be rooted in a confidence in the courts that survived the apartheid era. The difficulty with this proposition is twofold: First, as Ellmann indicates, a 1993 poll indicated a dramatic decline in this perceived legitimacy, the source of which cannot be adequately

[10] See, Haysom and Kahanovitz, 'Courts and the State of Emergency', above n 4, 187. See also D Basson, 'Judicial Activism in a State of Emergency: An Examination of Recent Decisions of the South African Courts' (1987) 3 *South African Journal on Human Rights* 28 and C Rickard, 'This Year's Message to Despondent Civil Rights Lawyers: Pack Your Bags', *Weekly Mail* vol 3 no 51 (24 December 1987–14 January 1988) p 8, col. 3.

[11] P Sidley, 'World Jurists Slam S.A. Courts', 2 *Weekly Mail* vol 2 no 45, (14 November–20 November 1986) p 2, col. 1.

[12] S Ellmann, 'Law and Legitimacy in South Africa' (1995) 20 *Law & Social Inquiry* 407, 425, concluded that public opinion surveys in South Africa find that 'Blacks expressed a substantial level of confidence in the legal system in 1981 and an even greater level in 1990'.

[13] Ellmann, 'Law and Legitimacy in South Africa', 409.

explained.[14] Second, to measure the legitimacy of the legal system on the basis of distinctions in attitudes between the apartheid courts, Parliament and police and then to verify its existence based on the turn to legalism in the democratic transition is methodologically confounding. While the empirical nature of poll results is extremely attractive, the qualitative data offered by Ellmann in his own reported interviews and an understanding of the role of the courts—particularly the lower courts where the vast majority of South Africans experienced the legal system—raise serious questions regarding a possible link between the standing of the courts in the apartheid period and the decision to adopt constitutional review as a central element of the post-apartheid political order.

Even the experience of the 1980s, where the courts were used as sites of struggle against unjust laws and to defend the rights of those engaged in resistance against apartheid, is unlikely to overcome the legacy of injustice meted out under apartheid laws. Rather, communities and individuals learned that the law and the judiciary were not necessarily at the whim of the executive, and that there was always the possibility—but only the possibility—of finding justice before the courts. For the majority of South Africans, the law and the judicial system were directly implicated in the construction and daily functioning of the apartheid system. This assessment of popular suspicion and limited legitimacy is reflected in the results of a study conducted in the late 1990s by James Gibson and Gregory Caldeira, who concluded that the 'Constitutional Court has not yet developed a broad stock of institutional legitimacy'.[15] They also concluded that 'courts are not always born with an endowment of legitimacy. Especially where legal institutions have been at the centre of political struggles, as they were in South Africa, newly created courts must earn the respect and trust of their constituents'.[16]

---

[14]   Ellmann, 'Law and Legitimacy in South Africa', above n 12, 427–28. In my view the problems of polling in South Africa during the 1980s and early 1990s cannot be rationalised away. Ellmann, for example, argues that the decrease in confidence expressed in the 1993 poll merely indicates disappointment following the elation experienced at the beginning of the democratic transition in 1990. Yet, another explanation may be that in 1993 those polled felt more inclined to offer their true feelings in a context where it had become clear that the democratic transition had become irreversible. Neither explanation is self-evident.

[15]   JL Gibson and GA Caldeira, 'Defenders of Democracy? Legitimacy, Popular Acceptance, and the South African Constitutional Court' (2003) 65 (1) *The Journal of Politics* 1–30, 23.

[16]   Gibson and Caldeira, 'Defenders of Democracy?', above n 15, 23–24.

Given this historical experience, it is difficult to conclude that the new Constitutional Court was in a position to draw upon either a vast reservoir of judicial legitimacy or respect for past law. It is easier to see how the new court would be able to use the past to distinguish itself as a completely new institution with a fundamentally different role in protecting individuals and promoting a culture of rights in a democratic South Africa. In fact, the Constitutional Court has treated the country's colonial and apartheid history (and its continuing legacy) as a constant backdrop and justification for its generous interpretations of rights. In its first major judgment striking down the death penalty, the justices made repeated reference to the country's recent history as a justification for their interpretative role and the purposive approach to interpretation. In his concurring opinion in *Makwanyane,* Justice Mahomed issued the most dramatic of these statements as he contextualised his reasons for striking down the death penalty:

> In some countries, the Constitution only formalises, in a legal instrument, a historical consensus of values and aspirations evolved incrementally from a stable and unbroken past to accommodate the needs of the future. The South African Constitution is different: it retains from the past only what is defensible and represents a decisive break from, and a ringing rejection of that part of the past which is disgracefully racist, authoritarian, insular and repressive and a vigorous identification of and commitment to a democratic, universalistic, caring and aspirationally egalitarian ethos, expressly articulated in the Constitution. The contrast between the past which it repudiates and the future to which is seeks to commit the nation is stark and dramatic. The past institutionalised and legitimised racism. The Constitution expresses in its preamble the need for a 'new order . . . in which there is equality between . . . people of all races'. Chapter 3 of the Constitution extends the contrast, in every relevant area of endeavour . . . The past was redolent with statutes which assaulted the human dignity of persons on the grounds of race and colour alone. Section 10 constitutionally protects that dignity. The past accepted, permitted, perpetrated and institutionalised pervasive and manifestly unfair discrimination against women and persons of colour; the preamble, section 8 and the postamble seek to articulate an ethos which not only rejects its rationale but unmistakenly recognises the clear justification for the reversal of the accumulated legacy of such discrimination. The past permitted detention without trial. Section 11(1) prohibits it. The past permitted degrading treatment of persons; section 11(2) renders it unconstitutional. The past arbitrarily repressed the freedoms of expression, assembly, association and movement; sections 15, 16, 17 and 18 accord to these freedoms the status of 'fundamental rights'. The

past limited the right to vote to a minority; section 21 extends it to every citizen. The past arbitrarily denied to citizens on the grounds of race and colour the right to hold and acquire property; section 26 expressly secures it. Such a jurisprudential past created what the postamble to the Constitution recognized as a society 'characterized by strife, conflict, untold suffering and injustice'. What the Constitution expressly aspires to do is to provide a transition from these grossly unacceptable features of the past to a conspicuously contrasting future founded on the recognition of human rights, democracy and peaceful co-existence and development opportunities for all South Africans, irrespective of colour, race, class, belief or sex.

The power of history is thus deployed by the justices of the new Constitutional Court as a way to repeatedly assert the Court's role in building a new culture of rights and to distinguish the past, including past law, as a counter-example or anti-model to itself.

III. CREATION OF THE CONSTITUTIONAL COURT

In stark contrast to the negative historical legacy of courts in South Africa, the origins of the new Constitutional Court as well as the quality of the justices appointed by the newly elected President Nelson Mandela, brought an extraordinary degree of legitimacy to the new institution.

A. The Court's Origins

Prior to the 1994 Constitution, the architecture of the South African high court system or Supreme Court was composed of a number of provincial and local divisions, which had both original and review jurisdiction with a final appeal to the Appellate Division. The executive appointed the judiciary, and as a matter of custom, its members were drawn from the ranks of senior advocates—the equivalent of barristers—in South Africa's divided bar. A number of senior advocates considered the apartheid judiciary to be tainted and were therefore reluctant to serve, and the apartheid regime tended to appoint judges that were sympathetic to its worldview. As a result, the integrity of some justices—particularly the extremely conservative Chief Justice Rabie—was increasingly brought into question. FW de Klerk's appointment of the more liberal Justice Corbett at the beginning of the democratic transition seemed to acknowledge the importance of shoring up the legitimacy of the judiciary in this period. At the same time, the liberation movement suggested a complete replace-ment, or at least vetting, of apartheid judges.

As attention shifted to the negotiation of a new Constitution, a debate began over the role of the judiciary in a new South Africa. While there was early agreement in negotiations at Kempton Park in 1993 on the principle that there should be a competent, independent and impartial judiciary that should have the 'power and jurisdiction to safeguard and enforce the Constitution and all fundamental rights',[17] the parties remained far apart in their proposals for the structure and functioning of a new court. While at first the parties seemed to agree that appointing new judges more rep-resentative of the population would be an important benefit of establish-ing a new Constitutional Court, a number of other issues continued to separate the parties. These issues included the following: whether a con-stitutional jurisdiction would be a parallel system of courts or integrated into the existing court system; whether the judges who would exercise this jurisdiction had to be senior judges from within the existing judiciary or possibly new appointees with little or no judicial experience; whether it would be a court of appeal or have first and final jurisdiction over the validity of laws; whether it would have sole jurisdiction or serve as the court of final appeal in a system of review that was integrated into the jurisdiction of the existing courts; and finally, whether the Chief Justice in an integrated court or the Constitutional Court itself as a separate body would decide if a particular matter was constitutional in nature or not, hence determining who would have the power to exercise jurisdiction in a particular case.[18]

Despite the South African Law Commission's earlier proposal that a specialist Constitutional Court be created to uphold a Bill of Rights, the government argued that such a court should not be a separate institution but rather a special chamber within the existing Appellate Division of the Supreme Court. The newly appointed Chief Justice Corbett strongly sup-ported this position. He felt that a separate Constitutional Court would undercut the prestige and authority of the Appellate Division. He was also concerned that a separate court would be considered political and thus would undermine the 'evolution of a human rights culture in South African and the legitimacy of the Constitution as the Supreme Law'.[19]

---

[17] *Third Report to the Negotiating Council, Kempton Park*, 28 May 1993, 2.

[18] See, R Spitz, and M Chaskalson, *The Politics of Transition: A Hidden History of South Africa's Negotiated Settlement* (Oxford, Hart Publishing, 2000) 191–98.

[19] Spitz and Chaskalson, *The Politics of Transition*, above n 18, 194.

Etienne Mureinik, an advisor to the Democratic Party, expressed another concern. He supported the creation of a separate Constitutional Court, but argued that 'the values of the Bill of Rights [should] permeate every corner of our law', building a 'culture of justification . . . in which every lawmaker and every official can be called upon to justify his or her actions in terms of the values for which the bill of rights stands'.[20] Despite these arguments, the two parties adopted the Technical Committee's Report and decided to create a separate Constitutional Court with final jurisdiction over constitutional matters. The existing high courts would be able to hear constitutional challenges and could decide that there was no constitutional violation in a particular case, but they would not have the power to declare a law or action unconstitutional; they would have to refer the case directly to the Constitutional Court for a decision on the constitutional issue. The Appellate Division was denied all jurisdiction in constitutional matters and was left as the highest court of appeal for all non-constitutional issues. This changed under the 1996 Constitution, which made what is now the Supreme Court of Appeals another step in the process of appeal, having the same jurisdiction as the High Courts, except as a court of appeal on all matters, including constitutional issues.

The Technical Committee proposed that Constitutional Court judges be nominated by an all-party parliamentary committee and be appointed by a 75 per cent majority of both Houses of Parliament. Initially, those involved in the multi-party negotiating process paid little attention to this suggestion. However, as the significance of the Constitutional Court became increasingly clear, a major political conflict exploded.[21] In fact, the conflict over this process brought the multi-party negotiations, once again, perilously close to deadlock. In the end, the solution was to combine the creation of a new Constitutional Court with the adoption of specific rules governing the appointment of new justices to ensure a presence of some sitting judges on the bench, thus simultaneously providing change and continuity.

---

[20] Spitz and Chaskalson, *The Politics of Transition*, above n 18, 194–95.
[21] See, E. Mureinik, 'Rescued from Illegitimacy?' *Weekly Mail & Guardian*, vol 1, no 5 (December 1993) 1; and N. Haysom, 'An Expedient Package Deal?' *Weekly Mail & Guardian*, vol 1, no 5, (December 1993) 1.

B. Appointment and Removal of Judges

Resolution of the conflict over judicial appointments to the Constitutional Court involved an elaborate compromise in which the newly elected President was required to follow three distinct processes in appointing members of the Constitutional Court for a non-renewable period of seven years.[22] First, the President appointed a President of the Constitutional Court in consultation with the Cabinet and Chief Justice.[23] Second, four members of the Court were appointed from among the existing judges of the Supreme Court after consultation among the President, Cabinet and the Chief Justice.[24] Finally, the President, in consultation with the Cabinet and the President of the Constitutional Court, appointed six members from a list submitted by the Judicial Service Commission (JSC),[25] a newly created body dominated two-to-one by lawyers.[26] Despite this inauspicious beginning, the resolution of this conflict was, with minor changes, essentially retained in the 1996 Constitution.

The final Constitution extended the period of non-renewable appointment from seven to 12 years, but also imposed a mandatory retirement age of 70 years. A subsequent constitutional amendment provides, however, that an Act of Parliament may extend the term of an individual justice.[27] Appointments to the Court are made by the President, either in consultation with the JSC and the leaders of the political parties represented in the National Assembly—in the case of the Chief Justice and the Deputy Chief Justice—or for the remaining positions on the Court, from a list of nominees prepared by the JSC after the President consults with the Chief Justice and the leaders of political parties. The JSC is required to provide three more nominees than the number of appointments to be made, and the President may refuse to appoint any of these by providing reasons to the JSC why the nominees are unacceptable; in this case, the JSC is required to provide a supplemental list. The President's power of appointment is further restricted by the requirement that 'at all times, at least four members of the Constitutional Court must be persons who

[22] Constitution of the Republic of South Africa Act 200 of 1993 [hereinafter 1993 interim Constitution] s 99(1).

[23] 1993 interim Constitution s 97(2)(a).

[24] 1993 interim Constitution s 99(3).

[25] 1993 interim Constitution s 99(3).

[26] 1993 interim Constitution s 105(1).

[27] Constitution of the Republic of South Africa Act 108 of 1996 [hereinafter 1996 Constitution] s 176(1), as amended by s 15 of Act 34 of 2001.

were judges at the time they were appointed'.[28] The President is required to remove a judge from office if the JSC 'finds that the judge suffers from an incapacity, is grossly incompetent or is guilty of gross misconduct' and the National Assembly votes by a two-thirds majority for that judge's removal.

Appointment to the Constitutional Court is also determined by the requirement that the person must be a South African citizen and that consideration must be given to the '[n]eed for the judiciary to reflect broadly the racial and gender composition of South Africa'.[29] In practice, the Constitutional Court has, despite its young age, experienced a regular change in the composition of its panel. This has occurred as a result of a number of developments, including the transfer of the first Deputy President of the Court to become Chief Justice (then head of the Supreme Court of Appeal exercising final appeal jurisdiction over non-constitutional matters), the death of Justice Didcott, numerous retirements and the fairly frequent use of acting justices when permanent members were either seconded to international organisations or on leave. The Judges' Remuneration and Conditions of Employment Act of 2001 now states that although they hold a single 12-year term of office, justices may continue until they have completed 15 years of total judicial service or reached the age of 75, whichever comes first, to ensure that those who have not previously held judicial office may still retire from the Court with a full judicial pension. Ten years after its inauguration, the justices of the Constitutional Court reflected the diversity of South Africa with two female, four white, six black, one Indian and two physically disabled justices on the 11-person panel.

While the Constitutional Court's first appointments were dominated by lawyers, judges and legal academics who had gained high stature during the struggle against apartheid—or whose integrity was recognised nationally and internationally—concern for the need to achieve or maintain racial and ethnic representation on the panel seems to have determined more recent appointments. In addition to the Constitutional Court, all other judges are appointed by the President on the advice of the JSC,[30] which must take into consideration the 'need for the judiciary to reflect broadly the racial and gender composition of South Africa'.[31]

---

[28]   1996 Constitution s 174(5).

[29]   1996 Constitution s 174(1) and (2).

[30]   1996 Constitution s 174(6).

[31]   1996 Constitution s 174(2).

Despite this constitutional admonition, constant debate continues regarding the need to transform the judiciary and what exactly a transformed judiciary would look like. For example, in 1990, no black judges served on the South African bench—outside of the apartheid Bantustans—and only one senior female judge served at that time. Today, more than 54 per cent of judges are black and non-white judges hold all the senior judicial leadership positions, including Chief Justice, Deputy Chief Justice, President of the Supreme Court of Appeal and all the Judge Presidents of the High Courts.[32]

The ANC weighed in on the debate over judicial appointments with a resolution at its National Conference at Polokwane in December 2007, which called for the establishment of '[a]ppropriate mechanisms . . . to pursue the priority of establishing an adequate pool of judicial officers who are steeped in and reflect the progressive values of our Constitution'. However, as Advocate Vuyani Ngalwana later argued in a speech before the annual conference of the Black Management Forum, 'the essence of judicial transformation lies not in packing the courts with black judges. It lies rather in packing the courts with judges who are genuinely beholden to the Constitution and the fundamental values thereof'. These 'progressive values . . . human dignity, equality and freedom', he noted, are foundational to South Africa's constitutional democracy and therefore senior judicial appointments should be based on a review of the prior judicial opinions of candidates that will reveal whether or not they are committed to these values.[33] Ngalwana emphasised the role of judicial opinions to argue that only serving judges should be considered for promotion to the Constitutional Court, which is formally open to the appointment of practising lawyers and legal academics as well as those with judicial experience. The idea that judicial appointments should be based primarily on the loyalty of the candidate to the progressive values of the Constitution as opposed to group identity or other political or social goals seems to demonstrate the distance that has already been traversed in the transformation of the judiciary from its colonial and apartheid origins.

However, the judiciary has not been immune from the sporadic internal conflicts and accusations of racism that have roiled many governmental institutions since the end of apartheid. The most public and

[32] Vuyani Ngalwana, 'Comment: How to Transform the Judiciary', *Mail and Guardian Online* (10 November 2008), available at www.mg.co.za/article/2008-11-10-how-to-transform-the-judiciary.

[33] Ibid.

contentious of these conflicts has revolved around Judge John Hlophe, Judge President of the Western Cape. From early in his tenure as head of the Western Cape High Court, Judge Hlophe became embroiled in public exchanges with members of the Cape Bar, with claims of racism and questions of propriety flung in both directions. These tensions soon led to Judge Hlophe being brought before the JSC, accused of failing to disclose business interests that may have resulted in conflicts of interest in cases he was called upon to decide. The JSC decided, however, by one vote in a racially divided decision, that he was not guilty of gross misconduct. This relatively high standard, requiring a showing of gross misconduct, is grounded in the constitutional protection of judicial independence implicit in the requirement that judges may only be removed from office if they 'suffer incapacity, [are] ... grossly incompetent or [are] ... guilty of gross misconduct'.[34] The President is required to remove the judge from office only if the JSC makes such a finding and the National Assembly adopts a resolution calling for the removal of the judge by a two-thirds majority.[35]

When all the judges of the Constitutional Court collectively lodged a complaint with the JSC in May 2008, claiming that Judge Hlophe had approached two members of the Constitutional Court and improperly sought to persuade them to decide a pending case in favour of Jacob Zuma, many observers assumed that he would be removed from office. In response to these accusations, however, Judge Hlophe brought a case before the High Court in Johannesburg. He claimed the Justices of the Constitutional Court had violated his rights to privacy, human dignity, equality, fair hearing and access to the courts and 'that their conduct failed to respect, promote and fulfil the rights in the Bill of Rights'. The premise of his claim was that the Constitutional Court had released its complaint to the media before he had had the chance to respond. Judge Hlophe also lodged a counter-complaint before the JSC in June 2008, making substantially the same claims; in this case, he asserted that the judges of the Constitutional Court were guilty of gross misconduct. When the High Court issued its decision on 25 September 2008, it divided along racial lines in Judge Hlophe's favour, by a three-to-two vote.[36] This decision

[34]   1996 Constitution s 177(1)(a).

[35]   1996 Constitution s 177(1) and (2).

[36]   See, *Hlophe v Constitutional Court et al*, in the High Court of South Africa (Witwatersrand Local Division), Case no 08/22932, Judgment of Deputy Judge President Mojapelo, issued 25 September 2008.

raised the spectre of a constitutional crisis, since any appeal would eventually have to come before the Constitutional Court, which, it was assumed, would have to recuse itself.

Amid a stream of public accusations and a growing political campaign by some of Judge Hlophe's supporters, the JSC conducted hearings and took evidence from judges of the Constitutional Court and Judge Hlophe in April and July of 2009. The JSC decided on 15 August 2009 that there was no need for a formal enquiry, since it had decided that none of the judges involved in either the complaint or the counter-complaint were guilty of gross misconduct; as a result, there was widespread condemnation of the Commission. In its decision, the Commission was careful to note that 'one of the hallmarks of a constitutional democracy is an independent judiciary' and argued that it was for this reason that the standard of judicial misconduct justifying removal was set so high.[37] While the Commission found that the behaviour did not amount to gross misconduct, it did acknowledge that Judge Hlophe had spoken to the two judges of the Constitutional Court about the pending case and that it was 'unwise and imprudent'. As the dust settled, it became clear that the JSC had not only averted a potential constitutional crisis, but also set a high standard for deciding whether a judge should be removed for gross misconduct; it had also, paradoxically, strengthened the independence of the judiciary by making it quite difficult to remove a sitting judge.

C. Jurisdiction and Relationship to the Courts of General Jurisdiction

Despite distrust of the old judicial order, participants in the political transition began to accept the idea of the Constitutional Court being the final interpreter of a new Constitution, although the exact parameters of the Court's power was left to subsequent negotiation. In fact, the Constitutional Court first created under the 1993 interim Constitution was initially placed in an equal position with the old Appellate Division of the Supreme Court of South Africa, which retained final jurisdiction over all non-constitutional matters but had no jurisdiction at all over

---

[37] See, Judicial Service Commission, Complaints of Judges of the Constitutional Court Against Judge President Hlophe and Counter-Complaint by Judge President Hlophe Against the Judges of the Constitutional Court: Decision and Reasons of the Judicial Service Commission, 28 August 2009, paras 24–27.

constitutional questions. The 1996 final Constitution retained this basic jurisdictional division; however, the Supreme Court of Appeals, which hears appeals from the High Courts, now has appellate jurisdiction over all matters, including constitutional issues,[38] with the Constitutional Court retaining original jurisdiction over direct constitutional applications[39] and serving as the final court of appeal on the Constitution.[40] Constitutional jurisdiction is, however, very far reaching; it deals with all government-related activity[41] and certain private activity[42], as well as fulfilling a duty to develop the common law and indigenous law in conformity with the requirements of the Bill of Rights.[43]

In practice, the Constitutional Court has applied rather strict criteria to those seeking direct access to the Court, preferring to allow a case to be argued up through the lower courts to get as full a development as possible of the facts and legal arguments before it reaches the Court. While the lower courts (including the Supreme Court of Appeals) may hear constitutional challenges to law and actions under the law—including legislative and executive acts—there is an express limit to their power in this regard. Any lower court decision declaring national legislation or an act of the President in violation of the Constitution must be forwarded to the Constitutional Court for confirmation before it can take effect. As a result, the Constitutional Court hears all challenges to acts of the President or national legislation. In addition to these cases, the Constitutional Court is also the final court of appeal on constitutional matters, including the question of whether an issue is a constitutional issue or not.

D. Early Decisions and the Triumph of Rights

In its first politically important and publicly controversial holding, the South African Constitutional Court struck down the death penalty.[44] Although there had been a moratorium placed on executions from the end of 1989, as part of the initial move towards a negotiated transition, possibly

---

[38] 1996 Constitution s 168(3).
[39] 1996 Constitution s 167(6).
[40] 1996 Constitution s 167(3)–(5).
[41] 1996 Constitution s 8(1).
[42] 1996 Constitution s 8(2)–(3).
[43] 1996 Constitution s 39(2)
[44] *S v Makwanyane and Another* 1995 (3) SA 391 (CC); 1995 (6) BCLR 665 (CC) [hereinafter *Makwanyane*].

as many as 400 people were awaiting execution at the time of the Court's ruling. By declaring capital punishment unconstitutional, the Court emphasised that the transitional Constitution established a new order in South Africa, in which human rights and democracy are entrenched and in which the Constitution reigns supreme. The Court's declaration of a new order based on constitutional rights was forcefully carried through in the adoption of a generous and purposive approach to the interpretation of the fundamental rights enshrined in the Constitution.

The unanimous opinion of the Court, authored by the President of the Constitutional Court Justice Arthur Chaskalson, was, however, judiciously tailored. Finding that the death penalty amounted to cruel and unusual punishment under most circumstances, Chaskalson's opinion declined to engage in a determinative interpretation of other sections of the Bill of Rights that may also have impacted upon the death penalty, such as the rights to life, dignity and equality. The individual concurring opinions of the remaining ten justices were not as restrained. Despite their concurrence in Justice Chaskalson's opinion, each of the remaining 10 members of the court went far beyond the majority opinion in their interpretation of other rights and in their prescriptions for the future trajectory of the Court's jurisprudence.

All 10 justices joined Constitutional Court President Chaskalson in giving explicit and great weight to the introduction of constitutional review. They emphasised that the Court 'must not shrink from its task' of review,[45] lest South Africa revert to parliamentary sovereignty, and by implication, to the unrestrained violations of rights so common under previous Parliaments.[46] Even the recognition that public opinion seemed to favour the retention of the death penalty was met with a clear statement that the Court would 'not allow itself to be diverted from its duty to act as an independent arbiter of the Constitution',[47] and that public opinion in itself is 'no substitute for the duty vested in the Courts to interpret the Constitution and to uphold its provisions without fear or favor'.[48] If public opinion were to be decisive, Chaskalson argued, 'there would be no need for constitutional adjudication'.[49]

---

[45] *Makwanyane*, above n 44, [22], quoting the South African Law Commission, *Interim Report on Group and Human Rights Project 58* (August 1991) para 7.33.

[46] *Makwanyane*, above n 44, [88].

[47] *Makwanyane*, above n 44, [89].

[48] *Makwanyane*, above n 44, [88].

[49] ibid.

The Court's blunt dismissal of public opinion was mediated, however, by a second line of argument that appears in a number of the concurring opinions. Here the Court grounded its approach to the death penalty in the recognition of a national will to transcend the past and to uphold the standards of a 'civilised democratic' society.[50] Society's will to break with its past and to establish a community built on values antithetical to the maintenance of capital punishment was evidenced, according to the Court, in the adoption of a new Constitution and Bill of Rights. As Justice O'Regan argued, the 'new Constitution stands as a monument to this society's commitment to a future in which all human beings will be accorded equal dignity and repect'.[51] In these arguments, the justices seemed to embrace the legal fiction of the 1993 Constitution's Preamble, which—despite its negotiated status and formal adoption by the unrepresentative tricameral Parliament—announced, 'We, the people of South Africa declare that . . . [and] therefore [adopt] the following provisions . . . as the Constitution of the Republic of South Africa'.[52]

The Court adopted a similarly strong stand in early cases that struck down legislation in violation of the equality clause and in numerous criminal cases involving both procedural and substantive rules that the Court found in violation of the Bill of Rights. In its first year, more than 64 per cent of the Court's caseload involved criminal matters, although this rate dropped to around one-third in the following two years. In considering the willingness of this new court to strike down legislation and reverse official decisions, it is important to note that the vast bulk of legislation struck down in this early period—as well as official decisions and Acts that were reversed—were based on laws and regulations inherited from the apartheid era. The old regime had insisted on legal continuity—the idea that all laws would remain in place until either reversed by new legislation or found to be inconsistent with the new Constitution by the Court—and the outcome of this approach was to indirectly empower the new Constitutional Court as it proceeded to strike down old laws and regulations without any resistance from the new democratic government. What might under other circumstances have been perceived as a counter-majoritarian, and hence anti-democratic, power was instead embraced as the triumph of human rights standards over the legacies of apartheid.

---

[50]   *Makwanyane*, above n 44, [199].
[51]   *Makwanyane*, above n 44, [344].
[52]   1993 interim Constitution, Preamble.

E. International Recognition and Constitutional Patriotism

This same boldness in upholding rights brought international attention to the new Court. From the moment the Court struck down the death penalty, it was held up around the world as a shining model, a new and progressive institution rising from the ashes of apartheid. When it first reversed a decision made by President Mandela, he welcomed the decision and publicly thanked the Court for doing its duty. By the time the Court was faced with making decisions at odds with the policies of the new government, it had garnered a significant amount of international support and recognition.

The symbolic stature of the new Constitutional Court further increased due to its project of renovating and transforming the site of a cluster of prisons, known as the 'Old Fort', located in the centre of Johannesburg. The Constitutional Court was first housed in a Johannesburg business park, but the building of the new Court building in the centre of the site of the Old Fort—along with the renovation of the Old Fort and related prison buildings into historical monuments to the history of the 'lawful' violation of rights—has placed the Constitutional Court in the midst of a project to build what has been termed in the German context 'constitutional patriotism'. This project, pursued more vigorously by some justices in particular, seems to be aimed at solidifying the historic role of the Court in the building of a new South Africa. Despite continuing social inequalities and, at times, blatant disrespect for rights by some government officials, government consistently and publicly asserts the notion that South Africa is building a culture of rights based on the new Constitution. As long as the political leadership in all branches of government continues to declare that the Constitution is South Africa's highest achievement in the transition away from apartheid, the Court will be able to pursue its public promotion of a culture of rights and constitutional supremacy, through its decisions and the articulation of a project of constitutional patriotism.

There can be little doubt that the Constitutional Court is one of the most successful institutions to emerge in post-apartheid South Africa. Not only is it the guardian of the political transition's most explicit symbol—the final Constitution—but unlike all other branches of government, the Court began its life as a brand new institution, its personnel largely untainted by apartheid. Its most explicit task is to uphold the promise of rights that embody the hopes and aspirations of those who struggled against apartheid. These attributes do not, however, guarantee power or authority, given the inherent institutional limits of an apex Court. Instead, the Court has used its symbolic authority to publicly engage in what has been termed a 'post-liberal' or 'transformative constitutionalism'[53]—a rejection of the negative past, a generous interpretation of rights and a commitment to 'inducing large-scale social change through nonviolent political processes grounded in law'.[54] Yet the Court has always wielded this power with a strategic eye to its own role, in what may be paradoxically viewed as a form of judicial pragmatism rather than the symbolic judicial activism that the Court's rights jurisprudence has led most international observers to applaud.

IV. STRATEGIC ENGAGEMENT AND JUDICIAL PRAGMATISM

Asserting a constitutional patriotism and declaring a culture of rights is all very well, but at the same time the Court has always been concerned about its own role in the new political order. Aware of their unique status within the new constitutional order, the justices of the Constitutional Court have been careful to define their own interventions as merely upholding the law and have denied claims that they might be substituting their own political decisions for those of elected officials in their roles as interpreters of the Constitution. The Court has, in fact, had to manage a number of quite explicit challenges to its role, including the demand in one case that all the justices recuse themselves because they were appointed by President Mandela; but it has remained quite conscious of the different ways in which it is responsible for ensuring the transition to democracy.

A. Jurisdiction and Authority

Despite the Constitutional Court's explicit authority to decide the meaning of the Constitution, the litigation of cases and the practice of constitutional interpretation will continue to test the bounds of this power. The universal acceptance of the Court's jurisdiction—or right to decide on the

---

[53] See, K Klare, 'Legal Culture and Transformative Constitutionalism' (1998) 14 *South African Journal on Human Rights* 146

[54] Klare, 'Legal Culture', above n 53, 50.

meaning of the Constitution—does not automatically imply agreement with the Court's decisions. While the Court has achieved a remarkable degree of legitimacy and acceptance of its authority in the first decade and a half of its existence, continuing controversy over judicial appointments and even disappointment over its limited acceptance of direct applications and some constitutional claims, keeps the question of its legitimacy and authority alive. These questions are in fact a healthy part of any constitutional order in which power to decide fundamental issues of governance is shared among a range of institutions with different degrees of democratic accountability. Although this tension may be considered an inherent aspect of constitutional democracy, the decision to have the newly created Constitutional Court decide whether the democratically-elected Constitutional Assembly had fulfilled its obligations to write a new Constitution within the bounds of the Constitutional Principles contained in Schedule 4 of the interim Constitution was an extraordinary, if not unique, grant of constitutional jurisdiction comparable only to the Indian Supreme Court's assertion of the basic structure doctrine in that Court's jurisprudence.

B. The *Certification* Judgments

Thrust into the unique role of arbiter in the second and final phase of the Constitution-making process, the Constitutional Court was faced with a number of distinct pressures. First, the democratically elected Constitutional Assembly represented the pinnacle of the country's new democratic institutions empowered with the task of producing the country's final Constitution—the end product of the formal transition. Given a history of parliamentary sovereignty and the failure of the courts to check the anti-democratic actions of the executive in the dark days of apartheid and during the States of Emergency, how was a newly appointed Constitutional Court going to stand up against the first truly democratic Constitution-making body in South African history?

Second, the credibility of the Constitutional Court was at stake. As the Court heard arguments on the certification of the Constitution, numerous sectors, including important elements within the established legal profession, openly speculated whether the Court had sufficient independence to stand up to the Constitutional Assembly, particularly over the key issue of the entrenchment of the Bill of Rights. For these lawyers it was clear that the provisions allowing the Parliament to amend the Constitution, including the Bill of Rights, by a simple two-thirds majority, were inadequate to protect the new rights guaranteed in the Constitution. From this perspective, failure to refuse to certify the text, on at least this ground—that the Constitutional Assembly had not included special amending procedures and had failed to entrench the Bill of Rights— would have amounted to a failure of the certification function, proving that the Court lacked the necessary independence to perform its role as the final arbiter of the Constitution.

Third, the Constitutional Court's certification powers were not only unique but were to be exercised on the basis of a set of Constitutional Principles negotiated in the pre-election transition. The Principles had, in the dying days of the multi-party negotiations and in the context of the COSAG rebellion, become the focus of unresolved demands leading to the incorporation of a number of contradictory Principles designed more to keep the contending participants within the process than to establish a coherent set of Constitutional Principles by which a future draft Constitution could be judged. Significantly, however, the basic framework of Principles—tracing their heritage from the ANC's *Constitutional Guidelines* of 1988, the Harare Declaration, the United Nations General Assembly Resolution on Apartheid and finally adopted by the major parties at CODESA—remained at the core of the Constitutional Principles. This basic framework, which guaranteed broad democratic participation, a justiciable Bill of Rights and an independent judiciary, provided the fundamental assumptions of the Constitutional Court's analysis of the content of the text and the Court's role in the certification process.

Fourth, the Constitutional Court's review of the text was permeated with the Court's own unarticulated assumptions with respect to the institutional implications of the new constitutionalism. These assumptions are exposed in the Court's response to those elements of the text that held implications for its own institutional role. In fact, many of the grounds upon which the Court declined to certify the text had institutional implications for the Court. For example, the Court's demands to strengthen the procedures and threshold for amendment of the Bill of Rights, its striking down of attempts to insulate the labour clause from judicial review, and the use of the presumption that a bill passed by the NCOP could be presumed to indicate a national interest overriding separate regional interests to tip the balance against the adequacy of the basket, or set, of regional powers. Thus, without explicit acknowledgement, the

Court's approach to the new text indicated a profound concern with guaranteeing the institutional prerogatives of the Court as the institutional repository of the power to decide who decides. It was this imperative to secure the role of the Court as guardian of a constitutional democracy based on the explicit foundations of constitutional supremacy that weighted the balance in the first certification judgment.

Despite its adoption after last-minute political compromises by 86 per cent of the democratically elected Constitutional Assembly, the Court declared that it was unable to 'certify' the new text of the final Constitution, in effect declaring it 'unconstitutional'. On its face, this action represented a bold assertion of the power of judicial review. Yet, the Constitutional Court's denial of certification was far more measured and subtly crafted than this bold assertion of 'unconstitutionality' implies. In fact, the Constitutional Court was careful to point out in its unanimous, unattributed opinion, that 'in general and in respect of the overwhelming majority of its provisions' the Constitutional Assembly had met the predetermined requirements of the Constitutional Principles. In effect, then, this was a very limited and circumscribed ruling. This analysis is confirmed with the benefit of hindsight, as the major political parties rejected any attempt to use the denial of certification as a tool to reopen debates; instead, the Constitutional Assembly focused solely on the issues raised by the Constitutional Court.[55]

The significance of the certification judgments thus lies in the degree to which the Constitutional Court was able to assert itself as the protector of constitutional democracy.

This role was reflected not only in the institutional confidence gained by the Constitutional Court in its first 18 months of operation, but also in the degree to which constitutionalism and the rule of law had been accepted by most South African political actors by the end of 1996. No historical precedent existed for a court to refuse to accept a national constitutional text drafted by a representative Constitution-making body; and the South African Court did so on grounds that emphasise clearly that the sovereignty of legislative bodies is to be subordinated. Yet none of the political parties questioned the legitimacy, either of the certification process itself or of the particular decisions issued by the Constitutional Court in that process.

[55] C Madlala, 'Final Fitting for the Cloth of Nationhood', *Sunday Times* (13 October 1996), p 4 col 2.

V. CONCLUSION: RIGHTS, POLITICS AND THE
MARGINS OF JUDICIAL POWER

The Constitutional Court has made many important decisions, yet some people express concern that it has yet to address a range of difficult issues that affect the majority of ordinary South Africans. Some of these issues hold the potential of confronting some of the more ingrained aspects of inequality and conflict that continue to pervade post-apartheid society. Most recently, the Court has decided a group of cases that hold profound consequences for the hopes and aspirations of the majority of South Africans. These cases include challenges to the 'customary' laws of succession on grounds of gender discrimination;[56] the KwaZulu-Natal Pound Ordinance, on the grounds that it denied cattle owners rights of equality and access to the courts;[57] and the Land Claims Court's decision that a community claiming land under the Restitution of Land Rights Act had failed to prove that their dispossession was the result of discrimina-tory laws or practices.[58] In each of these cases, the decision of the Court held important consequences for the relations of power: between men and women living under indigenous law; between land owners (usually white) and landless or land-hungry stock owners (usually black); as well as between land owners and land-claiming communities whose claims did not self-evidently fall within the terms of the Restitution of Land Rights Act.

In both the *Bhe* and *Richtersveld* cases, the majority of the Court acknowledged the constitutional status of indigenous law. In the first instance, the Court struck down a rule of customary law that discrim-inated on the basis of gender. In the second instance, the Court held that 'indigenous law is an independent source of norms within the legal sys-tem', but like all other 'law is subject to the Constitution and has to be interpreted in light of its values'.[59] The result in *Bhe* was for the Court to directly strike down—at least with respect to intestate succession—the

---

[56] *Bhe et al v Magistrate, Khayelitsha et al*, CCT 49/03, decided 15 October 2004 [here-inafter *Bhe*]

[57] *Xolisile Zondi v Member of the Traditional Council for Traditional and Local Government Affairs et al*, CCT 73/03 [hereinafter *Zondi*].

[58] *Alexkor Ltd et al v The Richtersveld Community and Others*, CCT 19/03, decided on 14 October 2003 [hereinafter *Richtersveld*].

[59] *Richtersveld* [51].

'customary' rule of primogeniture held by many traditionalists and others to be a key element of the customary legal system. In effect, the Court's decision will have a profound impact on the rights of wives and daughters who, until now, relied upon the system of extended-family obligation historically inherent in indigenous law but long since disrupted by social and economic change. On the other side, the Court's decision in *Richtersveld* recognised indigenous law as a source of land rights, thus strengthening the claims of those who have argued that their land rights—including rights to natural resources—were not automatically extinguished by the extension of colonial sovereignty over their territories. Their dispossession—through means other than the direct application of specific, discriminatory, apartheid land laws—will thus also be recognised for the purpose of claiming restitution of their land rights. Even if it is not as broad in its impact, the symbolic value of this recognition of indigenous land rights makes an important contribution to legitimising the new constitutional order among ordinary South Africans.

Finally, the *Zondi* case involved a challenge to a set of legal provisions that formed a central plank of the system of control and dispossession in the rural areas of apartheid South Africa. Under the Pound Ordinance, landowners were historically empowered to seise and impound animals trespassing on their land without notice to the livestock owner, unless the owner was a neighbouring landowner. Subsequently, the livestock would be sold if the owners could not afford the impounding fees and damages claimed by the land owner or could not be readily identified. Without notice requirements or judicial process, white landowners used these rules to exert power over members of rural communities who lived on the land as sharecroppers, labour tenants or wage labourers and held what little wealth or economic security they had in livestock. Although the rules were not racially based, they interacted with the racially based land ownership rules to structure rural social relations and to perpetuate a continuing process of dispossession as the ownership of livestock continually shifted at below-market prices from black to white farmers.

Because it was race-neutral on its face, the Pound Ordinance survived the dismantling of apartheid laws; but it nevertheless continues to have a predominantly racial effect because rural land ownership remains, even a decade after apartheid, largely in white hands. On the other side, as Justice Ngcobo noted in his opinion, are people such as 'Mrs Zondi, who belongs to a group of persons historically discriminated against by their government … which still affects their ability to protect themselves under the laws of the new order'.[60] With respect to the question of notice, the Court noted that the statute did not even require anyone to tell the livestock owners of impending sales and Justice Ngcobo pointed out that even a general public notice in government publications or newspapers is likely to be insufficient 'where a large portion of the population ... is illiterate and otherwise socially disadvantaged. Mrs Zondi is indeed illiterate. The thumbprint mark she affixed to her founding affidavit bears testimony to this'.[61] Furthermore, the statute permitted the landowner to 'bypass the courts and recover damages through an execution process carried out by a private businessperson or an official of a municipality without any court intervention'.[62] Holding the statutory scheme unconstitutional, among other reasons because its effect is to limit the right of access to the courts, Justice Ngcobo noted that the scheme removes

> from the court's scrutiny one of the sharpest and most divisive conflicts of our society. The problem of cattle trespassing on farm land ... is not merely the ordinary agrarian irritation it must be in many societies. It is a constant and bitter reminder of the process of colonial dispossession and exclusion.[63]

South Africa's experiment in constitutionalism is still young, and the conditions that gave rise to the new constitutional order—as well as the continuing problems of a post-colonial society facing the dual challenges of extreme inequality and a devastating HIV/AIDS pandemic—have brought domestic tension as well as global interest to the work of the Constitutional Court. Caught in the cross-hairs of struggles for the realisation of the extensive promise of rights entrenched in the Constitution and the limitations of governmental capacity and resources, the Court has thus far tread a careful path, avoiding the easy declaration of rights yet continuing to question government failings. At the same time, the courts themselves are undergoing transformation. Tensions over this process continue to simmer within the courts and among the courts, government and the legal profession.[64] Despite concerns that the ANC might attempt to stack the Court with judges sympathetic to the executive, two of Jacob

---

[60] *Zondi*, above n 57, [51].

[61] Ibid.

[62] *Zondi*, above n 57, [75].

[63] *Zondi*, above n 57, [76].

[64] See, 'National Judges Symposium' (2003) 120 (4) *South African Law Journal* 647–718. This is a report, including many of the speeches given, to the first plenary meeting of South African judges in 70 years and took place against a background of public controversy between senior judges and politicians.

Zuma's appointments should allay some of these fears: The first was the appointment of Judge Edwin Cameron—an openly gay, HIV-positive white jurist who publicly opposed President Mbeki's stance on HIV/AIDS. The second was Zuma's recent elevation of Judge Sandile Ngcobo—a fiercely independent jurist who is a strong proponent of democratic participation—to the position of Chief Justice. The more serious challenge facing the Court, as its composition changes and it becomes increasingly part of a 'normal society' will be whether it is able to continue to strike a balance between the need to address the legacy of apartheid—including the historic exclusion of the indigenous legal systems—and continue to uphold the claims of individual freedom and dignity that have become the hallmark of its first decade and a half.

FURTHER READING

Abel, RL, *Politics by Other Means: Law in the Struggle Against Apartheid, 1980–1994*, After the Law (New York and London, Routledge, 1995)

Bizos, G, *No One to Blame?: In Pursuit of Justice in South Africa* (Cape Town, David Philip, 1998)

Haysom, N and Kahanovitz, S, 'Courts and the State of Emergency' in G Moss and I Obery (eds), *South African Review* 4 (Braamfontein, Ravan Press, 1987)

Klare, K, 'Legal Culture and Transformative Constitutionalism' (1998) 14 *South African Journal on Human Rights* 146

Klug, H, 'South Africa: From Constitutional Promise to Social Transformation' in Jeff Goldsworthy (ed), *Interpeting Constitutions: A Comparative Study* (Oxford, Oxford University Press, 2006)

9

Co-operative Government, Regionalism and Local Government

———

Introduction – Origins and Principles of Co-operative Government – Interpretation of Regional and Concurrent Powers – Local Government and Service Delivery – Conclusion

I. INTRODUCTION

THE 1996 CONSTITUTION entrenches three distinct levels of government—national, provincial and local—and makes detailed provisions for their constitutional autonomy and inter-action. The inclusion of a specific constitutional chapter detailing the governmental structure of the country and laying down general principles of interaction among these different spheres of governance is unique in this regard.[1] The most significant of these principles is the provision requiring organs of state involved in an intergovernmental dispute to 'make every reasonable effort to settle the dispute' and to 'exhaust all other remedies before it approaches a court to resolve the dispute'.[2] Co-operative governance, in this sense, integrates the different geographic regions and discourages them from seeking early intervention from the courts; rather, they are forced into an ongoing interaction designed to produce interregional compromises through political negotiation—as has been the practice in Germany.[3]

---

[1] See Constitution of the Republic of South Africa Act 108 of 1996 [hereinafter 1996 Consitution] c 3: 'Co-operative Governance'.

[2] 1996 Consitution s 41(3).

[3] See, D Kommers, *The Constitutional Jurisprudence of the Federal Republic of Germany*, 2nd edn (Durham, NC, Duke University Press, 1997) 61–114.

South Africa's 1996 final Constitution is unlike traditional forms of federalism, which assume the relative autonomy of different political units—either formerly sovereign entities or newly created sub-divisions—and their exercise of certain specified powers. South Africa's Constitution creates a structure in which powers are simultaneously allocated and shared among different levels of government. A key aspect of this arrangement is a complex procedure for the resolution of conflicts over governance—between the respective legislative competencies, executive powers, and in relation to other branches and levels of government. Unlike its Indian and Canadian forebears, which retained central authority while allocating regional powers, South Africa's Constitution follows more closely in the footsteps of the German Constitution, placing less emphasis on geographic autonomy and more on the integration of geographic jurisdictions into separate functionally determined roles in the continuum of governance over specifically defined issues. Provision is made for some exclusive regional powers, but these are, by and large, of minor significance. All important and contested issues are included in the category of concurrent competence.

The basic structure of South Africa's 'constitutional regionalism' is reflected in the division of functional areas of legislative power into areas of concurrent and exclusive legislative competence, specified in Schedules 4 and 5 of the Constitution. And the substance of this constitutional design is contained in provisions that: (1) require joint or collaborative decision-making; (2) regulate inter-jurisdictional conflict, and; (3) secure limited fiscal autonomy. First, the Constitution provides for a second house of the national Parliament—the National Council of Provinces (NCOP)—which directly represents the provinces in the national legislative process through their provincial delegations, appointed by the legislative parties and Premiers of each province.[4] The Constitution then requires most bills to go before the NCOP, although the nature of the NCOP's role in each bill's passage will depend on the subject matter involved.[5] Constitutional amendment of the founding provisions,[6] the Bill of Rights[7] or those sections dealing specifically with the provinces—the NCOP or provincial boundaries, powers, functions or institutions—all require the support of at least six of the nine provinces. Ordinary bills must also go before the

---

[4] See 1996 Consitution ss 60–72.
[5] See 1996 Consitution ss 73–77.
[6] 1996 Consitution c 1.
[7] 1996 Consitution c 2.

NCOP, but procedure for their passage within the NCOP will depend on whether the bill involves a matter assigned by the Constitution to a particular procedure; is a matter of concurrent jurisdiction; or is an ordinary bill not affecting the provinces. Unless it is an ordinary bill not affecting the provinces, which may be passed by a mere majority of the individual delegates to the NCOP, the decision will be made on the basis of single votes cast on behalf of each of the provincial delegations. Furthermore, the Constitution requires an Act of Parliament to provide a uniform procedure through which 'provincial legislatures confer authority on their delegations to cast votes on their behalf'.[8] Conflicts between the National Assembly and the NCOP over bills affecting the provinces are negotiated through a Mediation Committee consisting of nine members of the National Assembly and one from each of the nine provincial delegations in the NCOP. This elaborate system of structures and processes seeks to create a system of enforced engagement integrating provincial and national interests at the national level. The requirement that provincial legislatures mandate their NCOP delegations serves in this context to further integrate the legislative process. In this way, provincial interests are projected onto the national agenda and regional bodies are required to debate nationally defined issues. Both processes were designed to limit provincial alienation.

Second, provision is made for the constitutional regulation of inter-jurisdictional conflict that may occur in the exercise of both legislative[9] and executive[10] powers. These provisions effectively denote the limits of this new 'regionalism'. In the case of executive authority, mirror provisions allow either the national or the provincial executives to directly intervene at the provincial and local levels, respectively, if a province or local government 'cannot or does not fulfil an executive obligation in terms of legislation or the Constitution'.[11] Although these provisions establish numerous safeguards against their potential abuse, they nonetheless pose an important limit to provincial and local autonomy. In the case of legislative authority, a whole section of the Constitution deals specifically with the circumstances under which national legislation will prevail over provincial legislation in areas where the two levels of government enjoy concurrent authority. Significantly, however, the default position is that unless the conflicting national legislation meets the criteria laid

---

[8] 1996 Consitution s 65(2).
[9] See 1996 Consitution ss 146–50.
[10] 1996 Consitution ss 100 and 139.
[11] See 1996 Consitution ss 100 and 139.

down in the Constitution, the provincial legislation will prevail.[12] This seems to grant more authority to the provinces, but in fact, the broad criteria establishing national authority over provincial competence—including where the national legislation provides for uniform national norms and standards, frameworks or policies[13]—means that provincial competence will provide a very thin shield against national legislative intrusion. It must be remembered, however, that the provinces will be significant participants in the production of such national legislation though the NCOP. Central authority is further privileged, however, by the inclusion of a provision establishing particular circumstances—including the need to maintain national security, economic unity or essential national standards—as the basis upon which national legislation may be passed, overriding even the exclusive subject matter competence secured for the provinces with respect to those areas defined in Schedule 5 of the Constitution.[14]

The third important feature of South Africa's 'strong regionalism' is the constitutional protection of fiscal distributions to the provinces so that they might, to some extent, fulfil their constitutional mandates and provincial policies independent of the national government. Again, however, this mechanism is characterised by an emphasis on integration through the Financial and Fiscal Commission (FCC)—an independent constitutionally created body that advises Parliament and the provincial legislatures on, among other things, the constitutional mandate that Parliament must provide for the equitable division of revenue among the national, provincial and local spheres of government.[15] Again, however, national government is privileged in that the taxing powers of the regional and local governments are constitutionally constrained[16] and made dependent upon national legislation.[17] And, as in the case of executive authority, the national government has a carefully constrained power through the national treasury to directly cut off transfers of revenues to the provinces—for at least 120 days at a time.[18] The outcome is a system of mediating sources of authority that aims neither to guarantee total

---

[12] See 1996 Consitution s 146(5).
[13] See 1996 Consitution sub-ss 146 (2) and (3).
[14] See 1996 Consitution sub-s 44(2).
[15] See 1996 Consitution 214.
[16] See 1996 Consitution ss 228 and 229.
[17] 1996 Consitution s 228(2)(b).
[18] See 1996 Consitution s 216.

regional and local autonomy nor to allow the national government to impose its will on these other spheres of government.

II. ORIGINS AND PRINCIPLES OF CO-OPERATIVE GOVERNMENT

Debate over the distribution of power between the different levels of government among the parties negotiating South Africa's democratic transition was both contentious and at times intractable. There were however significant changes in the understanding of the issues as claims for 'federalism' and local autonomy gave way to debates over the allocation of power and shared responsibilities of governance between different spheres of government. With the re-imaging of the ANC's initial demand for a unitary state as a claim of national sovereignty over the 1910 boundaries of South Africa, rather than its initial meaning of a central government with pre-emptive power over regional authorities, the debate became centred around the allocation and interaction of authority between the three levels of government. With this new emphasis, the issue of federalism—which the ANC had initially rejected because of its historic association in South Africa with the white opposition Democratic Party and the emasculation of governmental powers— became a central feature of the constitutional debate. Significantly, this shift was not inconsistent with the ANC's own internal organisational experience, in which its 10 regions were represented on the National Executive Committee and possess a certain degree of autonomy.

The adoption of the language of 'strong regionalism' by both the ANC and the National Party government also reflected the National Party's acceptance that the absolute veto powers of the upper house of the legislature would be limited to regional matters and its notion of political party-based consociationalism would be formally restricted to local government structures. Although the National Party government accepted the demise of its proposals for a rotating presidency and equal representation in the Senate, many of the provisions of the 1993 Constitution, and in particular its guarantee of a five-year Government of National Unity, satisfied many of the goals implicit in the apartheid government's earlier proposals. However, unlike the ANC and the National Party, the Inkatha Freedom Party (IFP) refused to concede its claim to regional autonomy, and its alliance with white pro-apartheid parties continued to threaten to disrupt the transitional process. Although factions of the IFP seemed ready to contest the elections for the KwaZulu-Natal regional government, the party's leader Chief Gatsha Buthelezi interpreted his party's poor showing in pre-election polls as cause to promote an even more autonomous position: encouraging and supporting King Goodwill Zwelethini in his demand for the restoration of the nineteenth-century Zulu monarchy with territorial claims beyond even the borders of present-day KwaZulu-Natal.

Although supporters of a federal solution advocated for a national government of limited powers, the interim Constitution reversed the traditional federal division of legislative powers by allocating enumerated powers to the provinces. This allocation of regional powers was included in a set of criteria incorporated into the constitutional guidelines and in those sections of the Constitution dealing with the legislative powers of the provinces. The IFP, however, rejected this solution, on the grounds that the Constitution failed to guarantee the autonomy of the provinces. Despite the ANC's protestations that the provincial powers guaranteed by the Constitution could not be withdrawn, the IFP pointed to the fact that the allocated powers were only concurrent powers and that the national legislature could supersede local legislation by establishing a national legislative framework covering any subject matter. This tension between provincial autonomy and the ANC's assertion of the need to establish national frameworks guaranteeing minimum standards and certain basic equalities led to an amendment to the 1993 Constitution before the Constitution even came into force. This amendment granted exclusive powers to the provinces in those areas in which they exercised legislative authority. In addition, the amendment granted exclusive jurisdiction to provincial legislatures in the following areas: agriculture; gambling; cultural affairs; education at all levels except tertiary; environment; health; housing; language policy; local government; nature conservation; police; state media; public transport; regional planning and development; road traffic regulation; roads; tourism; trade and industrial promotion; traditional authorities; urban and rural development and welfare services. Difficulty arose in distinguishing the exact limits of a region's exclusive powers and the extent to which the national legislature was able to pass general laws affecting rather broad areas of governance.

Although the provinces had the power to assign executive control over these matters to the national government if they lacked administrative resources to implement particular laws, the Constitution provided that the provinces had executive authority over all matters in which they had legislative authority as well as matters assigned to the provinces in the transitional clauses of the Constitution or delegated to the provinces by national legislation. The net effect of these provisions was continued tension between non-ANC provincial governments and the national government over the extent of regional autonomy and the exact definition of their relative powers.

A. Principles

Chapter 3 of the 1996 Constitution lays out the constitutional scheme of co-operative government. Most Constitutions rely either on the very structure of the Constitution to establish a 'federal' relationship between different regional units or provide specifically for a hierarchy of governments in which the national government allocates powers to the regions or the regions enjoy a degree of autonomy. South Africa's system of co-operative governance is unique in the way it defines different spheres of government and tries to constitutionally regulate their relative roles to facilitate intergovernmental relations across the different loci of governance in the country. Section 40(1) states that the 'government is constituted as national, provincial and local spheres of government which are distinctive, interdependent and interrelated'. The principles of co-operative government and intergovernmental relations listed in section 41(1) go on to define the specific duties that each level of government owes to the other as well as the duty of the legislature to adopt legislation creating institutions and mechanisms to facilitate intergovernmental relations and to resolve disputes between different levels of government.[19]

Apart from the general commitments to preserve peace and national unity, secure the well-being of the people and provide 'effective, transparent, accountable and coherent government', the key constitutional boundaries laid down in the Principles require each level of government to 'respect the constitutional status, institutions, powers and functions of government in the other spheres', and not to 'assume any power or function except those conferred on them in terms of the Constitution'.[20]

---

[19] 1996 Constitution ss 41(1)(a)–(h) and 41(2)–(4).
[20] 1996 Constitution s 41(1)(a)–(f).

These boundaries also require the different levels of government to 'exercise their powers and perform their functions in a manner that does not encroach on the geographical, functional or institutional integrity' of other governing authorities.[21] Instead, the Principles seek to promote an ethos of co-operation based on 'mutual trust and good faith'.[22] Finally, the Principles require an organ of state 'involved in an intergovernmental dispute must make every reasonable effort to settle the dispute . . . and must exhaust all other remedies before it approaches a court to resolve the dispute'.[23] This last element is strengthened by the provision that a court may refer a dispute back to parties involved if it is not satisfied that they have exhausted all non-legal remedies or made every reasonable effort to settle the dispute by other means.[24]

While these principles are called upon to play a symbolic and pedagogical role in shaping the behaviour of government departments and officials—both internally and in their relations with other governing units—the Constitutional Court has been called upon to apply them in related cases. Asked to confirm a High Court declaration of unconstitutionality, in a case in which district municipalities claimed they had been excluded from receiving equitable fiscal allotments by the Division of Revenue Act 1 of 2001, the Constitutional Court reviewed the Constitutional requirements of co-operative government in deciding whether to exercise its discretion to confirm the High Court's decision, despite the parties' settlement of the case.[25] In reaching its decision, the Court held that organs of state have a 'constitutional duty to foster co-operative government' and that the essence of Chapter 3 of the Constitution is that 'disputes should where possible be resolved at a political level rather than through adversarial litigation'.[26] In fact, the Court argued, the requirements of co-operative government include a duty to 'avoid legal proceedings against one another', a duty the courts must ensure is duly performed.[27] More specifically, the Court stated that 'apart from the general duty to avoid legal proceedings against one another', a twofold duty obliges organs of state in an intergovernmental dispute to

[21] 1996 Consitution s 41(1)(g).
[22] 1996 Consitution s 41(1)(h).
[23] 1996 Consitution s 41(3).
[24] 1996 Consitution s 41(4).
[25] *Uthukela District Municipality v President of the Republic of South Africa*, CCT 7/02 (2002).
[26] *Uthukela District Municipality* [13].
[27] Ibid.

'make every reasonable effort to settle the dispute by means of mechanisms and procedures provided for' and to 'exhaust all other remedies
before they approach a court to resolve the dispute'.[28]

III. INTERPRETATION OF REGIONAL AND CONCURRENT POWERS

As was the case under the interim Constitution, tensions between the
central ANC government and non-ANC controlled provinces soon
brought cases to the Constitutional Court in which the Court was called
upon to define the parameters of co-operative government. Although
wide-ranging in scope, these early cases addressed three issues central to
the question of legislative authority under the 1996 Constitution. First,
the court was called upon to define the constitutional allocation of legislative power in a case where a province claimed implied legislative powers to define the structure of its own civil service. Second, the court was
required to determine the scope of residual national legislative power in a
case where the national government claimed concurrent authority over
the establishment of municipal governments—despite the Constitution's
simultaneous allocation in this field of specific functions to different
institutions and spheres of government. Finally, an attempt by the
national government to extensively regulate liquor production, sale and
consumption—a field in which the regions were granted at least some
exclusive powers under the Constitution—required the court to define
the specific content of the exclusive legislative powers of the provinces.

One of the first such cases involved a challenge to national legislation
that sought to define the structure of the public service, including all
provincial public services. The Western Cape argued that the legislation
infringed 'the executive power vested in the provinces by the Constitution
and detracts from the legitimate autonomy of the provinces recognised in
the Constitution'.[29] The Court, however, pointed out that not only did
the national Constitution provide that the public service is to be structured
in accordance with national legislation, but also that the Western Cape
Constitution required its government to implement legislation in

---

[28] *Uthukela District Municipality* [19].
[29] *The Premier of the Province of the Western Cape v The President of the Republic of South
Africa and the Minister of Public Service*, CCT 26/98 (1999), 1999 (12) BCLR 1360 (CC) [4]
[hereinafter *Public Service* case].

accordance with the provisions of the national Constitution.[30] Describing national framework legislation as a feature of the system of co-operative government provided for by the Constitution, the Court noted that such legislation

> is required for the raising and division of revenue, the preparation of budgets at all spheres of government, treasury control, procurements by organs of state, conditions according to which governments at all spheres may guarantee loans, the remuneration of public officials at all spheres of government and various other matters.[31]

While the Court agreed that provincial governments are empowered to '"employ, promote, transfer and dismiss" personnel in the provincial administrations of the public service', the court rejected the idea of an implied provincial power depriving the national government of its 'competence to make laws for the structure and functioning of the civil service as a whole', which is expressly retained in section 197(1) of the Constitution.[32]

Turning to consider whether the national government's structuring of the public service encroached on the 'geographical, functional or institutional integrity' of the provincial government in violation of s 41(1)(g), the Constitutional Court considered the provisions of Chapter 3 of the Constitution, which deal with co-operative government. Interpreting these provisions, Justice Chaskalson, writing for a unanimous Court, emphasised that all spheres of government are 'distinctive, inter-dependent and inter-related'. He then pointed out that the 'national legislature is more powerful than other legislatures, having a legislative competence in respect of any matter' and the 'national government is also given overall responsibility for ensuring that other spheres of government carry out their obligations under the Constitution'.[33] The Court accepted that the purpose of section 41(1)(g) is to prevent one sphere of government from using its power to undermine other spheres of government and prevent them from functioning effectively. It also concluded that the section 'is concerned with the way power is exercised, not whether or not a power exists'.[34] The relevant question before the Court in this case, however, was whether the national government had the

---

[30] *Public Service* case [8].
[31] *Public Service* case [9]. .
[32] *Public Service* case [11].
[33] *Public Service* case [18] and [19].
[34] *Public Service* case [23].

constitutional power to structure the public service.[35] Justice Chaskalson argued that the power vests in the national sphere of government, emphasising that the Constitutional Principles

> contemplated that the national government would have powers that tran-
> scend provincial boundaries and competences and that 'legitimate provincial
> autonomy does not mean that the provinces can ignore [the constitutional]
> framework or demand to be insulated from the exercise of such power'.[36]

The Court did, however, strike down a clause in the law that empowered the national minister to direct a provincial official to transfer particular functions to another department (provincial or national) because such power encroached on the ability of the provinces to carry out the functions entrusted to them by the Constitution.

Although the Court seemed to come down strongly in favour of national legislative authority—at least when it is explicitly granted in the Constitution—the question of the allocation of legislative authority soon arose again. This time the case involved a dispute between the national government and the regional governments of the Western Cape and KwaZulu-Natal.[37] The provincial governments challenged provisions of the Local Government: Municipal Structures Act 117 of 1998, in which the national government claimed residual concurrent powers to determine the structure of local government, despite the provisions of the local government chapter of the Constitution, which set out a comprehensive scheme for the allocation of powers among the national, provincial and local levels of government. Considering this allocation of power, the Court recognised that the Constitution left residual legislative powers to the national sphere. However, at the same time, the Court determined that section 155 of the Constitution—which controls the establishment of local governments—allocates powers and functions among different spheres of government and the independent demarcation board so that:

> (a) the role of the national government is limited to establishing criteria
> for determining different categories of municipality, establishing criteria and

---

[35] *Public Service* case 23] and [24].

[36] *Public Service* case [25].

[37] *The Executive Council of the Province of the Western Cape v The Minister for Provincial Affairs and Constitutional Development of the Republic of South Africa; Executive Council of KwaZulu-Natal v the President of the Republic of South Africa and Others*, 1999 (12) BCLR 1360 (CC) [hereinafter, *Municipal Structures* case].

procedures for determining municipal boundaries, defining different types of municipalities that may be established within each category, and making provision for how powers and functions are to be divided between municipalities with shared powers; (b) the power to determine municipal boundaries vests solely in the Demarcation Board; and (c) the role of the provincial government is limited to determining the types of municipalities that may be established within the province, and establishing municipalities 'in a manner consistent with the [national] legislation enacted in terms of subsections (2) and (3)'.[38]

Applying this scheme to the challenged legislation, the Court found the attempt in section 13 of the Municipal Structures Act—which aimed to tell the provinces how they must set about exercising a power in respect to a matter that falls outside of the competence of the national government—unconstitutional. Despite claims by the national government that the provincial official was only obliged to take the guidelines into account and not to implement them, the Court argued that what mattered was that the national government legislated on a matter falling outside of its competence.[39] Thus, despite the Court's earlier recognition of the predominance of the national sphere of government in the scheme of co-operative government, here the Court drew the line and clarified that there was a constitutional limit to the legislative power of the national government.

Although these early cases seem on the whole to have rejected the autonomy claims of the provincial governments by recognising the commanding role of the national legislature, the Court was soon given the opportunity to explore the arena of exclusive provincial power after the national Parliament passed legislation that sought to regulate the production, distribution and sale of liquor through a nationally defined licensing scheme.[40] President Mandela refused to sign the Liquor Bill because he had reservations about its constitutionality and referred it to the Constitutional Court. The law sought in part to control the manufacture, wholesale distribution and retail sale of liquor—functions which, at least with respect to licensing, are expressly included as exclusive legislative powers of the provinces in Schedule 5 of the Constitution. Citing a 'history of overt racism in the control of the manufacturing, distribution and sale of liquor', the national government contended that the 'provi-

---

[38] *Municipal Structures* case [14].

[39] *Municipal Structures* case [20] and [21].

[40] *Ex Parte the President of the Republic of South Africa, In Re: Constitutionality of the Liquor Bill*, CCT 12/99, 11 November 1999, 2000 (1) BCLR 1 (CC) [hereinafter, *Liquor Licensing* case].

sions of the Bill constitute a permissible exercise by Parliament of its legislative powers'.[41] The Western Cape complained, however, that the

> Bill exhaustively regulates the activities of persons involved in the manufacture, wholesale distribution and retail sale of liquor; and that even in the retail sphere the structures the Bill seeks to create reduce the provinces, in an area in which they would (subject to section 44(2)) have exclusive legislative and executive competence, to the role of funders and administrators.[42]

The province went on to claim that the Bill thereby intruded into its area of exclusive legislative competence.

Faced once again with the issue of co-operative government, the Constitutional Court noted that

> [g]overnmental power is . . . distributed [at source] between the national, provincial and local spheres of government, each of which is subject to the Constitution, and each of which is subordinated to the constitutional obligation to respect the requirements of cooperative governance.[43]

Justice Cameron (serving as an Acting Judge) then proceeded to argue for a unanimous Court that co-operative governance includes the duty 'not [to] assume any power or function except those conferred on them in terms of the Constitution' and that the Constitution's 'distribution of legislative power between the various spheres of government' and its itemisation of functional areas of concurrent and exclusive legislative competence, must be read in this light.[44] Accepting that the national government enjoys the power to regulate the liquor trade in all respects because of the industry's impact on the 'determination of national economic policies, the promotion of inter-provincial commerce and the protection of the common market in respect of goods, services, capital and labour mobility', Justice Cameron concluded that the structure of the Constitution precluded the national government's regulation of liquor licensing.[45] He came to this conclusion by carefully defining three distinct objectives of the proposed law and distinguishing those functions that would apply predominantly to intra-provincial regulation as opposed to those aspects of the liquor business requiring national regulation because of their extra-provincial and even international impact. The Bill,

---

[41] *Liquor Licensing* case [33].
[42] *Liquor Licensing* case [37].
[43] *Liquor Licensing* case [41].
[44] Ibid
[45] *Liquor Licensing* case [58].

according to the Court, divided the liquor trade into three tiers and provided distinct forms of regulation for these specific aspects of the business. It provided first, for 'the prohibition on cross-holdings between the three tiers involved in the liquor trade, namely producers, distributors and retailers'; second, in an attempt to establish national uniformity in the trade, it provided for 'the establishment of uniform conditions, in a single system, for the national registration of liquor manufacturers and distributors'; and third, for 'the prescription of detailed mechanisms to provincial legislatures for the establishment of retail licensing mechanisms'.[46]

Having defined an aspect of the Bill that focused primarily on the provincial level, the Court then proceeded to define the primary purpose of granting exclusive competencies to the provinces as implying power over the regulation of activities 'that take place within or can be regulated in a manner that has a direct effect upon the inhabitants of the province alone'. In relation to 'liquor licences', it is obvious, the Court argued, 'that the retail sale of liquor will, except for a probably negligible minority of sales that are effected across provincial borders, occur solely within the province'. Given this fact, the Court concluded that the heart of the exclusive competence granted to the regions in the Constitution, in this arena, must 'lie in the licensing of retail sale of liquor'.[47]

Returning to an analysis of the 'three-tier' structure of the Bill, the Court argued that the manufacture or production of liquor, including wholesale trades in liquor, were not intended to be the primary field of 'liquor licences'.[48] The Court noted that the manufacture and production aspects have a national and international dimension, since little production is directed solely at the intra-provincial market.[49] This approach enabled the Court to simultaneously reject the Western Cape's claim of a right to regulate and control the production and distribution of liquor[50]—as these functions clearly fall outside of the primary basis for the defining of exclusive provincial competence—while framing a clear arena in which the constitutionally guaranteed exclusive competences of the provinces could be more vigorously defended. Distinguishing between licensing retail outlets, on the one hand, and manufacturing and distribution, on the other, the Court concluded that

---

[46] *Liquor Licensing* case [69].
[47] *Liquor Licensing* case [71].
[48] *Liquor Licensing* case [72].
[49] *Liquor Licensing* case [72]–[74].
[50] *Liquor Licensing* case [78].

if the exclusive provincial legislative competence regarding "liquor licences" in Schedule 5 applies to all liquor licences, the national government has made out a case in terms of section 44(2) justifying its intervention in creating a national system of registration for manufacturers and wholesale distributors of liquor and in prohibiting cross-holdings between the three tiers in the liquor trade.

However, as the Court pointed out, the national government had failed to make a case for the necessity of such national regulation in 'regard to retail sales of liquor, whether by retailers or by manufacturers, nor for micro-manufacturers whose operations are essentially provincial'. To this extent, the national Parliament did not have the competence to enact the Liquor Bill and the Bill was therefore unconstitutional.[51]

IV. LOCAL GOVERNMENT AND SERVICE DELIVERY

The early debates over regionalism in South Africa were overshadowed by reactions to the apartheid regime's policies of Balkanisation and a determination to achieve the unified state promised by the ideology of national liberation. However, many people recognised that local government was a key locus of potential conflict over social transformation. Early demands by the National Party for the protection of local community decision-making were criticised as attempts to privatise apartheid, yet the very spatial reality created by apartheid severely complicated the planning for local level democracy—distinct from the racially constituted character of local communities. As a result, the future of local government, imagined by most as the location where government is closest to the people, was sandwiched between the conditions created by local struggles and demands for effective governance. On the one hand, the negotiations over the future form of local government were left to those who had been at the forefront of the local struggles of the late 1980s. On the other hand, local government was tasked with resolving three of the most intractable issues facing the country: the delivery of public services, local economic development and democratic participation.

In order to understand the ways in which these three interrelated aspects of local government—service delivery, economic development and democratic participation—were given constitutional status and have shaped the legal structure of local government, it is important to first

---

[51] *Liquor Licensing* case [87].

focus briefly on the history of local government in South Africa.[52] Historically, municipal government in South Africa has been subject to regional authority. From before the establishment of the Union of South Africa in 1910, the four colonial entities that became the provinces of the Union had local authorities. The South Africa Act, which established the Union and served as South Africa's first colonial Constitution, gave the Provincial Councils responsibility for local authorities. This authority did not, however, apply to the African majority, which remained subject to the executive authority of the Governor-General and later the State President, with administrative power exercised by the Department of Native Affairs and its subsequent reincarnations (Bantu Affairs, Co-operation and Development, etc).

Apartheid's entrenchment of racially segregated communities—through the Group Areas Act 41 of 1950, other statutes and the policy of forced removals—created a system of spatial and governmental segregation in which nearly every 'white' municipality had one or more adjacent black urban areas or townships. The apartheid regime first attempted to create advisory bodies[53] and later elected 'Black Local Authorities' (BLAs)[54] within these communities, but these bodies were shunned, at best, and by the mid-1980s became targets of local resistance to apartheid. Elections in 1984 for the new BLAs were largely boycotted, and the subsequent attempt by these authorities to generate revenue by raising rents from the vast majority of black township residents—who were required to live in state-owned rental housing—ignited violent opposition. This urban uprising—supported by the ANC's call in January 1985 for the people to make the country 'ungovernable'—spread to approximately 155 townships around the country. The uprising led to black local councillors, police and informers being targeted as agents of apartheid. Twelve councillors were killed, and 'the homes of more than 300 were damaged and 240 resigned their posts. The BLA system set up the year before virtually ceased to exist'.[55]

[52] See, S Buhlungu and D Atkinson, 'Politics: Introduction', in S Buhlungu et al (eds) *State of the Nation: South Africa 2007* (Cpae Town, HSRC Press, 2007) 27–31 and JJN Cloete, *Central, Provincial and Municipal Institutions of South Africa* (Pretoria, JL Van Schaik, 1982) 241–81, 302–04, 311–14 and 317.

[53] Community Councils Act 125 of 1977.

[54] Black Local Authorities Act 102 of 1982.

[55] D O'Meara, *Forty Lost Years: The Apartheid State and the Politics of the National Party, 1948–1994* (Randburg, South Africa, Ravan Press; Athens, University of Ohio Press, 1996) 325–26.

In an attempt to counter these developments, the apartheid regime introduced a system of Regional Services Councils in 1985. The 47 councils created under this system attempted to provide bulk services across local racially constituted local government boundaries. This system was geared to work in tandem with the system of local security committees that had been established in 1979 to facilitate interaction between the South African Defence Force (SADF) and local civilian authorities as part of the regime's Total Strategy to defend apartheid. The jurisdiction of the 12 Joint Management Centres (JMCs) overlapped with the regional commands of the SADF. In addition to the JMCs, there were approximately 60 sub-JMCs and 448 mini-JMCs that served to integrate the military strategy with local authorities—the 12 city councils, 309 town councils, 114 village councils and 92 health committees or divisional councils that formed the basis of white local government in the apartheid era. On the other side of the political divide, the post-1979 period saw a dramatic growth in black civic associations, which came together in the South African National Civics Organisation (SANCO), and were an important part of the United Democratic Front that was launched in direct opposition to the regime's attempt to introduce a reformed form of apartheid with the 1983 'tricameral' Constitution.

The state's attempt to impose local authorities was the trigger for the 1984 uprising, which led to continuing states of emergency and the ultimate demise of the apartheid state. Yet it was also local politics that first turned to negotiations as a means to manage and eventually resolve intractable conflict.[56] Although it is true that the trade union movement, which had fought for recognition in the late 1970s, laid the basis for the later embrace of negotiations as a means of resolving South Africa's racial conflict, the local negotiations that began in response to local struggles— including rent boycotts and consumer boycotts against white business owners launched by township dwellers in towns across South Africa— served as a parallel track in the process of negotiations that led to democratic national elections in April 1994. These local negotiations and their subsequent coming together in the Local Government Negotiating Forum (LGNF) in 1993 empowered local participation in the negotiations for a democratic future. The negotiations also reflected the more restricted options available when conservative white authorities continued to

---

[56] See, E Pieterse, 'From Divided to Integrated City? Critical Overview of the Emerging Metropolitan Governance System in Cape Town' (2002) 13 (1) *Urban Forum* 3–35.

exercise local state power—even if the townships had become ungovern-able—as street committees and people's courts sought to establish alterna-tive forms of governance.

The results of these negotiations were both local and constrained. The LGNF reached early agreement on a three-phase process of trans-formation at its second plenary meeting on 30 June 1993, well before the national negotiators had reached agreement on the future of the country. However, this agreement embraced consensual decision-making and explicitly delayed the establishment of truly democratic local authorities until some undetermined time in the future. First, there would be a pre-interim phase in which members of local authorities would be appointed in equal numbers from what were termed the statutory and non-statutory sectors—that is, from those who were part of old government structures and those who were in opposition, usually activists from the local civic associations that residents had established. Second, there would be an interim phase, beginning after the first national elections, in which transi-tional local councils would be created throughout South Africa according to the provisions of the Local Government Transition Act (LGTA). These provisions were agreed upon at the LGNF; enacted into law by the undemocratic 'tricameral' Parliament; and incorporated unchanged into the 1993 interim Constitution. In addition to the LGTA, the negotiating forum produced a constitutional outline for local government that was later incorporated directly as Chapter 10 of the interim Constitution. Finally, there would be the establishment of truly democratic local gov-ernment in the final phase of the transformation, the details of which were left, in mid-1993, to a future Constitution-making process.

A. The Local Government Transition Act and the Interim Constitution

By keeping local government out of the national negotiations, the LGNF enabled local participants to engage in local bargaining and allowed them to formulate specific processes that reflected local patterns of conflict and relations of power. Yet it also constrained the pace of local transfor-mation by requiring a greater degree of co-operation than was possible to sustain at the national level. National negotiations were propelled by dra-matic events—such as the slaying of ANC and Communist Party leader Chris Hani. However, the mid-1993 agreements on local government set in place a more gradual transition, which was adopted into law and incorporated directly into Chapter 10 of the interim Constitution. The key element of this compromise was the acceptance of a form of consociationalism at the local government level, a form of governance the National Party demanded at the national level, but was ultimately rejected by the ANC. This consociationalism was manifested in the agreement to adopt forms of representation and decision-making that ensured that the white minority would have a veto when it came to decisions that would affect the distribution of resources among different parts of cities and towns. The result would ensure that the formerly white areas would continue to receive superior levels of municipal services. Tied together with the national agreement that guaranteed civil servants their existing positions for five years, it meant that there would be little redistribution of local government resources and services to the historically black and underdeveloped townships in the immediate post-apartheid era.

The initial pre-interim phase essentially formalised the existing local negotiating fora by providing that a local forum could be recognised as a transitional council if it was formed in accordance with schedule 1 of the LGTA. This statute provided that an equal number of members of a local forum be appointed from two separate sources: the so-called statutory component, which was made up of representatives from the former state-recognised local government authorities; and a so-called non-statutory component, representatives of organisations that were not formally recognised yet had an interest in the restructuring of local government. These participants were local activists, primarily members of the largely ANC-aligned local civic associations, which had come together in the South African National Civics Organisation (SANCO). Importantly, a local forum could not be appointed unless four-fifths (or 80%) of the combined statutory and non-statutory representatives in a local negotiating forum agreed to the appointment. As a result, the local white community retained a veto over the pace and nature of change in this period. Despite these limitations, the LGTA was incorporated into the interim Constitution both explicitly[57] and through the provisions of Chapter 10, which were themselves negotiated through the LGNF rather than the national Multi-Party Negotiating Forum that produced the 1993 interim Constitution.

---

[57] See, Transitional Arrangements: Local Government, s 245, 1993 'interim' Constitution.

A key part of the LGTA was the establishment of a demarcation process that began the task of redrawing apartheid's spatial map and created the basis for the democratic election of local representatives.[58] In April 1994 the government recognised 1,262 racially constituted local government entities; the demarcation process began the task of democratisation by shaping these into 843 geographically non-racial governmental units. Demarcation was also a prerequisite for the second phase of local government transformation, which required the election of 'transitional councils' based on a combined electoral system of local wards and proportional representation. While the interim Constitution stated that 'local government shall be elected democratically' and that the local government electoral system 'shall include both proportional and ward representation', there was no reference to the racial allocation of power that was embedded in the LGTA's provisions implementing these broad principles. Even within the LGTA the racial imbalances were disguised in bureaucratic language that required 60 per cent of each transitional council to be elected as representatives of wards while the remaining 40 per cent were chosen through a system of proportional representation based on party lists. The democratic imbalance in favour of minorities was, however, maintained with the requirement that wards be allocated evenly between those areas that had been within the formal system of local government prior to 1994 (Category A wards) and the former black townships in which the vast majority of the electorate lived (Category B wards). The first local government elections were held on a staggered pattern from October 1995 until June 1996 and produced an over-representation of white representatives, except in the Western Cape where the African minority were beneficiaries of this arrangement.[59]

While the ANC won the majority of elected local government seats in the 1995–96 local government elections, the pace of transformation was slowed by the structure of municipal decision-making, which was divided between management and elected officials. In addition, the requirement of super-majorities for budget decisions forced the contending sides to negotiate all major issues. Even though the national negotiators rejected the National Party's attempt to give voting rights to corporate entities that

[58]   See, LGTA s 11(1).
[59]   R Cameron, 'Local Government Boundary Reorganization', in U Pillay, R Tomlinson and J Du Toit (eds), *Democracy and Delivery: Urban Policy in South Africa* (Cape Town, HSRC Press, 2006) 78.

owned property at the local level,[60] they acquiesced to include constitutional provisions that required the following: a two-thirds majority to pass the budget of a local government;[61] an absolute majority for the adoption of town planning decisions;[62] and, when such decisions were delegated to an executive committee, the requirement that any failure to reach consensus be decided by a two-thirds majority of the proportionally appointed executive.[63] Finally, the interim Constitution also guaranteed the distribution of local government representatives in such a way as to ensure that 'irrespective of their numbers 30 % of ward-representation belong to these voters [white coloured and Indian]', thus extending the legacy of the Group Areas Act despite the formal abolishment of apartheid.[64]

B. 1996 Constitution and the Provisions for Local Government

Truly democratic local governments were established in South Africa after the local government election in 2000, which marked the end of the interim phases and the beginning of local government organised under the framework of the final 1996 Constitution. While Chapter 7 of the 1996 Constitution initially provided only broad principles for local government, the final text included a more detailed scheme after the Constitutional Court found that the original text failed to satisfy the commitments contained in the Constitutional Principles in Schedule 4 of the 1993 interim Constitution. Specifically, the Court held in its *First Certification Judgment* that Chapter 7 created no 'framework for the structures' of local government,[65] did not differentiate between categories of local government,[66] and failed to set out formal legislative procedures for local government.[67] The revised Chapter 7, by contrast, provided a detailed scheme for the creation and functioning of local government. It

---

[60] See R Spitz with M Chaskalson, *The Politics of Transition: A Hidden History of South Africa's Negotiated Settlement* (Oxford, Hart Publishing, 2000) 189–90.

[61] 1993 'interim' Constitution s 176(a).

[62] 1993 'interim' Constitution s 176(b).

[63] 1993 'interim' Constitution s 177(c).

[64] D Basson, *South Africa's Interim Constitution: Text and Notes*, rev edn (South Africa, Juta, 1995) 333. See also 1993 'interim' Constitution s 245(3).

[65] Contravening Principle XXIV. See *First Certification* Judgment [300–01].

[66] As required by Principle XXV. See *First Certification* Judgment [302].

[67] Required by Principle X, See *First Certification* Judgment, [301].

required that three categories of municipalities be established to cover the whole territory of South Africa[68] and that the objects and duties of local government include the following: providing 'democratic and accountable government for local communities';[69] ensuring the 'provision of services in a sustainable manner';[70] promoting the 'social and economic development of the community';[71] and, fulfilling the duty 'to give priority to the basic needs of the community'.[72]

Chapter 7 also included a number of provisions that required Parliament to pass legislation for the purpose of implementing the constitutional scheme for local government. To this end, Parliament passed a series of statutes addressing the delimitation, structure, administration and financing of local government. The first of these statutes was the Local Government: Municipal Demarcation Act 27 of 1998. This Act went into force on the same day as the second of the statutes passed to create a new system of local government, the Municipal Structures Act 117 of 1998. This Act established the criteria for defining the different categories of local government and created the mechanisms for establishing the different types of municipalities guaranteed in the Constitution.

In accordance with the provisions of the 1996 Constitution, the law provides for three general forms of local government: categories A, B and C. The six biggest cities in South Africa are categorised within category A. These metropolitan municipalities each have more than 500,000 voters and are responsible for coordinating the delivery of public services throughout their designated geographic areas. Category B includes all of the 231 local municipalities—medium-sized cities, small towns and villages—that fall outside of the six metro areas. In addition to these local municipalities, Category C provides for District Councils, which are usually constituted by between four and six small local councils, and include nature reserves and other rural areas where very few people live—called district management areas. District management areas fall directly under a district council and have no local council of their own. Elections for municipal councils vary slightly according to the category of municipal council; however, the basic notion of proportional representation of political parties underlies the local government electoral system.

---

[68] 1996 Constitution s 151(1).
[69] 1996 Constitution s 152(1)(a).
[70] 1996 Constitution s 152(1)(b).
[71] 1996 Constitution ss 152(1)(c) and 153(a).
[72] 1996 Constitution s 153(a).

There are two distinct variations from simple proportional representation at the local government level. First there is, in the case of most councils, the addition of direct representation based on the first-past-the-post election of ward representatives. In these cases, the council is made up of a 50:50 combination of directly elected ward representatives and representatives drawn from party lists to ensure overall proportional representation in the council, according to the vote received by the different political parties in the election. Second, the District Councils are made up of a combination of elected members and members chosen by and directly representing the smaller municipalities. In addition to these two structural variations, proportional representation of political parties in local councils was, in fact, skewed by the floor-crossing process, which was secured by constitutional amendment in 2002. This last variation will, however, be erased in the next local government elections as the floor-crossing provisions of the Constitution were rescinded by the Fourteenth and Fifteenth Amendments to the Constitution, adopted by Parliament in 2008 and assented to by the President on 9 January 2009.

In tandem with the emergence of democratic local government, there has been a resurgence of traditional authority in the approximately 10,000 chieftaincies across six of the nine provinces.[73] During the colonial and apartheid periods, traditional authorities constituted local government in areas of the country under tribal authority. However, the expansion of municipalities under the 1993 Local Government Transition Act and the 1996 Constitution's requirement that democratic local government be extended to all parts of South Africa effectively displaced chiefly control over local government. Meanwhile, traditional authorities continue to 'exercise a substantial influence and material patronage over communal tribal land'.[74] The demarcation of municipal boundaries that, at times, cut directly 'across traditional tribal land ... led to accusations that traditional leaders are never consulted on issues specifically relating to the well-being of their communities'.[75] While the roles of traditional leaders are explicitly recognised in Chapter 12 of the 1996 Constitution, customary law as well as the institution, status and role of traditional leadership is made subject to the Constitution. The Constitution does, however, explicitly provide that national legislation may provide 'for a role for traditional

---

[73] S Letsholo, *Democratic Local Government Elections in South Africa: A Critical Review*, EISA Occasional Paper no 42 (September 2006) 4.

[74] Letsholo, *Democratic Local Government Elections*, above n 73, 4.

[75] Ibid.

leadership as an institution at local level',[76] and states that in order to address issues relating to traditional authorities, 'customary law and the customs of communities observing a system of customary law',[77] legislation may provide for the establishment of houses of traditional leaders at both the national and provincial levels.

While the formal exclusion of traditional authorities has led to ongoing tensions between traditional authorities and local municipal governments, the legislature has tried to alleviate these tensions by providing explicitly for the recognition of traditional authorities within local government practice. In the interim period, traditional authorities were made ex-officio members of local municipalities that included their traditional areas of jurisdiction. However, with the advent of democratic local government their role has become even more attenuated. Although section 81 of the Municipal Structures Act of 1998 provides for the participation of traditional authorities in council meetings and requires a municipal council to allow the leader of a 'traditional authority the opportunity to express a view' on 'any matter directly affecting the area of a traditional authority' before the council makes a decision,[78] chiefs no longer have a formal role in local government decision-making. The only exception is if the Member of the Executive Council (MEC) for local government of the province—after consulting the provincial House of Traditional Leaders—explicitly regulates in the Provincial Gazette for traditional authorities to have a role in local government.[79] At the same time, the statute explicitly restricts the participation of traditional authorities to ensure that the number of traditional leaders participating does not exceed 10 per cent of the elected councillors in any particular municipality, and only one traditional leader may participate in any municipality with 10 or fewer councillors.[80]

C. Implementing the Final Phase: Demarcation and the 2000 Election

The 1998 Municipal Structures Act provided a legal framework for the establishment, election and functioning of municipalities. And the

[76] 1996 Constitution s 212 (1).
[77] 1996 Constitution s 212 (2).
[78] Municipal Structures Act 117 of 1998 s 81(2)(c)(3).
[79] Ibid.
[80] Municipal Structures Act 117 of 1998 s 81(2)(b).

Municipal Demarcation Act established a new institution to fulfil the constitutional guarantee that an independent body determine municipal boundaries.[81] The 10 members of the Municipal Demarcation Board (MDB) are appointed by the President for a term of five years, and have a constitutional mandate to determine municipal boundaries. They also have a number of statutory duties, including the authority to determine ward boundaries within municipalities, to declare district management areas and, most significantly, to access municipal capacity to perform the service and development functions allocated to local government under the system of co-operative government established by the Constitution. Significantly, the MDB is not an advisory body; it has final say in demarcation decisions. The independence of the MDB in this regard has been confirmed by the Constitutional Court, which stated in the *Municipal Structures case* that 'the power to determine municipal boundaries vests solely in the Demarcation Board'.[82] In restructuring municipalities in the lead up to the 2000 local government elections, the MDB pursued 'two broad objectives . . . to create more financially viable municipalities and secondly to make local government the focal point of delivery of essential basic services'.[83] The Demarcation Board implemented these goals by continuing the spatial reconstruction of local government, which had begun under the transitional law of 1993. And once again it consolidated the number of municipalities: from the 843 that took part in the 1995–96 elections to a final total of 284 municipalities covering the total territory of South Africa (later adjusted to 283 with the recognition of cross-boundary municipalities in 2000).

As a result of this spatial restructuring, the 2000 local government elections, which completed the final phase of local government transformation, produced a dramatically new landscape of local governance around the country. According to government policy crystallised in the 1998 White Paper on Local Government, the new system of local governance would initiate an era of developmental local government that would address the legacies of apartheid and ensure local democratic participation and economic development. Despite the overall reduction in elected

[81] 1996 Constitution s 155(3)(b).

[82] *The Executive Council of the Province of the Western Cape v The Minister for Provincial Affairs and Constitutional Development of the Republic of South Africa; Executive Council of KwaZulu-Natal v the President of the Republic of South Africa and Others*, 1999 (12) BCLR 1360 (CC) [14].

[83] Letsholo, *Democratic Local Government Elections*, above n 73, 3.

councillors—from 11,386 to 8,952—due to the consolidation of municipalities and reduction of wards, the ANC increased its control over
local government. It won 59.6 per cent of the proportional vote in 2000
compared to 58 per cent in the 1995–96 local government elections.
Meanwhile, the opposition Democratic Alliance won only 22.1 per cent of
the vote.[84] With the structural transformation essentially accomplished,
attention shifted to the achievement of the goals of service delivery, economic development and participation. While the White Paper 'made consultation a central pillar of democracy within local government',[85]
concerns over corruption and the capacity of local government to deliver
services and restructure the spatial legacies of apartheid have produced a
centralising dynamic. This has been described as 'centralized decentraliza-
tion' or 'joined-up government'[86]—in which public involvement is
expected to drive local governance, yet local initiatives are expected to
conform to a nationally constructed framework of policies and standards
that guarantee the goals of service delivery, development and participation. The best example of this dynamic is the combination of community
participation in the integrated development planning exercises required
by the Municipal Systems Act 32 of 2000 and the introduction of the most
cutting-edge notions of performance management in Chapter 6 of the
same statute. In addition, Parliament passed the Municipal Finance
Management Act 56 of 2003, which provided for extensive forms of
financial control and reporting as well as other mechanisms for financial
accountability in local governments. This national framework of legislation, along with the Municipal Property Rates Act of 2004, completed the
legal transformation of local government in South Africa.

For the ANC, progress made in the transformation of local government seemed to be reflected in the results of the 2006 local government
elections. In these elections, the ruling party increased its percentage of
the proportional vote to 65.67 per cent while the largest opposition party,
the Democratic Alliance, was reduced to 16.32 per cent. A significant
aspect of the 2006 elections was the ANC's decision to introduce a 50:50

---

[84] Letsholo, *Democratic Local Government Elections*, above n 73, 2–3.

[85] MM Khosa, 'Participation and Democracy, in R Calland and P Graham (eds),
Democracy in the Time of Mbeki (Cape Town, IDASA, 2005) 139.

[86] See, P Harrison, 'Integrated Development Plans and Third Way Politics', in
U Pillay, R Tomlinson and J Du Toit (eds), *Democracy and Delivery: Urban Policy in South
Africa* (Cape Town, HSRC Press, 2006) 186–207 and B Freund, 'The State of South
Africa's Cities', in S Buhlungu (ed), *State of the Nation: South Africa 2005–2006* (Cape
Town, HSRC Press, 2006) 303–32.

gender quota for its candidate lists. As a result, the percentage of women in local government bodies rose to 43 per cent of those elected from the proportional representation lists and 37 per cent of the ward representatives—a total nationally of 40 per cent of local government councillors.[87] Despite all these changes and the electoral dominance of the ANC, fundamental governance problems remain at the local level. As President Thabo Mbeki said in his 'State of the Nation' speech before Parliament on 11 February, 2005, '[w]e need massively to improve the management, organisational, technical and other capacities of government so that it meets its objectives'.

D. Role of Local Government: Service Delivery, Economic Development and Democratic Participation

The transformation of local government has been profound, yet the extraordinary levels of inequality between and within municipalities[88] has produced an uneven landscape in which contestation over resources, unfulfilled expectations and governance failures are reflected in ongoing—and at times violent—service delivery and other protests. Local protests increased after the 2004 national elections, grew to a crescendo of around 6,000 in 2006,[89] and have continued sporadically since then. While these forms of public resistance are clear evidence of local anger and disenchantment with ineffective delivery or unpopular government decisions—such as the redrawing of municipal and provincial boundaries—the vast majority of municipalities have been engaged in a protracted process of transformation with decidedly mixed results. Analysts have identified three underlying problems that they argue are the main causes of public anger: 'ineffectiveness in service delivery, the poor responsiveness of municipalities to citizen's grievances, and the conspicuous consumption entailed by a culture of self-enrichment on the part of municipal councillors and staff.[90]

[87] See, Letsholo, *Democratic Local Government Elections*, above n 73, 13.

[88] See, NS Makgetla, 'Local Government Budgets and Development: A Tale of Two Towns', in S Buhlungu et al, *State of the Nation: South Africa 2007* (Cape Town, HSRC Press, 2007) 146–67.

[89] See, Letsholo, *Democratic Local Government Elections*, above n 73, 6.

[90] D Atkinson, 'Taking to the Streets: Has Developmental Local Government Failed in South Africa?' in S Buhlungu et al (eds), *State of the Nation: South Africa 2007* (Cape Town, HSRC Press, 2007) 53.

Public protest appears to be the consequence of a range of municipal problems, which include failures in service delivery as well as lack of responsiveness, undemocratic decision-making, corruption and self-enrichment on the part of local councillors and staff. However, continued electoral support for the ANC reflects the complex relationship between local frustrations and the belief that government remains the most reliable source of development for local communities. Local government failures are particularly irksome to residents in a context in which the state has been engaged in massive infrastructure projects. The government has provided free basic water to approximately 18 million people and free basic electricity to communities within the jurisdictions of 165 municipalities. The provision of these services stands in stark contrast to the failure to deliver similar services to large numbers of people, maintenance problems, and ongoing issues related to providing supplementary services such as billing, responding to complaints and managing the waiting lists that exist for those still expecting the delivery of municipal services. On the one hand, poor communities have seen a dramatic increase in local government services, compared to the apartheid era. On the other hand, growing corruption and local frustration have increased national concern over local service delivery, which is supposed to be the key point of government activity in addressing public needs.

In response to these difficulties, the national government has introduced multiple layers of legal regulation aimed at creating uniform systems of planning and accountability across all municipalities. These governance techniques—from integrated development planning (IDP) to performance management—are designed to increase the effectiveness of local government while ensuring public participation and accountability. They have also placed an enormous burden on local government institutions and practices of governance. While the concept of integrated development planning was first introduced by an amendment to the Local Government Transition Act in 1996,[91] it became central to intergovernmental relations and the operation of local government with its inclusion in the Local Government: Municipal Systems Act 32 of 2000.[92] Described as providing the 'core principles, mechanisms and processes that are necessary to enable municipalities to move progressively towards the social and economic upliftment of local communities', the Act

[91] Local Government Transition Act, Second Amendment Act 97 of 1996.

[92] See, Harrison, 'Integrated Development Plans and Third Way Politics', above n 86, 187.

defined the 'core components' of a local IDP as reflecting the municipal council's long-term development vision; an assessment of local services as well as social and economic development; the council's development priorities and objectives for its term of office; local development strategies as aligned with provincial and national plans; a spatial development framework including guidelines for a land use management system; operational strategies; disaster management plans; a financial plan; as well as 'key performance indicators and targets'.[93] In addition to these core components, the Act defines a participatory process through which the IDP must be formulated and requires local governments to establish a performance management system to promote a culture of performance among its officials and administration as well as to 'administer its affairs in an economical, effective, efficient and accountable manner'.[94] In an attempt to bolster financial accountability in local governments, the national legislature adopted yet another piece of legislation in 2003 to promote local accountability by imposing national treasury norms and standards of financial management. The Local Government: Municipal Finance Management Act 56 of 2003 lays out a detailed scheme for the management of local government finances and budgeting and establishes a system of national and provincial oversight to monitor and intervene when local governments fail to follow the required reporting and other financial procedures established by the Act. The law creates an accountability cycle with explicit linkages among the IDP, annual budget, annual financial statements, annual reports, oversight reports and audit reports.[95] It also clarifies the roles and responsibilities of different local government actors including the mayor, executive and non-executive councillors and municipal officials, including the municipal manager.

Despite this attempt to link democratic participation and effective systems of oversight and governance, the experience of local government institutions remains highly contested and fraught with accusations of corruption and incompetence. The national treasury, in its review of local government budgets and expenditures for the period 2003–09 identified a number of problems related to financial management and capacity. First, the report identified a high degree of non-compliance with the legal requirements for updating the organisational structures of municipal

[93] Local Government: Municipal Services Act 32 of 2000 s 26(a)–(i).
[94] Local Government: Municipal Services Act 32 of 2000 s 38(c).
[95] National Treasury, *Local Government Budgets and Expenditure Review: 2003/04–2009/10* (2008) p 158, available at www.treasury.gov.za.

governments and the procedures for appointed municipal employees. It notes that 28 per cent of municipal employees are appointed to posts that are not part of the existing organisational structure and in the case of the province of Mpumalanga, more than 60 per cent of municipal employees are in positions that are not provided for within existing municipal staffing provisions.[96] Many of these might be 'political deployments' rather than skills-based appointments, although in some cases it is more likely a reflection of the fact that the municipality's organisational structure has not been updated.

Second, instability in senior municipal management exacerbates the problems of local government capacity and impedes its ability to address the growing challenges of accelerated urbanisation and poverty. By 2007, nearly 17 per cent of senior managerial positions—municipal managers and chief financial officers—were vacant. Many other officials were involved in political and other conflicts that resulted in suspension (on full pay) while they were being investigated or were involved in other legal controversies. Third, the report indicates that approximately '44 per cent of municipalities received an adverse or disclaimed audit opinion' over a significant portion of the period under review, indicating that 'fundamental principles of good governance, transparency and the accountable use of public resources and ongoing performance improvements, are being severely compromised'.[97] Fourth, local political parties have dominated the system of participatory democracy, including ward committees; ward councillor public meetings; IDP and development forums; and budget consultation meetings. Finally, the National Treasury noted in its 2008 review that despite unprecedented levels of support from national government, the efforts of municipalities were being hampered by 'councils distracted by political conflicts; poor governance practices; incompetence; and, corruption'.[98]

Government's attempts over the last decade to address these endemic problems have taken different forms. In 1997, the government adopted a set of eight principles for transforming public service delivery, entitled *Batho Pele* or People First. The principles apply to all levels of government, but they were primarily aimed at local government officials, since local

[96] Ibid p 181.

[97] Ibid p 169.

[98] National Treasury, *Local Government Budget and Expenditure Review, 2008: Meeting New Challenges of Growth and Poverty Alleviation*, 28 August,2008, slide 8, available at www.treasury.gov.za.

government is designated as the primary site of service delivery. The eight principles were framed as a citizens' guide to the obligations of government officials, and included the following requirements: consultation; service standards; access; courtesy; information; openness and transparency; redress; and finally, value for money.[99] In evaluating the impact of *Batho Pele* on service delivery, a South African Social Attitudes Survey study in 2007 found that respondents felt that 'government is improving delivery but not managing to communicate and respond to people's priorities'.[100]

Another approach has been the creation of a National Capacity Building Framework for Local Government, which seeks to coordinate its efforts to develop local capacity through a variety of 'stakeholders', including the non-governmental South African Local Government Association and national government programmes such as the Local Government Leadership Academy.[101] In addition, the framework makes a commitment to providing 'hands-on support' to increase local government capacity. In fact, this commitment to 'hands-on support' led the national government to use its constitutional and statutory powers to intervene directly in failing local institutions. In the period from 2004–07 the national government intervened 34 times in municipalities that experienced problems with their 'budgets, revenue collection, cash flow management, [or] internal controls', with the goal of improving 'internal reporting and timely decision-making, strengthening governance and oversight and developing operational skills to execute daily tasks'.[102]

E. Poverty, Local Government and the Promise of Democratic Participation

The problems of local government are compounded by the scale of the needs of the nearly 30 million poor people in South Africa as well as the

[99] Department of Public Service and Administration, Batho Pele 'People First': White Paper on Transforming Public Service Delivery, 18 September 1997, *Government Gazette* vol 388, no 18340, 1 October 1997.

[100] D Hemson and B Roberst, 'Batho Pele Season of Discontent' (2008) 6 (4) *HSRC Review*.

[101] See, National Capacity Building Framework for Local Government: In Support of the Five Year Local Government Strategic Agenda (2008–11) (Department of Provincial and Local Government in partnership with the SALGA), available at www.dplg.gov.za

[102] National Treasury, 2008 Local Government Budgets and Expenditure Review: 2003/04–2009/10, p 172, available at www.treasury.gov.za.

managerial and other problems within municipalities.[103] Even as the national government distributes an increasing share of the budget through local government, the transformation of local government— with its accompanying loss of experienced managers and the emergence of 'an organizational culture of incompetence and nepotism'[104]—provides the context in which these new institutions are being shaped. At the same time, the attempt to facilitate public participation through ward committees has been co-opted in many cases by the dominant local political party or undermined by the national deployment of senior municipal officials—such as executive mayors—who are thus less accountable to the local citizenry. As a result, some argue that 'open debate, the cornerstone of participatory democracy', has not taken place in a meaningful way at the local government level,[105] undermining efforts to achieve the goals of democratic participation, service delivery and economic development so central to the role of local government envisioned in the Constitution.

V. CONCLUSION

Despite the ideal vision of co-operative government in Chapter 3 of the Constitution, many people still question and debate whether the existing levels of government best serve the country. First, critics point out the cost of provincial government, particularly in the provinces where the provincial governments—as in the Eastern Cape and Mpumalanga— have gone from one administrative and political crisis to another. Second, observers argue that there is little role for provincial government in a situation where the national Parliament produces most of the legal framework and local government is responsible for service delivery. This is especially the case in the major metropolitan areas, which have the greatest capacity to govern themselves and include within their jurisdictions a large proportion of the country's population. Third, difficulties with municipal administration and the impacts of inefficiency and

---

[103] See, D Hemson, J Carter and G Karuri-Sebina, 'Service Delivery as a Measure of Change: State Capacity and Development', in P Kagwanja and K Kondlo (eds), *State of the Nation: South Africa 2008* (Cape Town, HSRC Press, 2009) 151–77.

[104] D Atkinson, 'Taking to the Streets: Has Developmental Local Government Failed in South Africa?', in S Buhlungu (ed), *State of the Nation: South Africa 2007* (Cape Town, HSRC Press, 2007), 62.

[105] Atkinson, 'Taking to the Streets', 65.

corruption on service delivery have led to a plan to create a single civil service for the country, thus taking the power to provide access to government employment out of the hands of local politicians.

There may be good arguments for consolidating the different spheres of government. And there might have been a strong possibility of achieving such constitutional and political restructuring when the ANC controlled all nine provinces and had a two-thirds majority in Parliament. This action seems much less likely since the 2009 national elections. The Democratic Alliance, the official opposition in Parliament, won a majority of votes in the Western Cape province, which allowed it to form a government there. In addition, the ANC fell just short of a two-thirds majority in the national Parliament, which would be required for any constitutional amendment. It was already unlikely that the ANC could have dramatically restructured the system of constitutional regionalism, since it would have had to overcome not only the political opposition of regional parties, such as the Inkatha Freedom Party, but also its own members' regional interests. Now, the fact that the Western Cape province would clearly contest any reduction in provincial powers makes this possibility moot. At the same time, it is clear that there are major differences in capacity between the metropolitan governments and the smaller municipalities, including most rural towns and districts. Yet it seems likely that the government will push ahead with its plan to create a single civil service. This will, it is hoped, create the opportunity for coordinated training and standards while also providing the national controls and opportunities that will divorce the administrative branches of the state from the worst elements of local politics, including local corruption and patronage networks.

Co-operative government is likely to dictate the overall structure of governance in South Africa for the near future. The challenge will be to find ways to improve coordination among the different spheres of government and to balance the tensions between local autonomy and the centralising tendencies of the national executive as it attempts to speed up service delivery. While the ANC completely dominates eight of the nine provinces, the emergence of the Congress of the People (COPE) as the official opposition in a number of provinces might mean that there will be an increase in demand for accountability at the provincial level. The end of floor-crossing will also mean that the ANC will no longer be able to attract opposition politicians with promises of political security and authority, thus destroying any real chance of opposition politics at all

284 Co-operative Government, Regionalism and Local Government

levels of government (the national, provincial and local). Thus, the future of South Africa's unique experiment in co-operative government seems secured, even if its practice and precise legal contours will, for some time, remain a work in progress.

FURTHER READING

Atkinson, D, 'Taking to the Streets: Has Developmental Local Government Failed in South Africa?', in S Buhlungu (ed), *State of the Nation: South Africa 2007* (Cape Town, HSRC Press, 2007)

Basson, D, *South Africa's Interim Constitution: Text and Notes*, rev edn (Cape Town, Juta & Co, 1995)

Freund, B, 'The State of South Africa's Cities', in S Buhlungu (ed), *State of the Nation: South Africa 2005–2006* (Cape Town, HSRC Press, 2006)

Hemson, DJ Carter and Karuri-Sebina, G, 'Service Delivery as a Measure of Change: State Capacity and Development', in P Kagwanja and K Kondlo (eds), *State of the Nation: South Africa 2008* (Cape Town, HSRC Press, 2009)

Letsholo, S, 'Democratic Local Government Elections in South Africa: A Critical Review', EISA Occasional Paper Number 42 (September 2006)

Makgetla, NS, 'Local Government Budgets and Development: A Tale of Two Towns', in S Buhlungu (ed), *State of the Nation: South Africa 2007* (Cape Town, HSRC Press, 2007)

O'Meara, D, *Forty Lost Years: The Apartheid State and the Politics of the National Party, 1948–1994* (Randburg, South Africa, Ravan Press; Athens, University of Ohio Press, 1996)

10

The Constitution of South Africa

Facing the Future

———➤•◀———

Introduction – Legacies of Inequality – The Future of Rights – Democracy – Conclusion

I. INTRODUCTION

THE FUTURE OF South Africa's constitutional order is intimately linked to society's ability to address the legacies of apartheid and colonialism that continue to dominate the daily lives of all the country's inhabitants. Despite the internationally recognised process of national reconciliation championed by President Nelson Mandela—and the highly regarded processes of the Truth and Reconciliation Commission—patterns of continued inequality and racism continue to plague the country. Meanwhile, those who benefited from the crime of apartheid (from large corporations to individual white citizens) persist in denying their complicity. These are the continued legacies of South African law and history. The Constitution's embrace of democracy and human rights serves as an inspiration, setting the highest goals for government, civil society and all citizens of the country. Yet economic and political competition has tended to reduce these aspirations to mundane realities. While the gravity of South African history has produced what might be defined as a 'unipolar democracy'—in which there seems to be little alternative to the electoral dominance of the liberation movement (as embodied by the ANC) for the foreseeable future—the realities of poverty and extreme inequality continue to produce serious tensions and, at times, violent confrontations. It is in this context that the Constitution must be understood.

II. LEGACIES OF INEQUALITY

After 15 years of democracy in South Africa, the legacies of apartheid—poverty, structural unemployment, limited government capacity, and criminal and domestic violence—remain an ever-present reality. In addition, the country has faced new challenges, including a devastating HIV/AIDS pandemic and increasing inequality.[1] While the ANC government has remained publicly committed to addressing these legacies, there have been dramatic shifts in policy choices. The implementation of government programmes has been mired in problems of local capacity, political patronage and varying degrees of corruption. In the face of these problems, the government has, in each post-apartheid election, emphasised its delivery of basic infrastructure in housing, water and electricity supply and promised to deliver even more in its next term in office. Despite these promises, South Africans remain frustrated by local government failures and corruption. The government has imposed national policy decisions in the face of local opposition—such as the redrawing of provincial boundaries to accommodate cross-border municipalities—that have led to violent demonstrations by local communities. The explosion of xenophobic violence in a number of poor and marginalised communities in 2008 highlighted the degree of anger and frustration of those who continue to suffer under the legacies of inequality and marginalisation South Africa's new constitutional democracy inherited.

In order to understand the post-apartheid constitutional order and its possible futures, we need to first trace the founding vision of how the democratic government sought to overcome the multiple legacies of inequality and oppression within the bounds of a rights-based constitutionalism. Many anti-apartheid activists imagined that the end of apartheid would lead to a dramatic redistribution of wealth, aimed at erasing the 300-year legacy of colonialism and apartheid. But the negotiated transition took place within a post-Cold War global context, which framed the conditions under which the democratically elected government took power.[2] The embrace of democratic constitutionalism in this context fundamentally reshaped the revolutionary imagination of the

---

[1] See, J Seekings and N Natrass, *Class, Race and Inequality in South Africa* (Scottsville, South Africa, University of KwaZulu-Natal Press, 2006).

[2] See, H Klug, *Constituting Democracy: Law, Globalism and South Africa's Political Reconstruction* (Cambridge, Cambridge University Press, 2000).

liberation movement and led the ANC's Constitutional Committee to adopt a complex vision of democratic rule and a rights-based constitutionalism that sought to address the legacies of apartheid while simultaneously establishing a rule of law that would ensure a measured process of change—one that would guarantee the security of those threatened by the transition and the goals of the democratic majority.

As the ANC explored the possibility of a negotiated transition from apartheid in the mid-1980s, it produced a set of Constitutional Guidelines that articulated an inherent tension between a democratic future—in which the privileged white minority would lose all political power—and the idea of legal and constitutional guarantees that would guarantee individual rights and provide continuing legal certainty to all South Africans. While the black majority expected a dramatic redistribution of resources long denied them, representatives of the white minority sought the protection of rights—both group and individual rights—as a means to ensure that there would be no dramatic change in the opportunities that community had long enjoyed. As the prospect of violent revolution and an accompanied forceful redistribution of resources ebbed, the task of finding an alternative means of addressing the expectations of the democratic majority and the legacies of apartheid gained urgency. What emerged from the ANC was a constitutional vision of collective action to overcome South Africa's legacy of racial domination and inequality. That vision assumed a broad interpretation of the notion of equality and incorporated a strategy for realising the proposed constitutional duty to actively eradicate 'the economic and social inequalities produced by racial discrimination' that was included in the ANC's Constitutional Guidelines.[3] In its first draft proposal for a Bill of Rights, the ANC's Constitutional Committee placed the achievement of formal equality at the centre of this vision. It also recognised that an active programme of affirmative action and other direct policy interventions designed to eradicate accumulated poverty and marginalisation would be necessary to provide a basis for the recognition and practice of formal equality. In the years since 1994, the ANC has embraced a number of different policies—from the Reconstruction and Development Programme to Broad-based Black Economic Empowerment (BEE)—as means to address the legacy

---

[3] African National Congress, *Constitutional Guidelines for a Democratic South Africa* (Lusaka, 1988), reprinted in (1989) 12 *Hastings International and Comparative Law Review* 322 [hereinafter ANC Constitutional Guidelines].

of inequality and economic disempowerment that continues to reflect the colonial structure of South Africa's inherited political economy.

While the ANC's Constitutional Committee's original vision included a broad range of mechanisms for addressing apartheid's legacy, the basic assumption of the liberation movement was that with democracy the peoples' representatives would be able to use legislative and budgetary authority to address historical inequalities. This assumption did not take into account the complexities of governance the post-apartheid state would confront. These complexities included the global political economy of the post-Cold War era as well as the more mundane issues of bureaucratic inertness, resistance and incompetence. The limited capacity of the new government to replace senior bureaucrats and policy makers within the state—as well as the temptations of power and wealth that saw the corrupt but legal practices of the old regime being replicated in the new government—has also undermined the goals of ANC policy and electoral promises. These issues have transformed the nature of the policies and goals of the original vision even as the government has dramatically extended public services and resources to communities and sections of the population that were explicitly denied equal access under apartheid.

The first attempt to take up the challenge of apartheid's legacies was the ANC's 1994 election manifesto and the Mandela government's initial policy of Reconstruction and Development.[4] Even though the Reconstruction and Development Programme (RDP) was framed in the terms of the ANC's original constitutional vision to address the inequalities inherited from apartheid, it also represented a subtle shift in focus that came with the ANC's preparation for assuming power. Not only was the programme designed to address the legacies of apartheid, but it also represented a change in view from an oppositional stance to that of a government-in-waiting. Significantly, this included a change in emphasis from a focus on rights to that of delivery, development and democracy. With the demise of the RDP in 1997 and the shift in emphasis to economic development through the government's new policy of Growth, Employment and Redistribution (GEAR), the government began to focus on a more dispersed set of policy tools, including employment equity and service delivery, as the key means of addressing the needs of the majority.

---

[4] See, African National Congress, *The Reconstruction and Development Programme: A Policy Framework* (Johannesburg: Umanyano Publications, 1994).

Passage of the Employment Equity Act (EEA).[5] and the Skills Development Act[6] in 1998, as well as the Preferential Procurement Policy Framework Act in 2000,[7] served as a significant bridge from the original constitutional vision of collective action to overcome apartheid's legacies to a more individualistic understanding of how equity might be achieved. The EEA represented an important legislative implementation of the promise of anti-discrimination and affirmative action that was included in the equality clause of the 1996 Constitution. But the very nature of the employment relationship meant that it would mainly apply at the individual level, even if it were oriented to benefit communities that had historically suffered racial discrimination. The scope of individual discrimination covered by the Act was also dramatically expanded to include, in addition to race, 'gender, sex, pregnancy, marital status, family responsibility, ethnic or social origin, colour, sexual orientation, age, disability, religion, HIV status, conscience, belief, political opinion, culture, language and birth'.[8] Significantly, the statute shifted the burden of proof in cases of discrimination and included robust affirmative action measures 'designed to ensure that suitably qualified people from designated groups have equal employment opportunities and are equitably represented in all occupational categories and levels in the workforce of a designated employer'.[9] Enforcement of the Act is also rather robust, including a range of mechanisms from administrative reporting functions and a Commission on Employment Equity, to dispute resolution through the Commission for Conciliation, Mediation and Arbitration. Finally, the Labour Court is given 'exclusive jurisdiction to determine any dispute about the interpretation or application of this Act'.[10]

After the 1999 election, another significant shift in focus occurred, as newly elected President Thabo Mbeki articulated the idea of an African Renaissance and with it a more nationalistic orientation in public policy. A significant aspect of this shift was the idea of BEE. The private sector had moved fairly swiftly after 1990 to incorporate a small number of prominent black political and business leaders into the higher echelons of

---

[5] Employment Equity Act 55 of 1998.
[6] Skills Development Act 97 of 1998.
[7] Preferential Procurement Policy Framework Act 5 of 2000.
[8] Employment Equity Act 55 of 1998 s 6(1).
[9] Employment Equity Act 55 of 1998 s 15(1).
[10] Employment Equity Act 55 of 1998 s 49.

the economic elite[11]—mainly by appointing individuals to boards of directors and granting shareholdings structured to increase black owner-ship through loans and directors' compensation deals. However, the modus operandi of this initial phase of BEE was to rely on corporate social responsibility through the adoption of voluntary codes, charters and other agreements. As the government's own self-study of October 2003, entitled, *Towards a Ten Year Review*, noted, progress in extending black ownership of public companies was extremely slow, having grown from 3.9 per cent in 1997 to only 9.4 per cent in 2002.[12] Control, on the other hand, measured by participation in boards of directors by previ-ously disadvantaged people, had increased only slightly from 1.2 per cent (13 individuals) in 1992 to 13 per cent (438 individuals) in 2002.[13] As a result, Mbeki's administration decided to simultaneously expand this initiative and create a legal framework to regulate its implementation.

The idea behind the 2003 adoption of Broad-based BEE was to use gov-ernment procurement and legislative pressure to expand black parti-cipation in ownership and control of the economy.[14] The Broad-Based BEE Act[15] created a legal framework within which a Black Economic Empowerment Advisory Council, led and appointed by the President, would seek to 'promote economic transformation' in order to achieve 'a substantial change in the racial composition of ownership and manage-ment structures and in the skilled occupations of existing and new enter-prises'.[16] There is little doubt that this legislation has had a profound effect on the South African economy. It has, however, served primarily as a key driver of corporate merger and acquisition activity, which, according to a Moody's rating agency report, accounted for R200-billion worth of busi-ness transactions in the decade between 1998 and 2008.[17] Success in the

---

[11]   See, S Bridge et al, *Trailblazers: South Africa's Champions of Change* (Lansdowne, South Africa, Double-Story Books 2007).

[12]   The Presidency, Policy Coordination and Advisory Services, *Towards a Ten Year Review: Synthesis Report on Implementation of Government Programmes* (discussion docu-ment) (October 2003) 41–42.

[13]   Ibid.

[14]   See generally, G Marcus, X Mangcu, K Shubane and A Hadland (eds), *Visions of Black Economic Empowerment* (Auckland Park, South Africa, Human Sciences Research Council, 2007).

[15]   Broad-based Black Economic Empowerment Act 53 of 2003.

[16]   Broad-based Black Economic Empowerment Act 53 of 2003, s 2(a) and (b).

[17]   'BEE Transactions Drive Domestic Corporate Activity', *South Africa: The Good News* (19 May 2008) available at: www.sagoodnews.co.za/bee/bee_transactions_drive_domestic_corporate_activity.html.

boardrooms did not, however, stem a growing criticism of BEE from both within and outside the ANC. While its supporters have justified it as a form of stakeholder capitalism and argued that it has had a positive effect beyond the small elite who have so visibly benefited from 'empowerment deals', a number of ANC members and allies believe it is 'more likely to blur the boundaries of race and class than to propel South African capitalism in a more inclusive, accountable and equalizing direction'.[18]

The election of Jacob Zuma and the restructuring of the Cabinet to emphasise a new commitment to job creation and rural development to conform with the decisions of the party's national conference in December 1997—which repudiated Mbeki's approach—introduced another shift in the ANC's efforts to address the legacies of inequality. Appointing a second Minister in the Presidency to head the newly created National Planning Commission, would, according to President Zuma, allow for a strategic planning process 'for the country to ensure one National Plan to which all spheres of government would adhere' and enable the government 'to take a more comprehensive view of socio-economic development in the country'.[19] At the same time, the government has continued to insist that delivery of public services through local government remains the primary vector through which development will take place. Even in the face of another surge in local protests against the failure of local government—including demands to abolish the Provinces and for direct national intervention—the government has continued to emphasise the importance of local government. Since taking office, President Zuma has repeatedly toured trouble spots and local communities and severely criticised corrupt local officials, promising greater emphasis on local delivery.[20]

Despite the institutional frustrations and policy changes that led to the abandonment of the Reconstruction and Development Plan's

[18] R Southall, 'Black Empowerment and Limits to a More Democratic Capitalism', in S Buhlungu (ed), *State of the Nation: South Africa 2005–2006* (Cape Town, HSRC Press, 2006).

[19] Statement by President Jacob Zuma on the appointment of the new Cabinet, 10 May 2009. Issued by Government Communications (GCIS) and available at www.info.gov.za.

[20] See, 'Zuma Repeats Warning to Lazy Public Servants', *Mail & Guardian Online* (8 June 2009), available at www.mg.co.za/article/2009–06–08-zuma-repeats-warning-to-lazy-public-servants, and 'Zuma Keeps Popular Touch in Face of Crisis', *Mail & Guardian Online* (7 August 2009) available at www.mg.co.za/article/2009-08-07-zuma-keeps-popular-touch-in-face-of-crisis.

project-based approach, the government has continued to see local initiatives as the best means of addressing local development needs. Despite an extended process of negotiations over the form and structure of local government, the ANC has embraced the idea that the implementation of its redistributive policies is best achieved by improving delivery of public services—whether in the form of new housing, water, electricity or employment opportunities. This emphasis represents in many ways a coming together of a number of disparate ideological trends shared both by the ANC and other political formations in South Africa. First, there is the sense that democratic participation can only effectively be achieved at the local level. Here, traditions of local democracy and autonomy—at times, more or less accountable to democratic institutions—are asserted as reasons for building local capacity and engaging with a range of new institutions, including the Municipal Demarcation Board, provincial governments and various statutory bodies designed to ensure accountability and provide the institutional capacity to most effectively address continuing patterns of inequality. Second, the many local interests, from within the ANC and among former local power brokers—whether traditional authorities or former white administrations—have found that they are able to reach local compromises or deals based on the sharing of resources available from national government. Finally, the emphasis on the delivery of public services has coincided with the enormous institutional and financial investments that have been made in restructuring local government so that each and every part of South Africa now falls within a municipality and has an explicit set of assigned functions and related resources.[21]

Along with the restructuring of local government, South Africa has seen the introduction of systems of governance based on the creation of ward committees, local development plans and other ways to ensure local participation in development. Even though local government has been the source of the greatest amount of patronage, corruption and incompetence, local activists and politicians often experience political engagement as an entrée to power and economic opportunities that they have long been denied. This has, at times, created enormous tensions between local officials and communities in desperate need of resources to address the vast infrastructural, social and economic problems that underlie the

[21] See, The White Paper on Local Government, 9 March 1998, available at www.info.gov.za. See also, Local Government: Municipal Structures Act 117 of 1998 and Local Government: Municipal Demarcation Act 27 of 1998.

entrenched poverty of so many South African communities. As a result, a whole range of new social movements has emerged, challenging local authorities and questioning the assumptions of many of the institutions and legal requirements that rely on local government and assume that development and democracy are intimately entwined.

III. THE FUTURE OF RIGHTS

South Africa's Bill of Rights and the jurisprudence of the Constitutional Court have been celebrated around the world. However, in South Africa, a domestic debate continues regarding the nature of constitutionalism in a post-apartheid society and the ruling party's attitude towards rights. This debate is reflected in different characterisations of the Constitution and the Court's jurisprudence as being either a form of liberalism or as a potentially transformative constitutionalism. The Court itself has asserted the importance of democracy to the new order and has been careful to acknowledge the legitimacy of the democratic institutions created and empowered by the Constitution. At the same time, political commentators have expressed concern that in the debate between communists and nationalists in the governing ANC tripartite alliance '[n]either the nationalists nor the communists are committed to the liberalism of our Constitution and it seems clear enough that under their full control it will be slowly eroded from above'.[22] From this perspective, the future of a rights-based constitutional order is premised on the continuing conflict between these different social and political factions within the ruling alliance and the new alliances they will need to establish to win political support and authority to govern.

In practice, the continuing realities of poverty and inequality and debates over government priorities and policies have led to the emergence of a number of post-apartheid social movements. The activists in these movements have complex relationships with the ANC and the government's administrative agencies at every level. They often stress the Constitution's provision of justiciable socio-economic rights and the government's duty to promote and fulfil these rights. When they have been unable to persuade government of the need to address particular

---

[22] I Baccus, '*Armani Elite v Unfree Masses*: Neither the Nationalists nor the Communists are Committed to the Liberalism of our Constitution', *Mail and Guardian* (18–22 December 2009) 26.

issues, these activists have increasingly sought redress in the courts, with the hope of redirecting government policies and resources. The most successful of the new social movements have adopted a multilayered strategy of appeals to government, public mobilisation and recourse to legal strategies. At the same time, the question of human rights and their enforcement has had a more political and rhetorical presence, compared to the specific instances in which lawyers have managed to get the question of the violation of particular rights before the Constitutional Court. Despite the complexity of this post-apartheid landscape, the adoption and development of constitutional rights, particularly social and economic rights, does represent a particular constitutional vision. This vision is inherent in the public celebration of the post-apartheid constitutional order and provides a legitimate conceptual space that enables social activists to pursue and transform this vision through strategies of political mobilisation, legal challenge and democratic politics.

The role of law and the courts in the ongoing struggle to address inequality in South Africa is best understood from this perspective as facilitating the interaction of different aspects of the multilayered strategies adopted by policy makers, government officials, social movements and activists. While the strategies of some social movements have proven relatively successful in advancing some social rights—as in the case of access to medicines in the context of the TAC and HIV/AIDS—the lack of immediate success does not preclude important transformations of the political and legal context in which these rights are pursued. Even absent successful political mobilisation or clear expressions of political will by the government or communities, legal frameworks and institutions, including courts, remain important means of keeping alive the possibility of developing these rights. Whether it is in challenges to ineffective government programmes or in the government's own formulation and development of policies, programmes, legislative mandates or institutions, the constitutional promise of rights sets an aspirational goal that focuses attention on the glaring problems of inequality that these constitutional provisions address. At the same time, the Constitutional Court's jurisprudence recognises that the Court has limited institutional capacity and must work with democratic institutions to achieve the consolidation of the constitutional order. This is most evident in the Court's practice—which human rights activists have criticised at times—of sending an issue back to the legislature for resolution within a constitutionally acceptable context or by showing deference to the policy choices made by government in its attempts to provide the socioeconomic resources the Constitution defines as central to the promise of human rights.

South Africa's legacy of deep inequalities poses a constant challenge to all sectors and institutions in the country. If government has battled to deliver the services it deems essential to addressing popular needs and concerns, the Constitutional Court has, until recently, enjoyed a charmed life: it has been held in high regard and the government has repeatedly acknowledged its authority and accepted its decisions.[23] Yet a period of heightening political tensions has seen the law increasingly used as a weapon in internecine conflict among government officials and within political parties. Along with this atmosphere of legal conflict has come increasing tension over the work of the judiciary, individual judges, and the process of judicial appointments itself. While the Ministry of Justice has proposed statutory reforms and constitutional amendments designed to improve the functioning of the courts and the administration of justice, these changes have raised fears that government is under-mining the independence of the judiciary. Even as the government was forced to withdraw some of these proposals, the Judicial Service Commission (JSC) publicly acknowledged that it was having difficulty attracting sufficient numbers of highly qualified individuals, acceptable to the members of the JSC, as candidates for judicial appointment. The complaint by the judges of the Constitutional Court against Judge John Hlophe dragged the JSC into the centre of the controversies over the role of the judiciary. However, the subsequent appointment of Chief Justice Sandile Ngcobo and the decision by the Zuma government to empower the Chief Justice's office to oversee the administration of the courts has, to a large degree, resolved concerns that government was bent on under-mining the authority or independence of the courts.

The courts alone cannot achieve the fulfilment of constitutional rights. This is a result of two related circumstances. First, the courts, and the Constitutional Court in particular, have been confronted by the failure of government officials to effectively implement court orders requiring public officials to resolve systemic problems of public administration and corruption, especially at the local level. This has been particularly evident in cases of the mismanagement of pensions and social welfare grants.

---

[23] See, *Minister of Health v Treatment Action Campaign (No 2)*, 2002 (5) SA 721 (CC), in which the Court stated that, 'The government has always respected and executed orders of this Court. There is no reason to believe that it will not do so in the present case', [129].

A large section of the population relies upon these streams of income, particularly in the underdeveloped rural areas of the former 'Bantustans', which are now part of the most poorly managed provinces. Second, the eruption of xenophobic violence across some of South Africa's poorest communities in the winter of 2008—which left many dead and injured and forced thousands of immigrants and refugees from other parts of Africa to flee their homes—dramatically illustrated the frustrations that exist between popular expectations based on the promise of rights and resources and the failures of democratic accountability and participation. The South African Institute of Race Relations said the violence was the result of poor and ineffective governance, which created a tinderbox of unmet expectations that exploded in Alexandra and spread to several other areas of the country. In May 2008, for the first time since the end of apartheid, the government sent the army into the streets of South Africa to quell the violence.

As a result of these confrontations, the government has begun to show greater responsiveness to local protests, despite an initial refusal to acknowledge the legitimacy of these claims. This was most evident in the case of residents of so-called cross-boundary communities, who had objected to being relocated—through constitutional amendments to provincial boundaries—to provinces they considered poorer or less effective at service delivery. When the Matatiele Municipality turned to the courts, it obtained a decision in the Constitutional Court to the effect that Parliament—and the National Council of Provinces, in particular— had failed to provide the necessary levels of public participation required by the Constitution before adopting a constitutional amendment that changed a provincial boundary.[24] Instead of reasserting its position by merely going through the motions of satisfying the procedural weaknesses in its prior decision, the government has now reversed itself. In a similar case, pertaining to the Merafong municipality in Khutsong, the government reversed its position in late 2008, to the delight of the local community. As a result Khutsong was reincorporated into Gauteng province, from which it had previously been excised.

This responsiveness is particularly significant in a context in which democracy remains the key ingredient in the struggles to achieve greater equality and to respect and promote the rights enshrined in the

---

[24] See, *Matatiele Municipality et al v President of the Republic of South Africa et al* 2007 (1) BCLR 47.

Constitution. The Constitutional Court has been prepared to boldly strike down national legislation and even a proposed constitutional amendment on the grounds that the legislatures involved in these particular processes had not allowed or provided the degree of public participation required by the Constitution. Yet the tensions between the courts and popular political leaders—and even the ruling party—demonstrate the institutional limits of judicial authority. Furthermore, the ANC's continued domination of the electoral vote (as demonstrated by the April 2009 elections) means there is little chance of a major political shift in either government policies or modes of implementation. Instead, the extraordinary levels of inequality and limited government capacity to address the needs of South Africa's poor majority threaten to exacerbate social conflict unless the government becomes more responsive.

IV. DEMOCRACY

After four successful democratic elections, the formal democracy entrenched in the Constitution seems to be well consolidated. However, the repeated, overwhelming victories of the ANC in these electoral contests has led to increased debate over the nature of South Africa's democracy and its future prospects. Some commentators have argued that the ANC's electoral dominance is too similar to other liberation movements in Africa and other post-colonial settings (such as the Congress Party in India). They believe this situation has led South Africa to become a single-party dominant democracy, with all the pathologies of patronage, lack of accountability and limited democratic participation or space that have characterised such polities. The Constitutional Court has itself held that both the national legislature and provincial legislatures have failed, in particular cases, to open themselves up to the degree of democratic participation promised in the Constitution. At the same time, the government's attempts to facilitate participatory democracy through the promotion of developmental planning exercises and other legislative mandates at the ward level in local government have floundered against the limits of local government capacity, graft and political intolerance. Do these failures mean that South Africa's democracy is purely formal and that a single party dominates the polity to the extent that there is no real political contestation?

What these critics fail to recognise is that the ANC has thus far not effectively transformed itself from a liberation movement into a political party with a single ideology or dominant political centre. Despite claims that the ANC functions today—as it once did in its underground structures—under the Leninist principle of democratic centralism, the ruling party (or ruling tripartite alliance of the ANC, Communist Party and Congress of South African Trade Unions) is better characterised as forming the core of what is functionally a unipolar democracy. This has meant that those who step out from under the banner of the ANC—and its historic role as liberator—or those who remain in opposition without viable claims to that legacy have been unable to attract significant electoral support. Even those who have significant individual histories of courage in opposing apartheid—such as some of the leaders of COPE, who broke away from the ANC a few months before the 2009 election—do not seem to be able to attract significant support away from the ANC. To the extent that this precludes the emergence of a democratic alternative to the ANC, it may be argued that South Africa's democracy is indeed unipolar. In any case, electoral support is tied, at least for of the time being, to a credible claim that the ANC and its leadership played a significant role and sacrificed for the cause of national liberation.

An enormous amount of political contestation does exist under the umbrella of the liberation movement. For example, members of President Zuma's Cabinet have publicly referred to the Mbeki government as a prior administration, as if referring to a completely different political entity. In many ways, this characterisation truly reflects the publicly stated changes in government policy goals from the Mbeki era. It also signals significant shifts in the internal political leadership of the ANC itself that resulted from Jacob Zuma's triumph over Thabo Mbeki at the organisation's National Conference at Polokwane in December 2007. At the same time, significant continuities exist in the leadership and even in the organisation's basic commitment to what it sees as the goals of the national democratic revolution. These continuities—and the contradictions they contain—have led to intense conflict between different sectors within the Zuma camp. For example, the government has attempted to sustain an economic model based on the need to attract foreign investment and export-led economic growth, while simultaneously trying to address the needs of a largely marginalised and poverty-stricken majority.While members of the Zuma camp could all agree to oppose Thabo Mbeki and his policies, fundamental disagreements have arisen regarding how best to address the difficulties facing the country, particularly in the context of the global economic crisis, which has undermined the country's reliance on commodity exports. One result of this tension has been increasing conflict between factions within the tripartite alliance and an ongoing political mobilisation geared towards reshaping the ANC at its centenary national conference, which is scheduled to be held by the end of 2012.

The removal of President Thabo Mbeki—first as President of the ANC in December 2007 and later as President of the country in September 2008—set an extraordinary example of political accountability within the context of the ruling ANC alliance. As a result, some fear that internal differences have become irresolvable and that the pattern of internal political contestation will become a continuous process. As Deputy President Kgalema Motlanthe, who criticised 'the factionalism that had taken a firm grip of the party' warned,

> You have a choice . . . The general election of 2009, the local government elections that will follow and the ANC centenary conference of 2012 can either be milestones down a greasy slope from which we can never return, or landmarks in the renewal of our movement.[25]

At the same time, the withdrawal of criminal charges of corruption against Jacob Zuma and the subsequent packing of sensitive government posts with Zuma loyalists—from head of intelligence to the head of the National Prosecuting Authority—has led to cries of foul and dark mutterings over the prospects of constitutional democracy in South Africa. Despite these concerns, it is also important to acknowledge that internal contestation within the ruling alliance and the government has led to more government officials and politicians facing suspension from their positions and legal action than nearly any other country in the world. In the period since Thabo Mbeki became President in 1999, a series of politically charged legal processes have taken place, including Commissions of Enquiry; criminal investigations and trials and suspensions involving the Deputy President; Judges, two consecutive heads of the National Prosecuting Authority; the head of national intelligence; the Chief Whip in Parliament; the Public Protector; the national Commissioner of Police; national Commissioner of Prisons, and a plethora of senior civil servants, municipal officials and local councillors.

---

[25] F Forde, 'Malema and Mantashe Lead the Charge Down the Greasy Slope', *Sunday Independent* (13 December 2009) p 14 col 1.

V. CONCLUSION

South Africa's post-apartheid Constitution offers a promise—that Constitutional rights, institutional restraint and formal democratic practices can provide an alternative to open conflict and violence. Despite growing levels of social tension, the institutions created by the Constitution have the potential—even in the face of intense political conflict and periodic malfunction—to mediate these conflicts. Over time, it may be possible to counter the inequality and deprivation that threaten to undermine South Africa's political and economic stability. Achieving this institutional stability will provide the basis for a more coherent response to the continuing blight of abject poverty and inequality that still haunts South Africa. And though some policies seem to be aimed at facilitating the achievement of individual wealth and empowerment, it may be more important than ever to recall the original vision of collective action— designed to confront the legacies of inequality and authoritarianism— which remains inherent in the rights and structures guaranteed in the South African Constitution.

Index